Breaking New Ground

Breaking New Ground

by JOHN N. COLE and CHARLES WING

Drawings by Charles Wing

The Atlantic Monthly Press BOSTON / NEW YORK

FIRST EDITION

LIBRARY OF CONGRESS CATALOGING-IN-PUBLICATION DATA

Cole, John N., 1923-
  Breaking new ground.

  Bibliography: p.
  Includes index.
  1. House construction—Amateurs' manuals.
  I. Wing, Charles, 1939-   . II. Title.
TH4815.C6497 1986   690'837   86-1211
ISBN 0-87113-019-X
ISBN 0-87113-028-9 (pbk.)

Published simultaneously in Canada

PRINTED IN THE UNITED STATES OF AMERICA

Contents

Introduction

When my wife, Jean, and I were fifteen years younger, and when our seven children were in the same chronological situation, we knew we either had to enlarge the house we were living in or start from the ground up and build a new one—a place designed for the times and for that awesome cluster of teenagers.

The times, if you recall, were parlous. The sixties and seventies had brought us not only conflict and rebellion but an energy crisis that gave every owner of an oil burner high anxieties. In tune with those times, we decided to keep our teens occupied with hammers and saws while they helped us build a new home designed to conserve energy and operate in gentle harmony with its environment.

Which decisions led to one of the most challenging and productive times of our lives. We found a splendid, south-facing building site on a Maine point overlooking Casco Bay, and we built one of the first large, passive solar homes on the coast. And although we used professional help to assist in installing complex items like auxiliary heating systems, plumbing, and electricity, we built most of the house ourselves (Jean, myself, our seven kids, and about forty of their friends). In November 1972, after two years of planning, preparing, and building, we moved in and celebrated a momentous Thanksgiving.

Many events of significance transpired during those tumultuous days, but few turned out to be more important than my meeting with Charlie Wing. Then a physics professor at Bowdoin College, Charlie applied much of his knowledge to a special, rather extracurricular course in house building—a course he had initiated. It met with stunning success and was constantly oversubscribed. Evidently, then as now, there were more folks than most of us realized who wanted to learn how to take matters into their own hands and design and build the sort of place they wanted to live in.

I was too committed to building our own place to find the time to take Charlie's course, but I milked him for as much information as I could. Like a hypochondriac who meets a doctor at a dinner party, I pressed Charlie with questions, questions about how thick a beam needed to be to support a roof, how deep the foundation posts should go, what sort of nails to use, what kind of insulation to select . . . there was no end to my need for technical information. Jean and I had the philosophy of our new home well in order; it was the conversion of those ideas to three-dimensional reality that we needed Charlie for.

And he came through, in superb style. After twelve years of year-round living in that house through every extreme of weather Maine could produce, each of Charlie's insights had been tested and proven. And although we didn't know how well his advice would hold up when we began, we knew he knew what he was talking about.

It was that quality of his, that eloquence about matters technological, that led to our partnership on the first book we wrote together, appropriately, *From the Ground Up*. It was a book about how to build a house, from the beginning, by a couple of people who had done just that. Its focus was Charlie's hard facts combined with my thoughts about that wonderful place on the bay and how much I, Jean, and every one of the children learned as we built it—not merely about construction, but about ourselves.

We came through it a stronger family and a more united family, as well as a better-housed family. During the happy years we lived there, the teenagers became adults and as adults sought their own identities, their own places to live, and their own companions to live with. It seemed that Jean and I had just gotten our gardens where we wanted them when we looked up from our hoes and rakes to find that the home built for nine now housed only two. Most parents of teenagers wonder if there is any end to the condition; yet when the end comes, those same parents wonder how the time could have flown so swiftly.

Just as we had known a dozen years before that the house we lived in then was too small, Jean and I knew as the eighties began to mature that our lovely place by the bay was too large for what, in the twinkling of a cosmic eye, had become a middle-aged couple schussing toward the Social Security years.

It was time for yet another change. This time, however, we wanted what I call a compact house; a place primarily for two, that doesn't cost too much, that's economical to run and maintain, and that will hold up through the years so its fixed costs will remain stable. A place, in short, for a couple, either a couple who are just getting started in their professional lives or a pair like Jean and myself—over fifty-five but energetic, with lives to live and careers to fulfill.

As I began doing preliminary research on our project, I learned there are close to fifty million Americans over fifty-five whose families have grown but whose lives are scarcely at their midway point, thanks to the ever-increasing life expectancies that modern medicine is so doggedly extending. Add to that number the bulge of baby boomers who have become today's young professionals and you come up with a robust slice of the population that shares the common dream of homeownership, especially if it's a home that not only meets their needs but does so for a modest price.

It was the recognition, and verification, of the relative universality of our needs as a couple that I took with me when I went to ask Charlie the first set of questions about our plans for a new, compact house. This time I wasn't going to pester Charlie with queries whenever I had the chance; this time I was going to get him involved from the beginning.

And the way I would get him involved, I decided, would be to suggest that we do another book together, this time about another house that Jean and I would build, but for a quite different set of purposes than our *From the Ground Up* house. I knew if I could acquaint Charlie with the significance of the numbers I had compiled, he would have no trouble defining the potential demand for the sort of information he and I could assemble. And not only that: We would be talking about a real house built for Jean and me, two real people with needs and life-styles shared by tens of millions of others.

Partly, I think, in self-defense and partly because he could visualize how the interchange might be adapted to a book, Charlie suggested I put my scores of questions in writing. He had learned from our previous experience that when I got him in a corner I not only inquired about what I needed to know but also dug for whatever information I could gather. Charlie is the sort of person who has never learned to say no, and I'm sure he contemplated endless sessions with me and my loosely organized (to say the least) areas of inquiry.

"Put it in writing," he said when we met to talk about the new house. "Once you know just what information you want, drop me a note and I'll answer it.

"That way," he explained with a smile, "by the time you and Jean finish the place, another book will be written."

And that is how this book came to be. It has been a learning process (another one) for us both. A great deal has changed since 1972. Building materials have been invented, modified, improved, or taken off the market to be replaced by others that can do the same job better and for less money. The energy crisis of the seventies has produced a new family of energy savers and energy systems that set new, high standards for efficiency. We needed to know more about them, and Charlie had the answers, as he almost always does, especially when it comes to saving money.

Because he does, and because his other qualities are strong where mine are weak, we make a good combination. And the sense of security, the snug-harbor feeling that Jean and I wanted our new home to capture, is a natural for Charlie. He has spent most of his life assembling wise budgets, making careful choices, and acquiring the precise information on which to base them.

The give-and-take between physicist and metaphysicist soon assumed a pattern, the pattern that unfolds on the following pages. I ask the questions and define the ends we seek. Charlie responds with precise definitions of the means to those ends.

It is, we hope, the sort of information that will answer the questions and meet the needs of millions of other couples who may be dreaming of or planning their own compact home. Sharing that information is the purpose of this book, and the back-and-forth format is used because that is how my questions and Charlie's answers truly evolved. It is how a compact home can come into being.

Charlie and I believe it is information that warrants sharing because, as *From the Ground Up* helped prove, there are countless Americans who want to live in a place of their own that is snug, secure, energy efficient, affordable, simple to maintain, in harmony with nature, and yet exciting enough as an aesthetic and stylistic statement to be a pleasure to live with, year after year after year.

I hope that when you finish this book, each of your questions is answered. If not, please contact Charlie.

John N. Cole

Breaking New Ground

1. *To Build or Not to Build*

Dear Charlie,

LETTER
1

Help! The place on the bay has been on the market for three weeks, and now it looks as if we have a serious buyer. He's dropping by tomorrow, and he says he'll bring a check, a deposit that will be the first step toward the day when Jean and I must move.

Now we need to make a batch of decisions about our next home. We know we don't want to leave this town. We are Yankees and will stay Yankees. We don't want to leave the region, and we are discussing building another home.

To build is what we hope you'll help us do, because we've already rejected the alternatives. Condos are not for us. Neither is an existing older place, because it needs care and retrofitting, and can never be tailored as precisely as one started from scratch.

And if we do build, then the place will need to be relatively inexpensive. (I'll never move to the supply-side economy if I don't keep a bit of the capital gain from the sale of our larger home.) It will need to be as energy-efficient as possible. Stability must be combined with comfort; in other words, we need to be reasonably warm or cool, but we must not depend on unstable systems to keep us that way. Heating solely with oil is not my idea of a stable system. What I want is a heating plan that has a low initial capital cost, is not hooked to products likely to escalate in price, needs little or no maintenance, and creates a dependable feeling of comfort.

A difficult combination, to be sure. But pondering it was what led us to ask questions. The process began when Jean and I considered space as part of the heating equation: the less space, the lower the demands on a heating system. "A compact house," I said. "That's what we need."

A need to conserve space, a need to conserve energy in a climate comparable to New England's, and a need to make the most from native building materials: Those are the realities that must be met by any designer of compact country homes. They are precisely the criteria Jean and I decided should be the controlling elements of the design of our new house.

Consider a few other decisions we made:

- Wood is going to be our primary building material, interior and exterior.
- Space actually enclosed will be kept to a minimum, so there should be no feeling of confinement. Every room should open on another, and most of them should have some access to the outdoors, either through a window, door, skylight, or reflection. Courtyards should be part of even the most modest urban and suburban homes; and rural buildings should pivot on a small garden that can be seen from nearly every room. No matter where a home is, its design should make use of the existing natural terrain — a "borrowed landscape" — or a courtyard to bring the outdoors in and make an ally of nature rather than an opponent.
- Every interior space should be flexible in the sense that it can serve multiple purposes. Shelves, cupboards, cabinets, closets, and built-in spaces under the stairs (or beneath the floor) should allow for storage of furniture and household accessories.
- The place should be framed much like the barns of our New England. Post-and-beam construction (with variations) can be the basic skeleton, and we'd like the boards used for sheathing to be fitted to the frame with cabinetmaker's precision and with a cabinetmaker's eye to grain, finish, and hue.
- The essentials needed for personal comfort should be provided; only a few nonessentials will be brought along.

The cumulative result of joining simple construction techniques and native materials with care and an eye to aesthetics should give us a low-cost home that has a lasting elegance. And, if we accomplish this within the minimum amount of enclosed space, while designing for the maximum sense of openness and contact with nature, our new home should demand minimum energy and maintenance to generate maximum comfort and contentment.

We hope for stability, and we seek economy. We want style, aesthetics, ease of maintenance, enough contact with nature to extend our horizons, and enough flexibility to allow for the return of some of those now-grown children when they visit. We also want a place that has a strong sense of order and simplicity, is easy to clean, and is convenient to put in secure limbo if we decide to take a trip for a week or so.

And, in addition to all that, we want a home that can respond to each of the definite seasons that bless us north of the fortieth parallel.

With a well-insulated, small, wooden house that is nonetheless well illuminated by natural light, our energy intake should be low and our heating system stable and comfortable. Regardless of what happens to oil prices or Social Security, our overhead and operating expenses will be so relatively low that shifts in the economy will have little effect.

We have set ourselves an arbitrary limit of 1,200 square feet, yet we hope it feels like 2,000 most of the time. Only when a storm is in full swing and we need to feel we are safe in our cave will we close the windows and doors that make the place such a happy surprise.

I am convinced that if we do a proper job of combining the best of current technology with an understanding of how to enclose the great within the small, we can have a moderately priced home that will keep us in comfort at a reasonably low energy cost. We hope it will require almost no maintenance, will be aesthetically pleasing, and will meet our yearnings for simplification.

What I need from you, Charlie (remember, I said at the start that I needed *help*), is some feedback on whether you think our dream home is possible or just pie in the sky. We have a pretty long list here of what's wanted, but nothing much about how we can begin to go about getting from here to there. That's where you come in. And there is a pile of questions.

Should we really think seriously about building?

If so, should we hire an architect? Any suggestions?

How much, really, will a place cost us if we do decide to go ahead?

Can we save money, really, if we do some of the work ourselves? You know me, Charlie — I'm not much when it comes to patience, and I'm no great shakes with a power saw either.

I'm not asking for much, am I? Nothing much, just the information that will help us make one of the most important decisions of our lives. But I think I've come to the right person. After all, from what I hear, you've been helping others with the same sort of information for years. So you ought to be able to help me, right?

I hope you'll give it a try. Will you? Can you?

Your friend,
John

Dear John,

And they shall build houses, and inhabit them . . . .
They shall not build, and another inhabit . . .
— Isaiah 65:21–22

Don't worry, I haven't caught religion. I just thought that was fair evidence that owner-building has been around for a long time.

In fact, until the standardization, industrialization, and homogenization of housing less than a hundred years ago, most people did build their own homes, with help from family and friends and an occasional outside expert stonemason. Plumbing, wiring, and central heating were rare. As a result there were few plumbers, electricians, heating and ventilating engineers, architects, or code enforcers. In short, human nest building proceeded in a most agreeable fashion.

But industrialization soon put an end to that. The unfamiliar technologies of plumbing and electrification invaded the home, requiring codes and enforcers to guarantee sanitary and safe installation. People of the industrial age worked away from the home but returned with a paycheck that allowed savings to accrue. The more they worked, the more money they could save — to pay others to do the work for which they no longer had time. Times were ripe for the emergence of the building professions.

The building industry was not unique. Almost without exception, household skills formerly considered basic turned into professions. Now, no one has a stronger instinct for survival than professionals, and nothing guarantees their survival better than the elevation of their professions to high mystery. Like their brethren in the field of human misery, the legal profession, architects found it immensely gratifying to obfuscate the obvious — to legislate and confuse ordinary people into thinking they could not and should not do what they had been doing so well all along.

But all is not lost. An estimated two hundred thousand homes are still built or contracted by their owners each year, most of them in rural backwaters like Maine, where common sense still prevails. The most commonly cited reason among the two hundred thousand couples who annually subject themselves to the most arduous task known to humankind — short of raising children — is money. The savings over buying a ready-made home range from 20 to 58 percent, depending on degree of owner involvement. Consider, for example, the average $80,000 home: 1,600 square feet of living space built professionally at $50 per square foot. The savings from three different levels of owner involvement would be:

20% by acting as contractor	=$16,000
44% by finishing the shell	=$35,000
58% by supplying all the labor	=$46,000

Studies show that when owner-builders supply all the labor, they typically spend two person-hours per square foot of living space. The same $80,000 house would then require 3,200 hours ($2 \times 1,600$) of the owner-builder's time. By saving $46,000 with 3,200 hours of labor, the owner-builder is effectively paying himself about $14 per hour. That shouldn't be too surprising, since the labor being displaced is currently charged out by the contractor at a national average rate of about $20 per hour.

But I don't believe money is the only reason people build their own homes. Cost cutting alone fails to account for a lot of the things I've experienced in my ten years of teaching owner-builders. It doesn't account for their building such large homes. It doesn't account for stained-glass windows, cherry kitchen cabinets, and solar greenhouses. And it doesn't account for people taking leave of jobs paying far more than $14 per hour to substitute their sweat for that of the anonymous professional.

Most of my students have something in common with you and Jean: They are in transition, either in identity or in life-style. Sometimes the house is important to their desired life-style. Sometimes the house is a badge of their newly claimed self-reliance. They cited other reasons for building their own homes:

For many, family togetherness has withered to sitting in front of the television together. Owner-builders often find that the experience of building a family shelter creates a strong feeling of family for the first time.

Many feel insecure about the world situation in general and energy supplies in particular. They build solar or superinsulated homes that require less than a cord of wood per year to heat.

Most homeowners are at the mercy of a professional when something goes wrong. Owner-builders can fix it themselves; they installed it in the first place.

And finally there is pride: pride in having done what no one, including their parents, thought they could do, pride in becoming one of what is now a special breed.

I still remember the four-hour lunch conversation we had a decade ago during which you convinced me to leave college teaching and start a school for owner-builders. How appropriate that you might finally become a student yourself! Apparently your idea was sound, because there are now about three dozen such schools. My own school, Cornerstones, is fairly typical, although of course I think it's the best. The typical course consists of morning sessions on theory, afternoon hands-on carpentry in the field, and evening sessions on design and drafting. The typical class has fifteen to twenty students, but there is no typical student. They come from all over the country, the age range is eight to eighty (one couple in their late seventies built a lovely log cabin!), and their professions range from truck driver to cabinet-level government official.

You're probably worried by now that I'm going to suggest you go to school and put in two years of hard labor building your own home. Don't worry, I wouldn't subject your brown-eyed friend to that. Jean has paid her dues. Living with you while building a house would be worse than Chinese water torture. Instead, I have a plan and an offer.

Plan. I don't know what you're getting for your existing 3,600-square-foot ark, but it should bring at least $40 per square foot, or $144,000. If you build a new, compact house of about 1,000 square feet at $50 per square foot, that should cost about $50,000. You are along enough in years to take the onetime capital-gain exclusion, and if you invest the $94,000 gain in a tax-free bond, that should net you around $10,000 a year in income. Without a mortgage, your annual operating expenses should consist of: fuel $200, maintenance $200, and taxes $1,000. So you should end up with a new house and a guaranteed tax-free annuity of about $8,500 per year.

Offer. I really think you should hire a contractor, John, but in recognition of your having given me the original idea for an owner-builder school, I'll give you and Jean a correspondence course on house building. It will be the same material I give to my owner-builder students and so will teach you how houses work and how to work with rather than against your contractor.

Your friend,
Charlie

P.S. I thought you'd be interested in the enclosed list of owner-builder schools compiled by my friend Ken Lelen of Home Again Publishing.

Building Resources
121 Tremont Street
Hartford, CT 06105
(203) 233-5165

Cathedralite Dome Seminars
820 Bay Avenue
Capitola, CA 95010
(408) 462-2210

Colorado Owner Builder Center
Box 12061
Boulder, CO 80303
(303) 449-6126

Cornerstones School
54 Cumberland Street
Brunswick, ME 04011
(207) 729-6701

Cosanti Foundation
6433 Doubletree Road
Scottsdale, AZ 85253
(602) 948-6145

Denver Owner Builder Center
5835 West Sixth Avenue
Lakewood, CO 80214
(303) 232-8709

Dome School
5955 Otter View Circle
White Bear Lake, MN 55110
(612) 429-1777

Domestic Technology Institute
Box 2043
Evergreen, CO 80439
(303) 674-1597

Dovetail Ltd.
Box 1496
Boulder, CO 80306
(303) 449-2681

Durango Owner Builder Center
Box 3447
Durango, CO 81301
(303) 247-2417

Earthwood Building School
Route 1, Box 105
West Chazy, NY 12992
(518) 493-7744

Eastfield Village
Box 145 RFD
East Nassau, NY 12062
(518) 766-2422

Georgia Solar Coalition
Box 5506
Atlanta, GA 30307
(404) 525-7657

Heartwood Owner-Builder School
Johnson Road
Washington, MA 01235
(413) 623-6677

Home Building Institute
6455 South Central Avenue
Chicago, IL 60638
(312) 735-3343

Lady Carpenter Institute
25 St. Mark's Place
New York, NY 10003
(212) 228-2520

Legendary Log Home School
Box 4150
Sisters, OR 97759
(503) 549-7191

Minnesota Trailbound School of
Log Building
3544½ Grand Avenue
Minneapolis, MN 55408
(612) 822-5955

New Homestead School
Route 1
Murphy, NC 28906
(704) 837-8873

Northwest Building Institute
5410 Southwest Dover Lane
Portland, OR 97225
(503) 244-8266

Northwest Owner Builder Center
1139 Thirty-fourth Avenue
Seattle, WA 98121
(206) 324-9559

Original Log House Construction
School
22203 State Route 203
Monroe, WA 98272
(206) 885-4972

Owner Builder Center
1516 Fifth Street
Berkeley, CA 94710
(415) 526-9222

Owner Builder Center of Fairfield/
Westchester Counties
335 Post Road West
Westpoint, CT 05880
(203) 726-7095

Owner Builder Center at Miami-
Dade Community College
11011 Southwest 104th Street
Miami, FL 33176
(305) 596-1018

Owner Builder Center Pacific
Box 10603
Honolulu, HI 96816
(808) 523-8056

Owner Builder Center of Southern
California
361 East Magnolia Boulevard
Burbank, CA 91502
(213) 841-1942

Riverbend Timber Framing
415 East Adnan
Blissfield, MI 49228
(517) 488-4566

Shelter Institute
38 Front Street
Bath, ME 04530
(207) 442-7938

Southwest Solaradobe School
Box 7460
Old Albuquerque Station
Albuquerque, NM 87914
(505) 842-0342

Tree House Design
15083 Manne Drive
White Rock, BC
Canada V4B 1C5
(604) 536-9624

Windstar Foundation
Box 178
Snowmass, CO 81654
(303) 927-4777

Yestermorrow
Box 76A
Warren, VT 05674
(802) 496-5545

Dear Charlie,

I like the money part best! I've never had a guaranteed tax-free annuity before. I'm not sure I know anyone who has one. In fact, I'm not sure I know what one is, except that the way you add it up, our future looks more secure than our present or any part of our past. If you can help us plan and build a place, and arrange my financial life so Jean doesn't have to worry so much about the grocery budget, you will have wrought a miracle. Which is what it would take to turn me into a prudent money manager. Nothing in my fifty-odd-year history indicates that such a change for the better is possible, but if you say the numbers can work as you have computed, then we would be fools not to build . . . with you as our guide, of course.

And that is the important part of your letter. (I know I'll never *really* have a tax-free annuity.) Since Jean and I read your latest, we have crossed the final barrier that separates intent from absolute decision. We don't talk in hopeful tones anymore about what a perfect compact home should be; we talk, for hours, about the kind ours will be.

Jean has sketched some rough plans. Together we've been looking through magazines and a couple of home-design books, and we've started a kind of mind's-eye measurement and evaluation of some of our neighbors' homes — trying to remember what we like best and trying to take note of the spaces that don't seem to work as well as they could. We don't want to repeat mistakes.

And that could be a problem. I don't know if I'm a failure at translating floor plans, but I have a difficult time converting those thin, straight lines in magazines into any sort of helpful reference. When I look at a 16′ × 20′ LR (I know that stands for living room) that takes up just a few square inches on a glossy page, I have a real problem trying to decide where our sofa will go, or if it will even fit.

And besides, I am very reluctant to get carried away by standardized plans for Mr. and Mrs. Average Couple. No one, in my view, is Mr. or Mrs. Average. Each of us has individual lifestyles, idiosyncrasies, or even (in my case) neuroses. I like to be able to see out some sort of window, no matter where I am in the house.

I'm certain my window compulsions are not taken into account by the folks who come up with the blueprints in *House Beautiful*. And I'm also sure there aren't too many mass-produced homes designed for a writer/editor who plans on having his office in his home — which, by the way, is not average. Less than 9 percent of the earning population is self-employed, so how many homes can you find that include a well-planned and well-designed work space for a person who needs reasonable protection from noise and interruptions?

If you combine my idiosyncrasies and neuroses with Jean's likes, dislikes, habits, and interests, you generate a unique combination in the sense that only this particular couple possesses them in the same degrees of intensity. That is why I believe so strongly in the owner-planned, owner-designed home . . . in the ideal.

When it comes to the reality of sitting down at the dining-room table with lots of paper and pencils, a T square, graph paper, rulers, and a couple of magazines for guidance, we are finding it difficult to come up with ways to take our combined personae and fit them into the criteria we've already established: you know, the notions of compact security, low maintenance, energy-efficiency, aesthetic quality, a feeling of space, and the others I outlined in my first letter.

I mean, it's great to have those ideals organized, but we're having trouble transforming them into a floor plan, a design that has enough informed significance to be taken seriously by a builder. We simply end each evening with a growing pile of sketches, and we say, "That's nice" or "I like this one," but we never seem to be convinced that we have solved the problems, that we're ready to take the next step — which is, I assume, finding a place to put the house we've decided we want.

Knowing you, Charlie, I feel pretty sure you have solved this problem for others like us. I'd bet a good part of that tax-free annuity you pulled out of the air that you're going to tell me there is a system for planning, that there are ways to account for our likes and dislikes, even our compulsions . . . like mine for windows.

So, now that we have absolutely and irrevocably made the go-ahead decision, now that we are fully committed (largely because we know you are there to help), we are asking for our first pivotal piece of information: How do we get a design organized?

Or perhaps that's not the correct question. It's also possible, I suppose, that you will suggest we accept a standardized, prefabricated plan and bend our personalities to it. Or you may recommend an architect, although as I recall you haven't made a habit of that.

We await your response with some impatience. Our enthusiasm peaks, but our performance lacks organization. I don't want to spend too many more evenings doodling with floor plans that I suspect from the start won't be translated into any of those fine lines on blueprint paper.

Your friend,
John

2. Designing Your Own Space

LETTER
4

Dear John and Jean,

I can't tell you how pleased I am that you've decided to go for it. It pains me to see how some of my friends live. They'd rather die than be caught in ill-fitting clothes, yet they live out stereotypical lives in ill-fitting houses designed for the "average" family. To the extent that each of us is different — that our lifestyle or the way we spend our lives is different — each needs an archetypal shelter. We need to be our own architects.

Henry David Thoreau said it better than ever I could:

There is some of the same fitness in a man's building his own house that there is in a bird's building its own nest. Who knows but if men constructed their dwellings with their own hands, and provided food for themselves and their families simply and honestly enough, the poetic faculty would be universally developed, as birds universally sing when they are so engaged? But alas! we do like cowbirds and cuckoos, which lay their eggs in nests which other birds have built, and cheer no traveller with their chattering and unmusical notes. Shall we forever resign the pleasure of construction to the carpenter? What does architecture amount to in the experience of the mass of men? I never in all my walks came across a man engaged in so simple and natural an occupation as building his house. We belong to the community. It is not the tailor alone who is the ninth part of a man; it is as much the preacher, and the merchant, and the farmer. Where is this division of labor to end? and what object does it finally serve? No doubt another may also think for me; but it is not therefore desirable that he should do so to the exclusion of my thinking for myself.

And again:

What of architectural beauty I now see, I know has gradually grown from within outward, out of the necessities and character of the indweller, who is the only builder, — out of some unconscious truthfulness, and nobleness, without ever a thought for the appearance; and whatever additional beauty of this kind is destined to be produced by a like unconscious beauty of life. The most interesting dwellings in this country, as the painter knows, are the most unpretending, humble log huts and cottages of the poor commonly; it is the lives of the inhabitants whose shells they are, and not any peculiarity in their surfaces merely, which makes them picturesque; and equally interesting will be the citizen's suburban box, when his life shall be as simple and as agreeable to the imagination, and there is as little straining after effect in the style of his dwelling.

We acknowledge food, clothing, and shelter as the basic necessities of life, but we give shelter short shrift. We say, and act as if we believe, "Clothes make the man" and "We are what we eat," yet we live in what amount to motel rooms with long-term leases. Our earliest adult lives are spent in the desperate scramble to achieve status in the community, beautiful children, and financial security. Fortunate are those who survive this age intact and go on to recognize that status is inside ourselves, all children are beautiful, and security is not equity alone.

I'm excited for you. I'm excited that you are ready to design a house that shelters not your bodies alone but your psyches as well; a shelter that expresses the character of its indwellers and encourages rather than hinders your lives.

And you're right, John, I do propose something of a system for getting an informed and practical start on your floor plans and space designs. I call it *activity analysis*, and I've learned over the years that it works well for most owner-builders, no matter what their life patterns or their idiosyncrasies, as you put it. This is how it works.

Activity Analysis

The Zen philosopher Alan Watts compared humans to the simplest of animals, worms, mere tubes that spend their lives taking in food at one end and discharging it at the other. One is tempted to agree, especially if the category *food* includes all that we take up and throw away. But on a more fundamental level I cannot agree. Human beings, all of us, do other things as well. We sleep, dream, listen to music, make love, bathe, sit around, come and go, work and play. Unlike the single-minded life of a worm, the life of a human consists of a series of *activities*.

These activities occur within *spaces:* big spaces, small spaces, shared spaces, solitary spaces. And they proceed regardless of the qualities of those spaces. The first step in the design of your own personal space is to realize that the qualities of your activities (and therefore of your life) are affected by the qualities of the spaces in which they occur. To stress this point I call the spaces within a house *activity spaces*. To the extent that your life is a series of activities, your house is a collection of activity spaces.

What are the determining qualities of these spaces? At the initial conceptual stage of design they are three: area, orientation, and degree of privacy.

AREA. No matter what the activity, there is always an area or size of space that feels best. It's frustrating to cook dinner in a too-small kitchen; it's equally frustrating never to achieve that wonderful intimacy experienced in a cozy dining room. So area is a psychological as well as a physical quality.

The average new house today contains about 1,600 square feet of living space, including three bedrooms and two baths. As you pointed out, John, the average family cannot afford it. But it's not the *house* they can't afford, it's the 1,600 square feet, three bedrooms, and two baths. Thus, area is also a financial quality.

How does one determine how large a space should be? Well, how does one determine how large a shoe should be? Unless you buy your shoes through the Sears catalogue, try one on! Of course you can't try on your space; it's yet to be built. But you can try on that of your friends and neighbors. The next time you're in your neighbor's house, pull out your 16-foot Stanley Powerlock and measure it up. Here's how it might go.

(To your neighbor) "Jeez, Dudley, we've always loved your living room; it's just right. Jean and I are thinking of building a new house. Do you mind if we steal your design?"

(To yourself) "Hmm — 12′ × 15′. If we just made this room 2 feet wider, say 14′ × 15′, we could spread the chairs out a bit so that jerk Dudley wouldn't keep stepping on Jean's feet."

(To Dudley) "What a great entrance hall, Dudley! I just love the formality, the sweep, the grandeur; don't you, Jean? Let's see here — 16′ × 20′."

(To yourself) "Boy, what a waste of space! I'm sure glad I don't have to pay Dudley's fuel bill. No wonder he drives that old Volvo. And I'll bet they have to change the plug on the vacuum cleaner twice just to do the hall rug. It looks to me as if all of us could fit into 8′ × 8′."

Trying on neighbors' houses is fun and gratifying. In no time flat you'll have the correct areas — unlike your neighbors — for all of your spaces.

ORIENTATION. We modern humans like to believe we are independent of the natural world around us. For example, we ignore the fact that somewhere in our subconscious there tick three clocks corresponding to the three dominant astronomical cycles: daily, monthly, and yearly. Of the three, the daily, or circadian, is the most powerful. We did not always wake to the sound of an alarm clock or the "Morning Pro Musica" show (although I think our ancestors would have greatly appreciated the latter). For at least 500,000 years we were gently wakened by the sunrise. Brain researchers have recently established the not-surprising fact that people who rise with the sun are generally happier than those jangled awake by alarm clocks.

What does this have to do with *orientation?* Regardless of the season, the sun rises in the east, passes south at noon, and sets in the west. Since most of our daily activities take place on a fairly regular schedule, there is often a strong correlation between our activities and the position of the sun. Orientation requires acknowledging the solar connection and deciding when each space should have sun. For example, since I detest alarm clocks, the windows in my bedroom face east; the orientation of my bedroom, or sleeping space, is therefore east.

DEGREE OF PRIVACY. When outside our shelters, we are on guard. Crossing the street, driving a car, even sitting at a meeting of the board, we are in our alert, public mode. Once we cross the domestic threshold, however, most of us drop our guard. The ambience and the comfort of the home draw us into more trusting, intimate states. Actually, between the boardroom and the bedroom lies a whole spectrum of privacy. Most people for whom boardrooms and bedrooms are daily events know the difficulty of the transition. Both time and space are required.

Here we are talking about space. Nothing gives a greater feeling of privacy than sheer distance, separation. Therefore, we must assign a *degree of privacy* to each of our activity spaces. If we arrange our spaces in order of privacy, then the most private will be remote from the most public, and privacy will be achieved most naturally. I suggest you assign degrees of privacy, with 1 being most public and 3 most private. In my house, kitchen and family room rate 1s, hallways and living room 2s, and bedrooms and study 3s. Arranging in order of degree of privacy would prevent juxtaposition of bedrooms and kitchen, family room and study.

EXAMPLE. Illustration 1 shows how to create a complete activity analysis in tabular form. First fantasize your day, from waking

ACTIVITY SPACE	AREA SQ FT	ORIENT-ATION	PRIVACY DEGREE
SLEEP	150	E	3
COOK	150	S & E	1
EAT	100	N or W	2
DECK	400	S & E	1
BATHE	50	S, E, or W	3
WORK	100	N or W	3
SIT/FIRE	200	N & W	2
ENTER	50	S or E	1

1. Charlie's example activity analysis

till going back to bed (after working, John — not immediately after waking up). In the first column list all of the significant activities that require space. Next try on your neighbors' spaces, adjust to your likes, and enter the desired areas. Third, relate each activity to the time of day. At the time of the activity, where is the sun? Enter the orientation of the activity space as the direction its windows should face to catch the sun. Finally, indicate the degree of privacy of each activity on a scale of 1 to 3.

When you have finished the table (and I would expect yours to be more extensive than the one in my example), you can add up the areas and get a rough idea of how large a house you really need for your life-style. Note that if the total area seems beyond your budget, areas can be combined. For example: Cook (Kitchen), Eat (Dining Room), and Sit/Fire (Living Room) could all be combined into one large room. Or Sit/Fire and Work (Study) might be combined.

After you have specified the areas, orientations, and degrees of privacy for all of your activity spaces, the next step is to see whether they'll fit and whether you can indeed have all that you want. Don't be dismayed at the list you have created. Most people fall into the trap of assuming that it can't possibly work out. In fact, it almost always does work out. The key to success is remaining loose; be general rather than specific about the details of your spaces. At this stage you are groping toward a finished design much like an artist or sculptor.

Like the artist beginning to draw a figure, you can use circles and ellipses placed so as to rough out the major features and masses of the body. I like to think of the circles as bubbles, because bubbles have a dreamlike quality and conform to the shape of available space while retaining their basic areas.

To construct a bubble diagram, assemble plenty of plain white paper, number-2 pencils, and a good eraser. In one corner draw an arrow pointing true south so that you can orient your bubbles to the sun. Next draw a circle or bubble representing the largest of your activity spaces. The size of this bubble represents the area of that largest space, and all other bubbles should be drawn proportionally. The rest of the process is like a game. It is as difficult to describe rationally as is the process of assembling a jigsaw puzzle. Your task is to find a configuration of bubbles that satisfies every relationship in the activity-analysis table. By allowing one or two minor discrepancies — such as letting an entrance foyer (degree of privacy 1) abut a bathroom (degree of

Bubble Diagrams

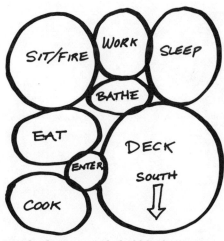

2. Charlie's example bubble diagram

3. Charlie's alternative bubble diagram

privacy 3) — you'll find not one unique solution but often three or four!

To prove my point, I've drawn two completely different bubble diagrams (Illustrations 2 and 3), both satisfying all of the criteria in my simple activity-analysis table. Both focus on the dominant feature of the house, the patio or deck. They are nearly mirror images of each other. I suspect there are several more solutions to be found by rotating or inverting the basic building shape. Furthermore, I haven't even tried adding a second floor. Often this will provide the solution to a privacy problem; nothing creates privacy more effectively than a stairway!

This has been a long letter, but it needed to be. This is the most important step in creating your house. Your homework assignment is to create your personal activity-analysis table and bubble diagram. Take your time; your list should be longer. First, there are two of you. Second, as Jean has probably already noticed, I've left out lots of small but important spaces, such as closets and stairways. Have fun!

Your friend,
Charlie

LETTER
5

Dear Charlie,

After a week or so of working with your activity-analysis system, we seem to have solved our problem of developing a solid base for our planning.

And I can tell you two more reasons I like your system: (1) I can draw ovals and circles well enough to produce diagrams that look almost as good as yours, and (2) I love what you say about orientation. I've always believed, as I've written many times, that humankind has managed to get too far removed from nature. Something pivotal is missing from our lives when we begin to ignore the compass, sunrises and sunsets, which way the wind blows, or what sort of weather the wind can bring. Technology may have given us the illusion that we can conquer or ignore natural presences. But we do so at our peril; the farther we try to pull away from nature, the more our lives lose texture and the more undernourished our spirits become.

So, as you will see on the enclosed activity-analysis sketches Jean and I finished and agreed on this morning (after working up and discarding nearly a dozen others), there are no living spaces in this compact house that are without windows. And each activity relates to the time of day, the position of the sun, and the propensities of the weather.

Both bedrooms, for example, have windows on the east and south; the morning sun will cheer and warm us when we awake, and it will follow us into the kitchen. From the living room and our dinner table we'll be able to see the sun set, and in summer we can stroll on the deck or patio to watch the full moon rise.

The patio, by the way, is important to both of us. As you know, Jean has a green thumb, or possibly two. She can make any plant grow, any flower bloom. That patio, in addition to the sense of space it offers, is also a fine place for plants, because it faces south, gets the best part of the sun, and provides a sort of shelter against the coldest winds from the north. What works so well for the plants, of course, also works well for us and our visitors.

About the only activity space in the house that doesn't have a fairly direct relationship with the sun and the cycle of days is my study, the place where I'll be working and trying to discover whatever became of that tax-free annuity you promised. But the office is where it is for a reason: I have always been captivated by what goes on outdoors in the country. I watch for birds, for the greening of the grass, or for the turning of leaves. It is quite possible for me to lose myself in these musings, and such voyages are not conducive to production, especially when I need all the self-discipline that can be encouraged.

So the study is on the northeast corner, upstairs, away from the traffic and the household action. No one will have to walk

ACTIVITY SPACE	AREA (Sq.Ft.)	ORIENT-ATION	PRIVACY 3 = most
Deck or Patio	400	S	1
Living Room	200	N, W	2
Dining Room	100	?	2
Kitchen	100	S, E	1
Bedroom 1	150	E	3
Bedroom 2	150	E	3
Bath 1	50	E or W	3
Bath 2	50	E or W	3
JNC's Study	100	N	3
BR Closets	16 + 16	?	?
Hall Closets	6	?	?
Formal Entry	50	S or E	1
Kitch. Entry	20	S or E	1
Stairways	40 + 40	?	?

1,088 sq ft heated area

NOTE: ? means we don't care

4. John and Jean's activity analysis

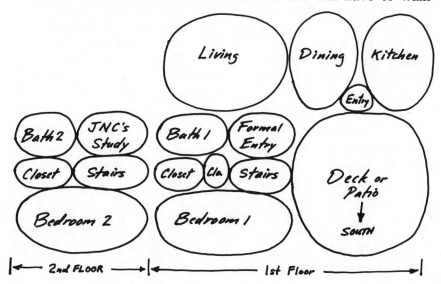

5. John and Jean's bubble diagram

through my work space to get anywhere, and my view of the great outdoors will be trimmed to a minimum. I am, however, just a step away from the necessities: the bathroom, and the stairs, so if Jean is out and the doorbell rings, I can answer with reasonable dispatch.

This process of imposing hypothetical situations on the arrangement of the activity spaces has worked for each of our other decisions. "What happens when I arrive with the week's groceries?" Jean wanted to know. That's why we added a door into the kitchen/dining space. It makes much more sense than having a single entry, a so-called front door that becomes more formal than perhaps it should be. The extra door to the kitchen also allows us easier access to the patio. Again, we think it's great to be able to step outdoors on a soft spring morning, to feel the sun's new warmth, to gather bright evidence that winter has truly made its exit.

What happened after we began working with your system is that we had fun. Like children moving furniture and dolls in a dollhouse, we moved ourselves and our guests from room to room. We stored clothes and food; we thought about dressing, cooking, and bathing. By the way, the downstairs bath is efficiently located to service those in the first-floor bedroom as well as visitors who stop in for a chat or a cup of coffee in the kitchen.

We tried to anticipate every sort of situation, every daily routine, and every special event that might occur in our home. This brought us around to the sort of self-analysis we went through when we built our first home by the bay fifteen years ago. I remember my realization then that planning and building a shelter is more than a structural exercise. It's an internal investigation, an examination of values, habits, personae, and relationships. And when every question is answered, every hypothetical situation posed, the owner-builder couple are likely to learn more about themselves, their family, and their marriage and its patterns than they do about joists or kitchen cabinets.

Jean and I have been together for more than twenty years; ours is a solid, warm relationship. But as we worked with your activity-analysis systems, as we each sketched our ovals and circles, we found ourselves sharing thoughts and ideas and insights we haven't talked about for years. It's been an altogether delightful and stimulating time.

And not only that — I think we've done a pretty good job. You'll note, I'm sure, that the approximate square footage thus far is still under the maximum 1,200-square-foot limit we imposed. I expect we may get closer to that before we convert this sketch to precise floor plans, but it's reassuring to know we have a bit of leeway as opposed to having to cut back.

I feel a bit like a student handing a paper to a professor. I can hardly wait to see what sort of a grade you give this activity analysis and bubble diagram, as you call them. I happen to think the circles and ovals are more substantial than bubbles. Less likely to float away or burst.

We assume the next step will be the conversion of this sketch to a more finished product, one with straight lines and precise dimensions . . . which won't be as much fun for me but must be done, I'm certain. Perhaps you can suggest some ways to help me get organized and to understand, for example, just how much relative space a stove or refrigerator will need in the kitchen.

I've never been that great when it comes to precision, as you know. But I now think of myself as an expert at space bubbles and activity analysis. Thanks to you.

Your friend,
John

Dear John and Jean,

LETTER
6

I see you've retained the idea of a deck or patio as a focus. Good! Decks and patios are not only inexpensive, but they also provide outdoor living space and tie the inside to the outside in a way that makes a small house seem much larger.

Aren't you amazed at your 1,088-square-foot total? When you design a house from scratch, you don't get stuck with extra bedrooms that collect old clothes and family rooms for which there is no longer a family. As I recall, your present house has 3,600 square feet. Do you realize what that means? Roughly speaking, your new house will cost a third as much to build, a third as much to heat and cool, a third as much to maintain, a third as much to insure, and a third as much in taxes as the old.

I'm impressed with your design. In fact, I can feel that primordial urge to build a nest again. It happens every time I get involved in a design, even if not my own.

The next task is turning your bubble diagram into a floor plan. That will involve two steps: (1) turning the oval bubbles into rectangles satisfying all *critical dimensions,* and (2) incorporating as many *architectural patterns* as possible. Since there is a lot of interaction between these steps, you'll find yourself working on both at the same time. They are, however, conceptually different, so let me describe them one at a time.

Critical Dimensions

Building materials, appliances, and many furnishings come in standard dimensions — at least the "standard," or lower-cost, versions do. In addition, experience has dictated certain minimum workable clearances for areas where people work and walk. Table 1 lists the most useful of those dimensions. If you need a dimension not given here, chances are you can find it in the architect's bible, the Sears catalogue.

Table 1
CRITICAL DIMENSIONS

1. Building dimensions (outside of frame): 2-foot increments
2. Exterior-wall thickness: R-14 wall — 4″
   R-19 wall — 6″
3. Interior-wall thickness: 4½″
4. Exterior door: 3′ wide
5. Patio-door set: 5′, 6′, or 8′ wide
6. Stairways: 3′ wide × 10′ long (for 8′ story) + 3′ landing
7. Hallways: 4′ wide
8. Closets: 2′ deep
9. Kitchen counters: 25″ wide including backsplash
10. Clearance between parallel counters: 3½′, or 42″ minimum
11. Kitchen range: standard — 25″ deep × 30″ wide
    apartment — 25″ deep × 20″ wide
12. Refrigerator: 26″ deep x 30″, 32″, 34″, or 36″ wide
13. Kitchen sink: 30″ wide
14. Washing machine, installed: 30″ deep by 30″ wide
15. Dryer, installed: 30″ deep × 30″ wide
16. Bathroom vanity: 22″ deep including backsplash
17. Bathtub: 2½′ wide × 5′ long
18. Shower stall: 32″ deep × 36″ wide, or 36″ deep × 36″ wide
19. Toilet (space for): 5′ deep × 3′ wide
20. Couch: 3′ deep × 5′, 6′, or 7′ wide
21. Chair, living room: 3′ × 3′
22. Beds: bunk — 36″ × 69″ or 39″ × 75″
    twin — 39″ × 75″
    full — 54″ × 75″
    queen — 60″ × 80″
    king — 76″ × 80″
23. Tables: kitchen — 36″ diameter plus extensions
    dining — 42″ diameter plus extensions
24. Clothes dresser: 17″ deep
25. Wood or coal stove: 36″ from combustibles, all sides

Humans have been around for at least five hundred thousand years. There is evidence they built log structures ten thousand years ago, and they probably leaned trees together over their heads long before that. Through the ages and across otherwise dissimilar cultures, certain patterns are found repeatedly in human habitations. It's as if the knowledge of these patterns were genetically encoded. At the very least, these patterns have been found to work — to please — and are therefore passed from generation to generation.

With increasing industrialization of housing, the push toward greater efficiency and lower cost constantly threatens these patterns. But the patterns should not be ignored; they are, quite simply, what make houses work. Therefore, study the patterns carefully and try to incorporate as many as possible into your design. If these patterns turn you on, you can find 214 more in an important and wonderful book, *A Pattern Language* by Christopher Alexander and friends.

TREE PLACES. Trees can define outdoor space. Next to a house or on a patio they create a roof. In a square pattern they define an outdoor room; a pair serves as a gateway; rows turn a driveway into a gallery. Even standing alone, a single tree can provide a focal point for a child's swing or a bench. Don't destroy trees thoughtlessly; they take a lifetime to grow back.

NATURAL GARDEN. Grow trees, bushes, flowers, ground cover, and grasses in a way that comes close to how they are found in nature. Form the boundaries with natural materials such as logs and stones. This "English garden" is a pleasing bridge between nature growing wild and the human compulsion to organize one's surroundings.

VEGETABLE GARDEN. Every home with land should have a vegetable garden. Vegetables are the only source of food capable of providing all of our needs. One tenth of an acre of good soil is sufficient to provide a year's worth of food for a family of four. But the benefits go beyond nutrition. Presidents of corporations do it, heads of state do it, mental patients do it: There is simply nothing more "grounding" to the body and soul than messing about in the soil.

SOUTH-FACING OUTDOOR SPACE. Except on a hot day in summer, given a choice, people will always sit in the sun. In fact, people detest shade so much that they will rarely cross a shaded

OUTDOORS

area to get to a sunny one. Therefore, in designing your house and its accompanying outdoor spaces, be sure to create a livable outdoor space such as a patio or deck on the south side of the house, as well as convenient access to it.

POSITIVE OUTDOOR SPACE. Positive space is defined, enclosed space; negative space is generally what is left over and provides no sense of being enclosed. People feel comfortable and secure in positive spaces but insecure in negative ones. The sheltering feeling of a house derives primarily from the positive enclosure of its rooms. In stark contrast is the negative emptiness of the spaces around typical tract houses. This needn't be; the wings of the building, the outbuildings, walls, fences, shrubs, and trees should all be used to create positive and therefore useful outside spaces.

OUTDOOR ROOM. We've all had fantasies of living in grass huts in the South Seas; large numbers of people well beyond adolescence still go camping. We have an urge to be outdoors and indoors at the same time. Many older homes have screened-in porches or trellis-covered patios. These spaces serve as outdoor rooms, spaces where the wind and birds can be heard and the flowers smelled, yet where people act as if they were indoors. What class!

SUNNY PLACE. This is a subpattern of the south-facing outdoor space. In any south-facing outside space there is a best spot, a sunniest corner against the building, a corner that is always protected from the wind. In the absence of wind and in full sunlight, I have experienced total comfort outside at 50 degrees Fahrenheit with no shirt in December. Make your sunny place attractive and usable. Mine is next to a sliding door, with a table, a chair, and a telephone jack. It makes winter shorter.

ZEN VIEW. I have heard various stories about the origin of this pattern's name. They are not important. The important point is that one should preserve the impact of a beautiful view by not boring the senses. Rather than gaping at it incessantly through a wall of windows, reserve the view for special times. My little house is on an ocean cove, but I built it in such a position that the cove can be seen only from my sleeping loft and from the path to my mailbox. Waking up and going for the mail have been transformed into special daily events.

THE ENTRANCE. How often have you been confused and frustrated in approaching a strange house for the first time? There is the formal entrance exactly in the middle of the main building, and there is the side door off the driveway, the door obviously used by the occupants. Which door are you expected to use? This is not a good way to begin a friendship! There are two keys to a successful entrance door. First, it must be obvious upon approaching the house which door you are expected to use. Second, the location of that door should place the visitor in an appropriate interior space of the house — not, for example, in the dining room or the bedroom. These situations are easily avoided at the design stage. I hope you won't have to resort to the extreme step taken by one of my neighbors, who contradicted the obvious with a sign on the front door that said, "This is not a door."

ENTRANCE TRANSITION. The outdoors is nonintimate. There our adrenaline is up; we are in a guarded state because the world is a dangerous place. Indoors we can be intimate, relaxed, civilized. A physical transition aids the required psychological transition: crunching up a gravel driveway, passing through a gate, walking under a grape arbor — all put us on notice that we are passing into a different space.

ENTRANCE ROOM. The actual point of transition between inside and outside is woefully neglected in most new houses. An entrance space should recognize the following needs: (1) a window through which to see who's knocking at your door; (2) shelter from wind and rain for the poor knocker; (3) an outside shelf or bench on which to rest packages while you grope for your keys; (4) space in which to gyrate while putting on your coat; (5) a bench on which to sit while donning or doffing boots; (6) storage space for boots, coats, and hats; (7) a clearly indicated point of departure so that you don't have to follow your guests to their car in a protracted and awkward good-bye; and (8) a temporary holding space from which to deny Bible salesmen and other riffraff immediate access to the intimacy of your hearth.

WINDOWS WITH SMALL PANES. Nothing is less aptly named than the picture window. The special talent of an artist is the ability to extract a picture from the ordinary. Large unbroken expanses of glass don't frame pictures; they take in the whole outdoors. Their frames don't limit the visual information streaming into the brain. When a window is broken up by muntins, however, each smaller pane frames a picture of less detail, a scene that the eye can comprehend. A further argument can be made for windows of smaller overall size. Narrow windows frame entirely different scenes when viewed from different points in a room.

LOW WINDOWSILLS. One of the primary functions of a window is to provide contact with the outside. Modern practice is to place the windowsill above the height of furniture (about 30 inches) so that tables and chairs can be placed anywhere along the wall. Since eye height when seated is only 36 inches, the immediate foreground cannot be seen while you are seated. (Don't you get the urge to stand up when you hear a noise outside?) A sill height of between 12 and 14 inches allows contact with the ground yet distinguishes the window from a door. For a sense of security, a sill height of 20 inches is recommended for second-story and higher windows.

NATURAL DAYLIGHTING **PLACE BY A WINDOW.** Two things that we tend to want when indoors are contact with the outside world and light. If a window creates a sitting place, both these desires are satisfied. If not, we'll find ourselves restlessly moving around the room between a comfortable seat and the windows. A window place can be as simple as a comfortable chair next to a window with a low sill. More elaborate and attractive are built-in window seats and window alcoves.

WINDOWS ON TWO SIDES. Given the choice between a room with windows on one side or a room with windows on two or more sides, people nearly always pick the latter. Nothing need be said about a room without windows. Windows on only one side have several disadvantages: They leave remote areas of a room dark and unpleasant, cause glare or high contrast between the window and the wall, and hinder communication by only partially illuminating the face and its expressions. If you have any doubt about this pattern, think about your favorite rooms; I'm sure they all have windows on two or more sides.

DORMERS AND SKYLIGHTS. A room with sloping ceilings needs windows built into the ceiling to satisfy the requirements for contact with the outside and natural daylighting. A window high up gives good lighting but no contact with the ground. A low window gives contact but poor lighting. The compromise is either a vertical window built out from the roof — a dormer window — or a skylight in the roof at eye height.

SHELTERING ROOF. A strongly sloping roof is symbolic of shelter; witness the phrase "a roof over your head." Children's earliest drawings are symbolic rather than realistic, so is it not significant that the houses they draw have pitched roofs, even when they themselves live in apartments? Furthermore, we like to see the rafters overhead that are protecting us. I believe that this symbolism derives from the fact that the first dwellings were nothing more than roofs, merely trees or timbers leaning against each other.

VARIED CEILING HEIGHT. The height of a ceiling has a powerful effect on the intimacy of a space. A public room such as a family room could have a height of 9 feet, a dining room a height of 8 feet, and a bedroom or sitting alcove a height of only 7 feet. Achieving different ceiling heights on the first floor of a two-story house is difficult. It is simple, however, when the house consists of more than one module. Other useful constructs are cathedral ceilings, lofts, and changing floor levels.

SPACE DEFINED BY STRUCTURE. Compare the intimacy of a restaurant in a former home that has many small rooms to the intimacy of a restaurant in a modern building where spaces are delineated by movable partitions. Spaces are not as well defined when formed by flimsy, clearly nonstructural partitions as when formed by the structural walls of a building. This becomes clear when trying to lay out spaces inside a timber-framed building.

SITTING ALCOVES. No single plain room can serve a group of people well all the time. There are times when all want to be together, but some desire at the same time to read alone or do homework or talk with one another. A room allows all these things if it contains alcoves, smaller spaces within the larger space. An alcove may be as simple as a small circle of chairs in a corner or as complicated as a small, three-sided room off the main room.

SITTING CIRCLE. When free to choose, people in a group will always arrange themselves in a circle. A circle attracts people, especially if it touches the main traffic paths through the house. The circle should be tangential to the traffic, however, and not cut by it. Arrange a variety of chairs, a couch, and cushions loosely in the circle so that people have a choice of where to sit according to their moods.

OVERHEAD

SITTING AROUND

FIRE. The Greeks believed the universe consisted of four elements: earth, air, fire, and water. Fire is the symbol for life, warmth, energy. When the fire in your body goes out, you're dead; when the fire in the home goes out, the home seems cold and dead. Nothing focuses a sitting circle better than the warmth of a fireplace or stove. A television screen is a poor substitute, in my mind.

COOKING AND EATING

KITCHEN LAYOUT. The efficiency experts have gone too far in the kitchen; it has reached the point where, for lack of counter space, dishes have to be prepared sequentially. I've yet to hear anyone complain about a kitchen being too large or having too many counters. Every kitchen consists of four major work areas: refrigerator, stove, sink, and preparation counter. Proper efficiency consists of: (1) no two work centers being separated by more than 10 feet, (2) appropriate storage and tools at each center, and (3) a total of at least 12 feet of free counter space.

OPEN SHELVES. I hate modern kitchens with Mediterranean fruitwood cabinets because I can never find what I'm looking for. The pot I want is always under three other pots under the kitchen sink with Mr. Clean. And it turns out, after a special trip to the supermarket, that I did have a can of tuna fish; it was behind the dog food. What's missing is the good old pantry where the pots hang on walls, the shelves are one can deep, and food is not something to be ashamed of.

WAIST-HIGH SHELF. Have you ever noticed how every waist-high horizontal surface in the house collects junk? There is a constant flow of objects too big to keep in our pockets, too transient to put away, too useful to throw away: pencils, notepad, newspapers, address book, telephone book, mail, keys. To make the best of a bad situation, provide a waist-high shelf in the kitchen just for these things. The same shelf can be used for unpacking the groceries.

FARMHOUSE KITCHEN. If a kitchen contains a table and chairs, it will soon become the social center of the house. The importance of eating together is ceremonially recognized in most religions. No less important are the joy of cooking together and the anticipation created by the sounds and smells of food in preparation. Provide enough room in the kitchen for a number of people to work together, a table and chairs for eating, and even one or more comfortable rocking chairs for the likes of John, who would rather watch.

A ROOM OF ONE'S OWN. No one can sustain intense intimacy without periodically reestablishing his or her personal identity. Lack of privacy will result in the construction of barriers. Establishing our own identity requires if not an entire room at least a corner that is ours alone, where whatever we leave will not be touched. This requirement applies to children as well as to adults. The identity of a couple requires similar private space. Nothing will destroy the intimate bond between a couple faster than inability to get away from the children.

DRESSING SPACE. Dressing and undressing and leaving clothes around are very disruptive unless space is set aside for them. Provide a dressing and clothes-storage space between the bedroom and bath. It can be part of bedroom or bath, but it should be at least 6 feet across with 6 feet of hanger space, 6 feet of open shelf, several drawers, and a full-length mirror.

WORK SPACE. Ongoing work requires a separate work space in order not to disrupt the rest of the house and to provide the proper environment for concentration. If the work involves mostly paperwork, a minimum floor space of 48 square feet is required. The space should be enclosed on two or three sides and should open out onto a larger space. The person working will be most comfortable with his or her back to a wall and looking into the larger space or out of a window.

WORKING AT HOME. Retirement is unnatural, very often leading to boredom, lack of direction, and rapid physical decline. The skills of the person being retired may be at their peak. We can personally avoid this crisis if we start working at home at an early enough age. With the advent of personal computers, information networks, and telecommunications, the number of jobs that can be performed at home is increasing. The goal is meaningful work that is inseparable from our daily existence, that we can do at our own pace, and that can never be taken from us by "the company."

PRIVACY

DOORS IN CORNERS. The location of doors dictates the traffic pattern through a room. Placing a single door in a corner or a pair of doors in adjacent corners frees the remainder of the room for the business of living and results in the most efficient use of space. The one exception is when a room is large enough to contain more than one activity space, in which case the door should enter between spaces.

MINIMIZE HALLWAYS. A hallway serves the single purpose of getting you from one space to another. As such, it represents a failure in the design process. If hallways comprise 10 percent of a heated space, then the overall living space costs 10 percent more than it should. An entrance hall or foyer can do double duty and thus escape the penalty.

CLOSETS. Don't let your closets be afterthoughts. And don't place them on outside walls for thermal insulation. With exterior walls already thermally insulated, closets are more valuable when placed between rooms for acoustic insulation or for thick walls as transitions into private spaces.

STAIRCASES. The failure of most owner-builders-designers to include a staircase in the original conceptual design usually results in disaster. Stairs between floors require a volume of two stories and an area on each floor of about 40 square feet. However, properly placed and integrated, a stairway open to a living space can serve as a series of sitting places and as a stage for some of life's little dramas. The next time you're at a party, watch what happens on an open staircase.

STORAGE. Don't forget the need to store things that are "temporarily" not being used. Some things need heat; more often they just need to be kept dry. Attics are drier than basements. Provide a minimum of 15 percent of the heated space for dry bulk storage.

Wow, I didn't know I had that much to say. Patterns are important, though, because they are the things that make a good house work and a bad one fail.

Now the ball is in your court. Use the critical dimensions and patterns to turn your bubble diagram into a floor plan. Go to the stationery store and buy a pad of 8 × 8 gridded tracing paper. The lines on the paper are straight and at right angles. The 1/8-inch grid translates to 1 foot in the real house, so you can use an ordinary ruler (¹⁄₁₆ inch = ½ foot, ⅛ inch = 1 foot, ½ inch = 4 feet, etc.), and the whole house should fit nicely on a single sheet of 8½″ × 11″ paper.

This is the most time-consuming step of all, but it should also be the most fun. Expecting great things, I am —

Your friend,
Charlie

Dear Charlie,

Well, here it is. Jean is better at making neat little things, so I gave her the graph paper and ruler. But I still find it difficult to believe that such an apparently direct and simple diagram could have been cause for so much head scratching, table pounding, and even a few moments when I thought Jean was about to slap me up the side of my head.

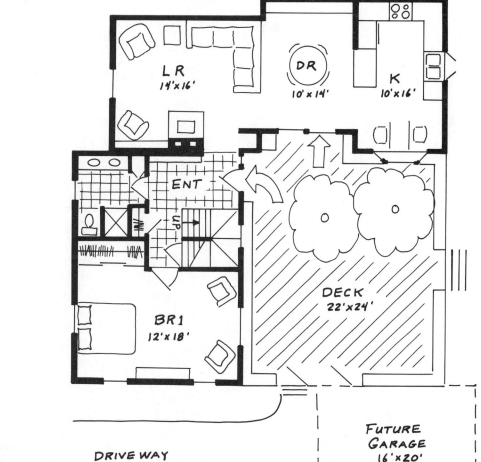

6. Jean's floor plan

Part of the problem with blueprints, if that's what this can be called, is our unfamiliarity with dimensions. I know you said the Sears catalogue could help, and your standard measurements — your table of critical dimensions — for everyday household items were of some use. But it's amazing to me how Jean and I could spend most of our lives looking at the same easy chair and footstool (Daddy's chair) or the same sofa we've had since we were married without ever really understanding their dimensions. It's not only that we don't know the feet and inches — how high, how long, how wide, etcetera — but that we cannot compute what I call the living dimensions. My easy chair, for example, may be about a 34-inch cube. (I know that's right because I just measured it.) But it has to have legroom, preferably a place behind it for magazines and old newspapers, and perhaps a table beside it for the evening drink and snacks. Thus the living dimension becomes more than the absolute, and it is the living size that needs to be figured into the blueprint if the spaces are going to make any sense.

Which is why, when we went through the process of producing this small but excruciatingly important bit of paper you now have in your hands, I went wandering through the house with my arms about half-outstretched, like Moses wandering in the wilderness. I was trying to get some idea of the spaces that feel right and comfortable, that give you room to move yet aren't so vast you begin to lose the sense of orientation, of place.

Jean said I looked like a comic imitation of the Frankenstein monster, but I kept at it. And, for me anyway, it works. It helps me relate to some of the more precise numbers you so helpfully included in your table. In my Frankenstein configuration, as it turns out, my arms span about 5 feet, give or take a few inches. When I walk along a hallway (in someone else's home or in a public building) and my hands touch both walls, I know the hall is a bit narrow to fit my personal living dimension.

Once I got this point across to Jean, the back-and-forth talk over the sketches for blueprints became a bit more civilized. We switched from arguing about the length and breadth of things to a more productive discussion of your architectural patterns.

I've got to say this, though. You can get in trouble introducing concepts. These architectural patterns, for example, are a whole new way for us of looking at shelter space, of considering the outdoors as an integral part of the whole. For a while there we got carried away with the recognition that every element of a home must relate. Trees, the garden — all the outdoor spaces tie in with the entrance on the outside, yet the entrance must also make sense on the inside. It must bring visitors into a place they recognize as welcoming, as moving them toward the center and the people within, as opposed to making them feel as if they've stepped into a waiting room in a tax examiner's office.

All this has led to some modifications to the basic bubble diagram we were so satisfied with just a couple of weeks or so ago. I'm sure you expected this; you've been through it before. But I'll tell you, I was so delighted after Jean and I finally agreed on where to put the bubbles that I had to grit my teeth and promise myself to be flexible when I realized the bubbles were merely a guide, not the absolute definition. You know me; once I think I've got a job done, I hate learning I've got to go back and do more of it.

But there was no standing pat after we shared your insights about architectural patterns. You'll note, I'm sure, the two trees that appear to grow right through the deck, which someday they will. You could say you planted the seeds for those trees when you talked about tree places and how trees can define outdoor space. No sooner had Jean read that but, wham, she had two of them growing through the deck.

I tucked the wood box into the far corner of the living room. And I did it in spite of what you had to say about not putting closets on outside walls for thermal insulation. The wood box is where it is because it can be filled so easily. When I carry wood in through the door, I'm just a step away from where it needs to be stored. In our last house I came through the door and along the entrance hall, turned a corner, and went all the way across the living room before I got to the hearth. As you can guess, I left a fine trail of pine needles, bark, and several crawling creatures among the muddy footprints each time I made the journey. This is not a practice I recommend unless you happen to like being berated as a slob and other epithets too ungracious to mention.

This tale about the wood box is, in a way, a parable of architectural patterns. Except that I would phrase it a bit differently, if I were as clever as you. My terminology would concern daily activities, the patterns of routine, the practice of living. Each of these terms involves an image in my head, a collection of the details that make up a day and a night in a home: the twenty-four-hour spans that, for most of us, vary only slightly. We eat, sleep, read, wash, work, talk, listen, and go to get the mail in pretty much the same ways every day.

I think that it's important to have a realistic and detailed understanding of these routines when you start making hard decisions about the details of a blueprint. Jean, for example, never likes to be caught short when unexpected visitors arrive. And, with seven children plus their spouses and close friends out there, given to dropping by whenever the spirit moves them, she has good reasons for her storage compulsion. Therefore there's plenty of cabinet space in the kitchen and more under the entire length of the storage space that runs along the dining room's outer wall.

And what you don't see in the blueprint (and believe me, there is almost as much left out of a blueprint as there is included) is the cellar under the bedroom / entrance hall area. That underground space, that wonderful space the earth keeps from freezing, is a superb storage area as well as a place for the backup furnace, the washing machine, and my collection of fishing lures.

With well-designed shelves and perhaps even some cupboards to help keep the dust out, a cellar adds a significant amount of storage space for all the sorts of supplies Jean feels compelled to keep on hand. You remember, I'm sure, that our previous home had no cellar; it was built on concrete posts, as you recommended. That was about all we could do (within financial reason) at that particular site. We built on a whaleback, a bulge of glacial granite sprung from the center of the earth. Blasting solid rock and spending solid hunks of money was the only way we could have had a cellar there.

We kept telling ourselves we didn't miss it, but we did, Jean far more than I. We missed it so much that we've already decided that this, our compact home — our snug, secure, and sensible place — must have a cellar. So when we decide on a site (which raises more questions), we're going to be certain we choose one that can be dug, not blasted.

The major problem I have with blueprints, Charlie, is my inability to transpose lines to actual space. I cannot, as I hope most builders can, look at a set of lines and put myself within them — not easily. I have, on occasion, taken strings and small stakes, gone out to the yard, and inscribed dimensions on the sod. However, I've learned that a bit of string on the ground is not the same as a wall. And there is no ceiling, which further distorts the true nature of the interior dimensions that will exist.

It's a learning process I'm still involved with, this transposition. I'll give you an example. The second story of the home you see on these blueprints is a dandy place for a bedroom. Jean and I like the sense of privacy; we love the skylights. The prospect of lying in bed and looking up at the stars is enough to send me racing up the stairs to get to bed early.

But check out the study. It measures 6′ × 8′. I did the string thing on our living-room floor, and I found I could sit inside a 6′ × 8′ space with enough room left over for a typewriter. And that's how I make my living: sitting at a typewriter. There wasn't, however, enough room left for much else, and over the years I've learned I accumulate a great deal of "else." Newspapers, magazines, notebooks, photographs, books and more books, even a few rocks collected from beaches I visit . . . it's all "else," and it gets brought to my study because I collected it and I want it close by.

Okay. The "else" is one problem. Then take a look at the upstairs bath. If I'm meditating, as I usually do after breakfast, and someone opens that bathroom door, both my knees are likely to be fractured.

What I'm saying — and this is my first disagreement with you — is that even though your space formulas may tell you that 6′ × 8′ is enough for a study, and 6′ × 10′ enough for a bath, I find that by understanding how to transpose those dimensions, they are too constricting for me. "For me" is the key element. The space could be fine for someone else, someone without my pack-rat eclecticism, but after a bit of work with my transposition theory and process, I've been spattered with the first seeds of doubt.

And since we completed this blueprint, they have sprouted. Which is what I mean about the problems involved with trying to circumscribe lives and concepts with straight lines on a two-dimensional piece of paper. I don't like to lock every option within those lines.

I like to stay loose, a bit flexible. I like to allow for change even as construction proceeds. This, I realize, is not an attitude highly regarded by mortgage lenders or the folks who issue building permits. So we'll let this blueprint stand . . . for now.

I guess I feel somewhat the same way about blueprints as a Maine carpenter I was told about. The fellow doing the telling was one of the several young, would-be carpenters we had working on our first place. I met him on Main Street a few years later, and he told me he had liked working with wood and hammers so much that he decided to make carpentering and building his career.

"I've still got a lot to learn," he said, "but I've been apprenticing to an old-timer, and I can tell you, working alongside someone who knows what he's doing is one of the best ways I know to get educated."

We talked on awhile, and he told me a story about blueprints I'll always remember, perhaps because it fits my notions of them.

He and his senior partner were building an addition to a restaurant, a kind of closed-in porch that was going to give the owner more space for tables with a view.

"When I got to the job," my young friend said, "I noticed the old-timer didn't have any blueprints around. But I followed his instructions and figured he must have a set of plans somewhere. But days went by, and still no blueprints. And he was building in spaces for windows as we put together the framing for the outside wall. I kept asking myself, How does he know where the windows are supposed to go?

"I got so I couldn't stand it any longer, and one morning as he was about to start framing another window, I asked him: 'How do you know where these windows are supposed to go? I haven't seen a set of blueprints since we started this job.'

" 'Well,' the old-timer said, 'I just keep building this wall until I feel a window coming on. When the feeling gets real strong, I put one in.' "

I'm not saying *we* should build our home that way, Charlie, but let me tell you what's in the back of my mind about how I might change this blueprint as we go along.

Knowing how much Jean values her storage space, and how much "else" I seem compelled to collect, I'm thinking of moving my study. Charlie, don't get upset. Not that much will change. Just as the cellar doesn't show on the blueprint, neither does the space over the garage.

But there is space there, under that peaked roof. All we have to do is put a basic floor over the garage rafters, put a window on the east end and a skylight in the south slope of the roof, and I'll have a dandy work space, even more quiet, more private, and more remote than that small space upstairs in the house. What's more, I'll have all sorts of room for my "else" under the eaves, where the roof slope gets too low for anything but storage.

If we make this change, the upstairs bath can grow enough to eliminate the risk of bruising the knees of someone reading on the throne, and Jean can use the space left over for the storage she never seems to have enough of.

Blueprints are not etched in stone. That's my point, Charlie. Not even this one that Jean and I have worked on for so long. Staying loose (just a bit), understanding individual compulsions and idiosyncrasies, and being able to translate lines into a sense of space — these are also elements that must be considered and reconsidered if a blueprint is going to come alive, is going suddenly to be able to be "seen" as the living space it will someday become.

The process is fascinating to me and Jean. It's more fun than television, more entertaining than crosswords or backgammon, and more challenging than anything else you can do indoors with a pencil and graph paper. I think most people will find themselves totally and delightfully preoccupied with drawing blueprints of *their* personal home, even if they aren't planning to build right away. Once they get to know some of the rules, once they are able to understand the blueprint vocabulary, and once they have been informed about critical dimensions and architectural patterns, they can produce a blueprint that's as appropriate and sensible as any done by an architect.

We have, with your help. We have the light, the sense of the outdoors, the snugness, and the efficiency that we want. We have a consciousness of the weather, a variety of windows, a harmony with the sun's travels, and a space pattern that works . . . almost. I'm still reserving the right to move my study.

That is what I believe blueprints are all about. They get as many ideas in place as they possibly can, which is not the same as saying they eliminate the possibility of adding other ideas as they occur, if they do. I hope you agree, Charlie. If I don't get a loud phone call or a nasty letter, I'll assume so.

Your friend,
John

3. Site and Climate

Dear Charlie,

More than a week has passed, and you haven't called to tell us that our blueprint, or any part of it, is a disaster. From which we can only conclude that it meets with your approval, although I'd bet a pair of World Series tickets that you'll show up at our door one of these days with a "few" suggestions for improving the floor plans. That's okay. Your suggestions have always been provocative. They make us think, even though they don't always persuade us to agree and/or acquiesce.

Not having heard from you (by the way, are you feeling in good health? I'll have to call to make certain you don't have the flu), we just couldn't wait any longer to start looking for land. The "site" is how you refer to it; most of us amateurs simply call it a piece of land.

For weeks we've been collecting clippings from the Land for Sale sections in the local papers' classified ads. They consistently read as if the property being sold is a working diamond mine that the owner is forced to abandon for a fraction of its real value. Now, Jean and I know not every piece of land is as perfect as its marketers claim, but we are also certain that we do not know how to evaluate properly each building site we've looked at or plan to look at.

There is, however, a basic point of view I take with me each time we go exploring a site. It was put there some thirty years ago by one of my fishing partners and close friends I met during those years I spent working on the water as a commercial fisherman. Hurricanes were routine autumnal visitors on eastern Long Island, and whenever the warnings came through those Septembers, Jim and I would have to move our boat, skiff, and dory to the places we considered safe in any storm. The first of my fishing Septembers, I was surprised when Jim took the 42-foot "big" boat up a small saltwater creek, around a sharp turn in a marshy canal, and into a small cove — a place so confining that we could reach the large oak trees on the shore with our bow and stern lines. Once we had finished the job of making the boat fast, it was obvious that a hurricane would have to obliterate the entire county before our prize possession could be significantly damaged. Yet, looking at the cove casually, I had always assumed it would be too shallow to float a 42-foot boat. Jim had made no assumptions; he had measured the depth.

"Pick your spot, Cap," he said. "Always pick your spot."

The criteria for that particular spot were: enough water to float the boat, protection from winds around the compass, places to tie the four lines from each of the craft's quarters, and an absence of other watercraft that could break loose and ram ours.

I never forgot that episode. When Jean and I do choose our site, it will definitely be "our spot" — one that fits our personal lives as well as it meets the needs of the compact home that will be built there.

As I've said in earlier letters, we want a snug place, one that consumes a minimum of energy but still allows us a sense of comfort. Living twenty (or even ten) miles from the nearest community that offers the basic services is not, in our opinion, energy efficient. Round-trips to the store can roll up a considerable amount of mileage, and Jean's new career would just about mandate that we continue to be a two-car family.

But if we find a place within reasonable walking distance of essential stores and services, we will save both energy and money. And with a bonus: If I do more walking every day, I'm sure my body will be grateful. Writing is such a sedentary occupation! My waistline and my muscle tone cry out for some regular exercise.

Fine. We locate a site close to town. But there's a catch. I'm still enough of an iconoclast and nature lover to want the place to have a bit of ground, a view, and a sense of the country, even though it's close enough to town to meet our energy criteria.

Now this is a combination that we have learned isn't easy to find. We don't, for example, want a long driveway. We had one at our former place and loved the privacy it assured. But it also assured considerable snowplowing and shoveling, which wasn't all that bad when we had the boys to help. They are men now, and while I'm not averse to shoveling a considerable amount of snow, I'm not looking forward to coping with a drive that is more than a half-mile long while Marshall is in Detroit (in a condo, by the way) and Sam is in Bangor.

If you're still with me, Charlie, you begin to sense the dimensions of our current search. What we want, in so many words, is a place that offers all the amenities and privacy of that former home on the point that was miles from town, except this time we want none of the inconvenience or expense of the distance that guaranteed our solitude and our daily contact with natural presences.

The only sensible strategy seems to be to keep looking, no matter how discouraged we may be at the end of a day that began with good leads and finished with dead ends.

But, as my grandfather used to say, all things work for the best. So let's assume he was correct, and these months of pondering and weeks of searching do lead us to the location we want. Location in these terms being a spot, not a site in the technical sense that you use the word.

We'll locate, but we may not know all we need to about the site. I mean, how can we tell by looking at what we consider a fine location whether the soil will allow us energy-efficient waste disposal (if we are not supplied with town sewerage lines)? And what do we look for in terms of our solar orientation, our protection from the weather? How can we tell if we'll be relatively cool in the summer, naturally air-conditioned, as it were? And will the winter snows pile higher beside our home than they do at our nearest neighbor's?

There are, as you can see, Charlie, a great many questions about site details that Jean and I will have trouble answering. That, my friend, is the reason I hasten to get this in the mail before we make a decision on a location. Knowing you, I'm sure you'll respond with what we need to know about a site.

Meanwhile, wish us luck as we follow every good lead. One of these days we'll find a trail that goes to just the spot we want, and not a dead end.

Your friend,
John

LETTER
9 *Dear John and Jean,*

What are the qualities of a good site? Oh boy, this is going to be a long letter! Landscape architects say you can't build a good house on a bad site. Believe it! "Good site" does not refer to purchase price or proximity to schools or distance to the nearest fire hydrant; it refers to *habitability* and *comfort*.

Few subjects excite me more, so put another log on the fire, get a cup of tea, and settle into your favorite reading chair.

First of all, what is comfort? Physiologists have devised a diagram they call the human comfort zone (Illustration 7). It is defined as the range of air temperatures (vertical scale, on the left) and relative humidities (horizontal scale, on the bottom) over which the average person in ordinary indoor clothing is neither too hot nor too cold when sitting. You'll be amused at one of the "objective" ways these scientists obtained their highly subjective data. Without informing their subjects, they measured the production of widgets by factory workers while varying temperature and humidity in the factory. When productivity fell off, they assumed the workers were uncomfortable. Sounds gross, but I can't fault their logic!

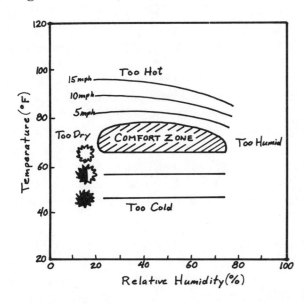

7.

All married couples know that when two people sit in the same area, one can be comfortable while the other complains of the cold. Obviously there is a certain amount of variability between individuals. There are also cultural, regional, and seasonal differences; witness Darwin's observation of the natives of Tierra del Fuego sweating by the fire Darwin had lit to stay warm. Closer to home, 50 degrees Fahrenheit seems frigid in July but absolutely balmy in January. So take the comfort zone as an indication of relative comfort. The principle still holds true.

According to Illustration 7, the average person is comfortable within the temperature range of 65 to 78 degrees Fahrenheit and the relative humidity range of 20 to 80 percent. Beyond these limits we generally turn on the furnace, the fan, the humidifier, or the air conditioner.

However, we may not always have to turn to mechanical devices for comfort outside the core comfort zone. The sets of lines above and below the core zone indicate how the entire zone can be pushed upward by a breeze (either mechanical or natural) and downward by radiation received by the body (either artificial or solar). The effect of a breeze is to lower the felt temperature by about 1 degree for each mile per hour of speed, so in a steady breeze of 7 miles per hour the average person should be comfortable from 72 degrees (65 + 7) to 85 degrees (78 + 7). The effect of radiation is to lower the comfort zone by approximately 20 degrees per solar equivalent (20 degrees for full sunshine or its equivalent). In full sunshine, the average lightly clothed person should be comfortable from 45 degrees (65 − 20) to 58 degrees (78 − 20). I have personally confirmed this effect by sitting comfortably in my shirtsleeves in a windless spot on my deck in December when the air temperature was 45 degrees.

Similar effects can be achieved with a fan and a wood stove. What excites me, however, is the possibility of achieving comfort over the incredible range of 45 to 85 degrees without heavy clothing or energy-consuming heating or cooling systems. Our 500,000-year evolution has equipped us, like the other warm-blooded animals, to deal with significant temperature variations. Much of what I'll describe further on has to do with the selection and use of building sites that capitalize on nature's climatic variability.

Climate

Climate is measured by the same four variables that define the human comfort zone: temperature, humidity, wind, and radiation. The ranges of all are so great that it is useful to break them into two distinct categories: macro (large) and micro (small).

It was long ago discovered that placing meteorologic instruments at least 6 feet above ground resulted in more consistent readings among locations. So all of the data of the National Weather Service come from instruments placed to represent large geographic areas. These are the data given in your daily weather report; they describe the macroclimate. On the other hand, instruments placed close to the ground record surprisingly large variations resulting from such effects as ground moisture, vegetation, and topography. These data describe the microclimate of the specific spot.

A climatic study in Ohio illustrates the difference between macroclimate and microclimate. The macroclimate was represented by 88 weather-bureau observation points distributed throughout the state of Ohio, an area of roughly 40,000 square miles. The microclimate was measured at 109 close-to-the-ground spots within an area of only a quarter of a square mile in the Neotoma Valley. Look at the results in Table 2; need I say more?

Table 2

MACROCLIMATE VS. MICROCLIMATE
(TEMPERATURES IN DEGREES FAHRENHEIT)

Variable	Macroclimate (entire state)	Microclimate (within valley)
Maximum temperature	91° to 102°	75° to 113°
Variation	11°	38°
Minimum temperature	−6° to −20°	14° to −26°
Variation	14°	40°
Growing season	138 to 197 days	124 to 276 days
Variation	59 days	152 days

TEMPERATURE. I have enclosed four macroclimatic temperature maps. The first (Illustration 8) shows the summer design temperature, or temperature exceeded during only 2½ percent of summer hours.

The Macroclimate

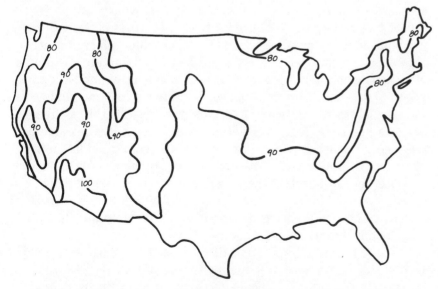

8. Summer design temperature (level above which temperature rises during 2½ percent of time in summer)

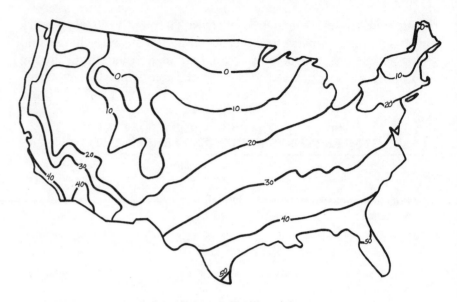

9. Winter design temperature (level below which temperature falls during 2½ percent of time in winter)

The second (Illustration 9) shows the corresponding winter design temperature, or temperature below which the mercury dips during only 2½ percent of winter hours. This map shows a lot more variation, which explains why more northerners go south every winter. The variation is due primarily to the lower angle and less even heating effect of the sun in winter. Both coasts reflect two strong macroclimatic effects. The first is the *adiabatic* (without addition or subtraction of heat) cooling effect of altitude. You probably enjoyed the cooling effect of letting air out of people's tires when you were a kid, John. When air expands, it cools. When air rises in the atmosphere, it similarly expands and cools, though not so dramatically. This natural cooling rate is about 6 degrees per 1,000 feet of elevation, explaining why the same people who go south in the winter go to the mountains in the summer. The second effect is the moderating influence of large bodies of water on adjacent shores. Looking at the coast of New England, you can see why people play golf all winter on Cape Cod and why the pea-planting date is nearly the same for New York City as for Halifax, Nova Scotia.

The third map (Illustration 10) lists annual cooling-degree days. Under the vastly oversimplified assumption that people will turn on the air conditioner whenever the average daily temperature exceeds 65 degrees, cooling-degree days are the annual sum of the daily excesses over 65 degrees. (For example, if the average temperature on a summer day is 75 degrees, 10 degrees of cooling

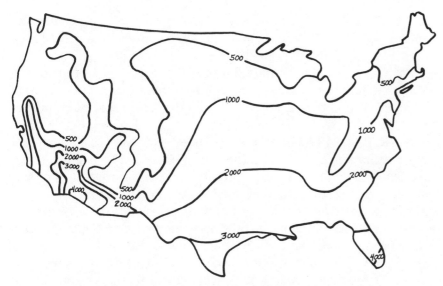

10. Cooling-degree days, base 65 degrees Fahrenheit

are necessary, which counts as 10 cooling-degree days.) But any-one who has lived in Hartford, Connecticut, or Washington, D.C., can tell you that humidity is a factor as well.

The fourth map (Illustration 11) shows annual heating-degree days, the annual sum of the daily deficits of the average daily temperature below 65 degrees. The analogous theory, of course, is that heating fuel will be burned when the average outdoor temperature dips below 65 degrees.

Both cooling- and heating-degree days are pretty fair indicators of the relative costs of cooling and heating identical houses in different climates. In other words, don't move to either Houston or International Falls, Minnesota.

11. Heating-degree days, base 65 degrees Fahrenheit

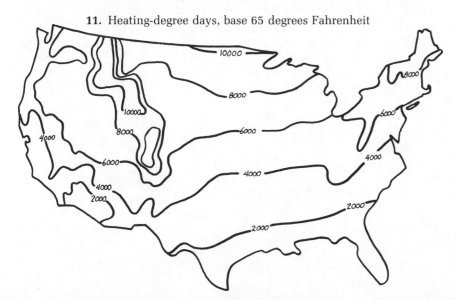

HUMIDITY. Relative humidity — the actual moisture content of air compared with its maximum possible content, expressed as a percentage — is of greatest interest in summer, when it frequently exceeds the comfort limit of 80 percent. Note the curved upper limit of the human comfort zone (see Illustration 7); this means that a breeze has less cooling effect at higher humidities.

SOLAR RADIATION. It may surprise you that the amount of solar radiation received at the outer edge of the earth's atmosphere is actually 7 percent greater in winter than in summer because the earth is then closer to the sun. (Remember *that* the next time your pipes freeze.) The average radiation for the entire year is called the solar constant and amounts to 429 Btu (British thermal units) per square foot per hour (1 Btu is the amount of energy that will heat a pint of water by 1 degree). What happens on average to that solar bonanza is shown in Illustration 12. Of the 429 Btu, 16 percent is absorbed and turned to heat by air molecules; 28 percent is reflected back to space by clouds; 26 percent is scattered or reflected but ultimately finds its way to the earth diffusely (from all directions); and 11 percent is similarly scattered but back into space. Only 19 percent reaches the earth uninterrupted as direct radiation.

Therefore, less than half of all extraterrestrial solar energy ever reaches the earth's surface. Unfortunately, like income, the distribution is uneven. Illustration 13 shows how much solar energy falls on the earth during January. People living in Phoenix are getting more than their fair share; people living in Buffalo should move.

12. What happens to solar radiation received at outer edge of atmosphere

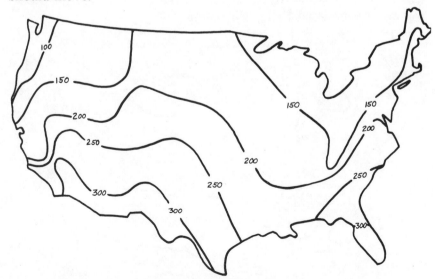

13. Solar energy received at surface of earth in January, in langleys

WIND. In winter, moving air is called wind; in summer, it is fondly referred to as a breeze. Our differing feelings about the identical phenomenon are due to the effect of moving air on the comfort zone. In winter we are too cold already, so the windchill increases our discomfort; in summer we are too hot, and the same cooling effect is welcome.

Fortunately, the winter wind and the summer breeze are very often from differing directions. The enclosed maps (Illustrations 14 and 15) show average wind directions for January and July.

Here on the coast of Maine, the prevailing winter wind is from the north and northwest, while in summer the prevailing breeze is from the south and southwest. Your house should take

14. Average wind direction in January

15. Average wind direction in July

advantage of nature's changeability by turning its back to the winter wind and opening up to the summer breeze. Trees planted as a shelterbelt to the northwest would block the wind but not the breeze. More about that when I describe the microclimate.

The Microclimate

If you're getting drowsy, get another cup of tea, because what follows should knock your socks off. The microclimatic effects I'm about to describe have the potential of "moving" your house 1,000 miles north or south.

TEMPERATURE. The most powerful microclimatic temperature effect is cold-air ponding. You've probably witnessed the phenomenon but not understood it. Here's what happens.

All objects in nature continually give off heat by radiation. The rate at which an object radiates heat energy is strongly (to the fourth power) proportional to its temperature. Since all objects in the universe continually radiate in all directions, all objects are both radiating and receiving at the same time. Whether an object receives more heat than it radiates and thus warms up or suffers a net loss and cools down depends on the relative temperatures of the object and its surroundings. The net flow of heat energy is always from warmer to cooler surfaces.

On a clear night the surface of the ground faces outer space, and boy, is that cold — 459 degrees below zero! Clearly, the surface of the ground cools, and it does so rapidly. The air near the ground cools by contact with the surface. Cool air is heavier, more dense, than warm air. Therefore, the heavy cold air acts like water in seeking the lowest level. If on a hillside, it will flow downward and stop only at the lowest point.

In this way, cold-air ponds tend to accumulate in low-lying areas on clear nights, especially when there is no wind to mix the layers of air. You've seen these ponds; you drive over a hill, and there before you in a low spot is a ghostly pond of fog. The air that has settled into the depression has cooled to below its dew point, resulting in fog. If the temperature is below freezing, what is produced is not fog but frost.

The most dramatic example of this phenomenon I've read of is the Gstettneralm sinkhole in Austria. Illustration 16 shows the temperatures measured there on a clear January night just before sunrise, when the pond had built to its maximum extent. At the top of a nearby hill 400 feet above the bottom of the depression the air temperature was 29 degrees, but at the bottom of the

16. Temperatures on a clear January night in the Gstettneralm sinkhole in Austria

hole the temperature was −20 degrees! Sounds like a good place to build one's mother-in-law a home.

Illustration 17 shows what happens in the similar geometry of a valley over a twenty-four-hour period. The curves represent hourly temperatures at three points in a valley. I'm sure Jean can relate this to her garden. From the curves it is clear that the slope is the best garden spot: It gets warmer than the peak, but it runs far less risk of frost than the bottom of the valley in spring and fall. This illustration also shows why so many early European villages and monasteries were located on mountain slopes rather than in valleys.

One might discount the last two illustrations due to their extreme topography, but here's one closer to home no one can ignore. Illustration 18 shows the lowest overnight temperatures at three points in a field that most people would consider flat. A slight depression of 5 feet across a 300-foot-wide field collected a pond of air 4 degrees colder than the air at the high ground, in this case producing a frost.

Now you know why the weatherman says, "There may be frost in some of the low-lying areas tonight." Just be sure you didn't plant your garden in one of them.

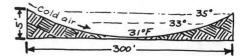

17. Temperatures over a twenty-four-hour period at the bottom, on the slope, and at the peak of a valley

18. Distribution of minimum overnight temperatures across a "flat" field

SOLAR RADIATION. Our word *climate* is derived from the Greek *klimat*, meaning inclination in relation to the sun. Those Greeks were no fools. I'm going to show you three instances in which microclimate is altered by the ground's inclination to the sun.

Southern slopes. Earlier I explained that 19 percent of the total extraterrestrial radiation reaches the earth's surface directly. *Directly* means in the form of parallel rays, as if from a flashlight. Illustration 19 shows a bundle of such rays striking three different surfaces: (A) tilted 20 degrees south toward the sun, (B) horizontal, (C) tilted 20 degrees north away from the

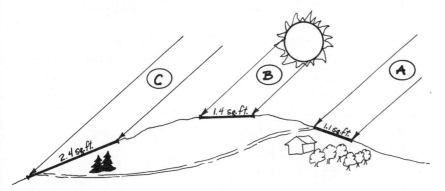

19. Areas covered by 1.0 square foot of solar radiation at slopes of 0 degrees and 20 degrees north and south

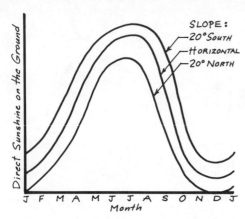

20. Annual variation in direct solar radiation on level and sloped ground surfaces at 48 degrees north latitude

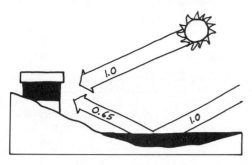

21. Increased winter solar radiation through windows of a house north of a body of water

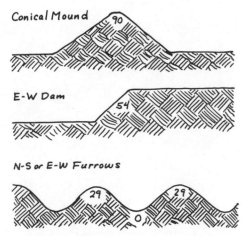

22. Increased solar-heat gain (Fahrenheit degrees × hours) of various earth mounds relative to flat ground

sun. Since the very same bundle of rays — and therefore the same amount of energy — strikes all three surfaces, the heating effect on each is inversely proportional to the areas of the surfaces. The intensity, or heating effect, on the south slope is twice that on the north slope.

Illustration 20 shows the relative amounts of direct radiation received each month of the year at 48 degrees north latitude for similar slopes: (A) 20 degrees to the south, (B) horizontal, (C) 20 degrees to the north. The differences are most striking in the winter months, when the rays of the sun are received from the lowest angles. In fact, during the month of December the north-facing slope receives no direct radiation at all, and the south slope receives twice as much as the horizontal surface. This effect has nothing to do with the radiation received by the walls or windows of a house, but it sure makes the yard more pleasant!

In terms of the heating effect of the sun on the ground, locating on a 20-degree south slope is nearly equivalent to moving your house to flat ground 20 degrees, or 1,360 miles, to the south!

Reflection from water. Both water and ice are highly reflective of solar radiation at the low angles typical of winter. Illustration 21 shows the benefit of placing a house just to the north of a body of water. Measurements show an increase of up to 65 percent in radiation received through south-facing windows due to the reflected component, and with no increased heat loss at night.

Solar gardens. Back to Jean's garden. Ever since I first helped in the family garden as a toddler, I remember squash, cucumbers, and corn being planted in conical mounds, while beans and potatoes were planted in furrows. I thought the mounds discouraged bugs, who wouldn't want to climb the hills. Not so. Long before agricultural engineers unraveled the mystery, plants were observed to germinate earlier and grow faster when planted in these raised earthworks. Now science has provided the answer: solar heating.

Illustration 22 shows three different soil-mounding techniques and the advantage of each over flat ground in terms of degree-hours; i.e., the accumulated hourly differences in temperature between the mounds and level ground at a depth of 2 inches. The conical mound is clearly best; assuming the excess temperature to be spread over ten daylight hours, the mound would average 9 degrees warmer than level ground. The drills shown are oriented north–south. Drills oriented east–west show 25 percent less gain than those oriented north–south.

WIND. Thinking of wind in terms of water helps in visualizing its motion and resulting effects. Although we see wind indirectly in the motion of falling leaves and snowflakes, our perceptions are warped by the falling motion of these relatively dense objects. Likewise, the rising of a warm buoyant plume from a smokestack disguises the natural motion of the wind.

Water, on the other hand, is closer in density to its suspended objects. The motion of tea leaves and the "snow" in those little glass paperweights is very close to the motion of the water itself. Therefore, try to think of the effects I'm about to describe as occurring in water, and I'm sure you'll come away with a better feel for the motion of air.

Illustration 23 shows what happens when wind blowing from the left encounters an obstacle. The fact that air is compressible relative to water is not an important factor at the wind speeds we are dealing with. The wind cannot go through the barrier, so it goes over or around. As the wind rises to clear the barrier, it drags the air close to the barrier on the windward side into a circular eddy. Once over the barrier, the moving air produces frictional drag on the relatively stationary air behind the barrier and thus causes similar circular eddies. Finally, at a typical downwind distance of about ten to fifteen barrier heights, the wind returns to its full strength. As you'll see as you read on, the degree of penetrability of the barrier has a large effect on the back eddies, since air moving straight through the barrier will counter and diminish their backward motion.

Shelterbelts. Illustration 24 shows the effects on wind speed of four types of shelterbelt (strips of forest). The vertical scale is in percent of original undisturbed wind speed. The horizontal scale represents horizontal distance: upwind (to the left of the shelterbelt) and downwind (to the right of the shelterbelt), measured in average tree heights.

Shelterbelt B, made of dense evergreens, is so dense throughout its height that the wind intensity is reduced to essentially zero within the forest. Belt C is semipenetrable at the bottom so that some air moving through the lower forest level emerges to counter the first reverse eddy downwind of the belt. A minimum wind intensity occurs where the opposing air currents meet, at a distance of about five tree heights downwind. Belt D is quite open beneath, with the result that the higher wind intensity pushes the minimum point downwind to about eight tree heights. Finally, Belt A, a deciduous forest in winter, is penetrable throughout its height and blocks the wind the least of all.

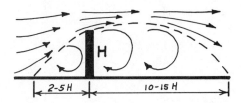

23. Air currents around a solid barrier

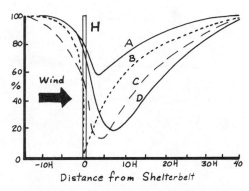

24. Wind-speed reduction due to four types of shelterbelt: (A) penetrable throughout, (B) dense throughout, (C) semipenetrable beneath, (D) open beneath

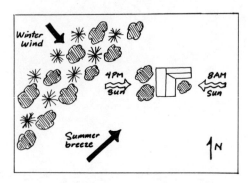

25. Planting to block both winter wind and summer sun

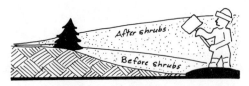

26. Snow accumulation (snow drift) downwind of shrubs of height H

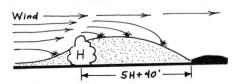

27. Charlie's friend Ralph before and after planting a snow fence of shrubs

Before jumping to the conclusion that the place to be is inside the forest, however, consider what the wind does in summer. If the wind were to blow from the opposite direction, as it does here in Maine in summer, you would have no ventilating breeze either. If you instead placed your house five tree heights downwind of the winter wind, you would find yourself also five tree heights upwind of the summer breeze. You'd therefore get only 10 to 15 percent of the winter wind but 80 percent of the summer breeze. Illustration 25 further shows how you could place your house to block winter winds from both the north and northwest, but not block breezes from either the south or southwest.

Snow fences. A snow fence is a small-scale artificial shelterbelt. A row of shrubs performs the same job as the highway department's stick-and-wire version but looks better and never wears out. Illustration 26 shows how wind-driven snow is stopped by such a barrier. Loose, freshly fallen snow is picked up and carried by a strong wind. Encountering the fence or shrubs, the wind speed drops, as shown in the illustration. With a drop in speed, the wind must drop the snow. Some snow is dropped upwind of the fence, but most is dropped at the point of minimum wind intensity. The empirical formula in the illustration shows how far upwind of a road or driveway you should place your snow fence. For example, a 4-foot-high fence or a row of 4-foot-high shrubs should be planted 60 feet upwind ($5 \times 4 + 40 = 60$).

I'm sure I'll forget $e = mc^2$ long before $L = 5H + 40$, thanks to poor Ralph, who bought my old place ten years ago. The first winter Ralph was annoyed, as I had been, by the way the snow piled up in the driveway just downwind of a small embankment. The next spring Ralph set about curing the problem with his own version of a snow fence, a dense row of shrubs. Unfortunately, he had not observed snow fences as keenly as he might have (didn't ask the locals either, due to their lack of college education), and so he planted the shrubs so that the point of maximum snow drop occurred precisely on his driveway (Illustration 27). He never did figure out what happened. He moved the next year, and his snow fence continues to be a money-maker for the local snowplower to this day.

Your friend,
Charlie

4. Site Services

Dear Charlie,

Hey, guess what? We have a piece of land, a site, a place to put our new home . . . however you want to express it.

I'm not certain of its macroclimate or microclimate, but I do know it can have the proper solar orientation, and it already has a sort of shelterbelt, if that's what you can call the line of trees between our land (yes, we already bought it, and without consulting you further) and our neighbor to the north.

Looked at through the eyes of a scientist like you, our primary reasons for deciding may not hold up as objective or even informed. But they are our reasons, and they do have their basis in the thinking we've done about where and how we want to live.

I suppose I'd better tell you where it is, before I go much further. We've been there so many times since we first decided it might do the job that I'm assuming everyone already knows we've made a choice. But, of course, no one does; no one except the realtor and the seller.

The property is on the River Road, about three-quarters of a mile off Pleasant Street, which, as you know, puts us less than 2 miles from the center of town. And the distance from our place to that small market (and a couple of eating places) on Pleasant Street is less than a mile.

So our first requirement is more than satisfied: We are, as we wanted to be, close to town.

And meeting that requirement was not easy. Many of the ads we answered were either too sketchy ("Land for sale, call . . .") or too overwritten (the "stream" turned out to be drainings from a culvert under the road), leaving us a bit desperate about whether we could ever find what we wanted.

And, as I've said before, some of the realtors weren't much help. Even though we told them we wanted a location close to town, they spent much of their time and mileage money driving us around the countryside. Actually, it was on a trip back from one of those fruitless searches that we first noticed what is now our land.

On the way in from the farm country, as we slowed for the more heavily settled area of the River Road, Jean happened to notice this rather spacious lot with a small For Sale sign in its roadside corner. There was no phone number on the sign, nor any indication of how a prospective buyer might go about getting more information. So we asked the real estate salesperson at the wheel if she knew anything about the land; by that time we'd already gone by.

"Oh, that lot," she said, as if she'd known of its availability for some time. "Yes, I know the land," she went on, "but I'm not certain of the price. It's changed once or twice during the year. I'll check on it and call you tonight."

What I wondered was how come we hadn't been taken to the lot before. I mean, if the realtor knew about it, why hadn't we been shown it? Because, I suppose, people are inclined to make assumptions about other people, and the realtors had made some about us. Knowing we had sold a large house out in the country, they assumed that another place like it was what we *really* wanted, in spite of our talk about how and why we'd decided to live in town.

It could have taken another month or more for us to convince our friendly, local real estate brokers if Jean hadn't seen that sign. What I'm saying, Charlie, is that you never gave us any scientific insights about how to deal with realtors and their assumptions — although I'm sure you would have if we'd asked. Well, my advice is: Tell them fifteen different times and in fifteen different ways just what it is you're looking for, whether it be land or house, and you'll have a better chance of finding it. Better yet, keep your own eyes open and do as much of your own looking as you can.

We did, though, get a call that evening, and the price seemed right. So the next morning we were back, where we should have been all along, checking out some of the other points you have told us to keep in mind.

I have a feeling that a couple of generations ago, before this part of the country experienced the most intense growth rate in its history, our land was part of a small farm. It looks like a pasture that has only recently been allowed to go untended. There are no mature trees, just some scrubby stuff, the sort that is always the first to take over what was formerly a hay field or stock pasture.

In that sense, it's not quite what we wanted. We both had told each other a hundred times we didn't want to give up on trees altogether. Well, we compromised; there aren't any oaks or maples on the property proper, but there is a clump of 20-foot poplars in one corner and plenty of lovely tall oaks on the property line. And, on the eastern edge of the lot, where the land slopes fairly steeply to a tributary of the Androscoggin River, there is what amounts to a suburban forest. That hillside is too steep for building, and the valley is too wet. So I guess we'll have a woodsy view for a long time to come.

The news about the scarcity of trees isn't all bad, however. If we build the house in the northeast corner of the lot, we can save several poplars for the patio and otherwise have a clean sweep to the south and east. Our home will catch all the solar energy there is to be caught. And, if your numbers are correct (only joking, Charlie), the trees that line the north boundary will be our shelterbelt, exactly where it's needed.

But there are problems — problems you left unresolved in your last letter. Because this has always been a pasture, there is no existing road to the corner where we think you will agree the house should go. The lot is about 150 feet deep by about 130 feet wide, so if we put our new home near the back line, we'll have to build a new entrance road, or driveway, about 100 feet long. How much will that cost, Charlie? And how do we know the land can support a road? Will we have to truck in rocks as a road base?

I know it's a bit late to be worrying about the answers. We're like most land buyers, I suppose. We got so carried away with finding what *looked* like just what we wanted that we forgot to check on some of the nitty-gritty details, like how much it will cost to build a driveway.

I'm sure you can tell us, Charlie. I'm not so sure I want to hear the answer.

Assuming that we do build in the back corner, where we'll also have more privacy and be that much further removed from the moderately heavy road traffic, we then have to decide what to do about sewage disposal and water. When we were 10 miles from town, we had no choice. Now, if we choose, and want to pay the quarterly bills, we can run underground pipes to River Road and tie in to the town water and sewage systems. How much will that cost? Will it be more or less than we'll have to pay for our own well, and our own sewage disposal system, provided we can get one approved and have the sort of soil that makes one feasible?

You forgot to give us any of this information, Charlie. Or

maybe you didn't. Maybe you assumed we knew what we needed to know. That's an assumption you shouldn't make again. For example, I don't know what the latest policies are at the Central Maine Power Company. Will we have to pay to have electrical power hooked up to the house? How much will it cost to have the wires put underground? Can the telephone lines go in the same ditch?

What we are saying again, Charlie, is "Help!"

You know the River Road. You know the size of our home. You have the floor plan right there in your office. Now you know the size and basic features of our new site. You can visualize it almost as a square of open land in your mind's eye, with nothing there now except scrubby shrubs and tall grass, along with a delightfully private yet open southern exposure.

Got that? Okay. Now tell us everything we need to know before we decide to put in a driveway, before we commit to town water or drilling a well, before I call Central Maine Power and ask foolish questions. And, while you're at it, you might also tell us if we should use a dowser, if you also tell us we'd be better off drilling a well.

Anxiously,
John

LETTER
11

Dear John and Jean,

Your land sounds great. I once thought finding a perfect house site or a design that worked perfectly was a matter of luck, but in retrospect it always seems to happen to people who like themselves and each other — people who are "centered." I now believe it's simply a matter of being open to what is right. Rightness is all around us; we simply need to be receptive to it, whatever form it may take.

As it turns out, I'm familiar with your land. It has been on the market for more than a year without a bite. Many uptight, "uncentered" people have looked at it and, restricted to the accepted definition of a house lot, have rejected this perfectly marvelous spot! Congratulations on your discovery.

Those things you have questions about are euphemistically termed site improvements by real estate brokers and land developers. I'm not so sure they're always improvements over nature, but they do make life a good deal easier. I call them site services, and I'll deal with each in the order in which you will be needing them.

Road

We generally look for land in good weather, when the earth is dry and free of frost. We'd be better off if we looked during blizzards and the mud season, when the qualities (or absence thereof) of a good road are more obvious. Listing the qualities we seek will probably evoke memories of some not-so-successful roads from your past. Are we not looking for a road for all seasons that is:

- Inexpensive to build
- Maintenance free
- Hard-surfaced all year
- Easy to plow
- Easy to navigate in snow and ice
- Pretty, if not beautiful?

BUILDING A PROPER ROAD. Illustration 28 demonstrates in cross section the building of a proper road. Your contractor (found in the yellow pages under Excavating Contractor) will go through most if not all of the following steps:

Step 1. Remove all loose organic material, putting aside the topsoil, which will be very useful later. The ability of a road to support the weight of well-drilling rigs, concrete trucks, and other assorted indignities depends upon the bearing capacity of the soil. Topsoil has been turned over by worms, if not Rototillers, and therefore has little bearing ability. The soil below the "organic horizon," in contrast, has had thousands of years to compact. If the topsoil is sandy, gravelly, or very thin, however, your contractor may elect to leave it in place.

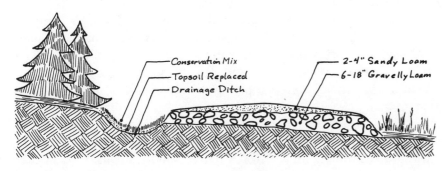

Conservation Mix
Topsoil Replaced
Drainage Ditch
2-4" Sandy Loam
6-18" Gravelly Loam

28. Ingredients for a successful dirt road

Removing large trees yourself can save a lot of money. Bull-dozer operators conform to my definition of successful people, which is to say they are doing exactly what they would as children, regardless of remuneration. They hate to get off their Mighty Dozers, especially to chain-saw trees. They are more likely to simply push 40-foot oaks over, leaving you with a hell of a mess. Instead, take the trees down yourself and cut them into firewood immediately, removing the wood to a good drying spot for next season. Have the bulldozer remove the tree stumps. This task will be a lot easier and cleaner if you leave the bulldozer 4 feet of trunk for leverage against the roots.

Step 2. The contractors will already have considered the most trouble-free route for your road (consulting with you, of course, if you had the sense to be there when they laid it out). But now they'll create drainage ditches to dispose of rain and meltwater from up slope before they spill over and erode the road surface. At the lowest points they may install culverts to pass the water from one side to the other. Contractors have uncanny built-in spirit levels and can sense where water naturally wants to go. Their ditches and culverts simply aid the natural flow rather than forcing it to spill destructively over the road. The ditches are also convenient places to push snowbanks. Elevated roads catch less snow, especially drifting snow.

Step 3. Next, a foundation of gravel thick enough to support the expected traffic without giving way and to fill the holes of the ground surface is laid. Over a sandy, well-drained soil or bedrock this foundation may not be required; on the other hand, a marshy condition may require 18 inches or more of bony gravel (mixed gravel, including large stones). The best material is generally gravelly loam, which contains just enough clay to make it hang together.

Step 4. The saved topsoil is then spread over the raw, exposed ditches, and conservation mix — a mixture of fast-growing rye and more permanent clover — is immediately seeded and covered with hay to prevent erosion.

Step 5. Contractors may at this point suffer from a compulsion to finish the job. Try to dissuade them. The road will look and perform better in the long run if allowed to age a bit. Let the well driller, concrete truck, and rain compact the foundation to its ultimate density before applying the finish coat of uniform sandy loam.

I'm sure you've noticed the crown in most roads, the slope to each side from the middle. That crown is built in not to land you in the ditch during an ice storm but to shed rainwater as quickly as possible. Nothing is more destructive of a road than standing water. On a dirt road, each passing tire mixes the water and gravel and then throws water and gravel together out of the puddle. The result is ever-deepening potholes and washboards, eventually requiring expensive regrading.

A MATTER OF AESTHETICS. The preceding steps deal with only the practical aspects of owning a road. An aesthetic consideration is shown in Illustration 29. The common approach for a driveway would be straight on in, shown in Option A, with the result that everyone can see you and you can see everyone. And since the power company likes to run its lines where it can service them by road, you will be looking at power lines as well.

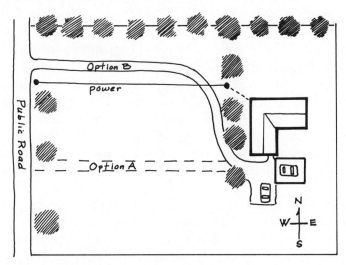

29. Two options for the layout of a driveway

I like Option B better. It's a prettier approach to the house; it pulls the power lines to one side, leaving a larger front yard; and it gives you privacy from the passing traffic. I've drawn it to suit your particular site, but the example perfectly illustrates the general principles: approach the house indirectly to afford privacy from the street; incorporate both gentle curves and straight, tree-lined stretches (beautiful in fall foliage or winter snow); consult with the power company to make sure they'll place their poles where you wish.

The price for all this beauty? A measly extra 25 percent.

Electricity

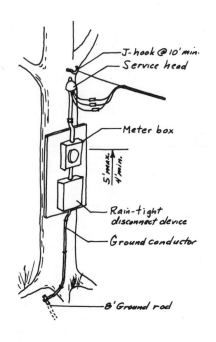

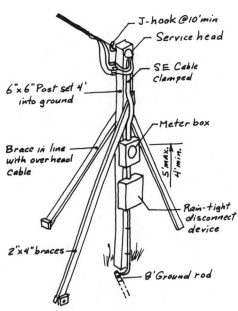

30. Temporary electric service during building

It may surprise you to learn that dealing with electric utilities has been one of the pleasures of my life. As you know, I'm invariably their opponent when it comes to building new power plants, because I simply can't see why the same investment in conservation wouldn't solve the problem in a cleaner way. But when it comes to one-on-one customer relations, they can't be beat. They arrive at your house wearing freshly ironed uniforms, bright yellow hard hats, and smiles that make John Glenn look like Attila the Hun. They apparently have no other purpose in life than to make electricity safe and convenient, if not economical. Although it was against his work rules, one fellow literally rewired my botched service entrance for free, humming all the while.

Your utility, Central Maine Power Company, is fairly representative of utilities across the United States. Because they have to conform to the standards set by the National Electric Code (more about that when I tell you about wiring your house), specifications for getting service are quite uniform. I dropped in on the line department at the local district office and picked up the booklet called "Distribution Standards." The line department is who you deal with up to the meter box. From the meter box on the outside to your service-equipment box (fuse box) on the inside, you'll be dealing with the meter department. Don't worry about your antinuclear reputation; they don't bite!

TEMPORARY SERVICE. You'll find it convenient to install a 60-ampere temporary service before the house is ready for the permanent service. You'll need a meter box (Central Maine Power provides the meter) and a rain-tight disconnect device with a ground fault interrupter. All the necessary parts are available at the hardware store, but look around first. After your house is built you'll no longer need the whole setup. You can generally buy a used system from an owner-builder, or perhaps your contractor has one. You can install the service on either a braced 6" × 6" post or on a sturdy tree, as shown.

PERMANENT SERVICE. After your siding is on — at least where you plan to install the meter — you'll be glad to get on to permanent service. It is sometimes less expensive, and it's always more convenient for the carpenters. Illustration 31 shows, but fails to explain, a few critical points. First, although the cable leading to the meter is pretty much free to run all over the outside of the house, the distance from the point of wall entry to the service-equipment box inside the house must be an *absolute min-*

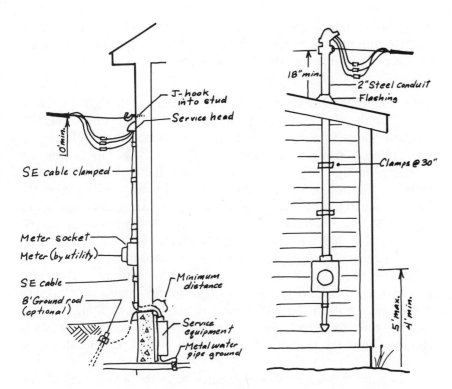

31. Installations for permanent electric service

imum. Failure to observe this rule could cost you megabucks. A friend of mine wired up thirty circuits to a service box that he had located on an inside wall rather than the outside wall directly behind the meter. The smiling man in the yellow hat made him move the box and, since electric cable doesn't stretch, *rewire* all the circuits.

The service-drop clearances (minimum height of wires) are: 10 feet over the ground, 15 feet over driveways, and 18 feet over the street. Finally, grounding can be accomplished with a number-8 copper wire connected to either a metal incoming water pipe or a copper-clad steel rod measuring ½ inch × 10 feet driven into the ground.

If the wall of your house is too short to give the required ground clearances, then install a rigid steel conduit mast, as shown in the illustration.

THE UNDERGROUND OPTION. Some people consider power and telephone lines hanging off a house unattractive. The power company offers an alternative, although usually at greater cost. It will run underground cable a maximum of 150 feet from the last pole to the meter on the house. Since you undoubtedly want your telephone in the trench also, the cable is buried at a depth of 30 inches minimum. Wherever the cable runs under a driveway or walk, it must run through a Schedule 40 polyvinyl chloride plastic pipe and at a minimum depth of 36 inches.

THE GETTING-ELECTRICITY DEAL. Okay, what's it going to cost? The deal is different for different utility companies, but the Central Maine Power deal for a new installation is as follows.

Primary power-line extension. The utility will extend its primary, or high voltage, line up to 2,000 feet per new customer (meter). Up to 1,000 feet of the total can be on private property. There is no charge for the first 300 feet. For the remainder up to 2,000 feet, the customer pays 4 cents per foot per month for 60 months, in addition to the cost of the electricity consumed.

For example, suppose your driveway is 400 feet long and starts 1,200 feet from the last electric pole on the highway. The total line extension is then 1,600 feet. (The 400 feet along your private driveway is within the 1,000-foot private-property limit.) Therefore we only have to consider the cost of 1,300 feet of line, since the first 300 feet are free: $.04 \times 1,300 = $52 per month for 60 months.

Beyond 2,000 feet, the customer pays the actual cost of the installation (estimated at $2.60 per foot for the simplest installation) plus an annual maintenance fee of 11 percent of the cost. For each additional 1,000 feet, then, the added cost would be $2,600 plus $286 per year for maintenance.

Service drop. There is no charge for an overhead service drop from the last transformer, again at a distance of up to 150 feet. For underground service, however, the customer pays for the trench, all conduit, backfilling of the trench, and a onetime charge of $125 plus $1.35 per foot. On that basis I estimate it would cost you an extra $500 for underground service. You have to decide whether it's worth it.

Telephone   I'm sorry, but I'm not getting involved in this one! I couldn't communicate with them when they were all one company. Do you imagine things have gotten better? I'm sure of just one thing: You should call the *power* company first, because the least expensive deal is for them to piggyback on the electric service.

A Surface water
B Natural spring
C Dug well
D Driven-point well
E Drilled well

32. The hydrologic cycle and sources of drinking water

HOW AND WHERE IT OCCURS. Illustration 32 shows the hydrologic cycle wherein pure water evaporates from the surface of lakes and oceans, rises into the atmosphere, and falls again as condensed rain or snow in another place. As the rain falls, it dissolves carbon dioxide from the atmosphere and becomes slightly acidic (containing carbonic acid). With more pollutants being added to the atmosphere from industrial and power plants, rain downwind of these sources is becoming increasingly acidic.

Some of the rain and snowmelt runs off the surface and collects in streams and surface ponds (A). What doesn't run off or evaporate again sinks into the ground as groundwater. The dashed line shows the water table, or level at which the ground is saturated with water. Due to the extremely slow horizontal movement of groundwater, the water table tends to follow the surface of the ground, although it rises and falls with rain and drought. Water below the minimum level of the water table, and therefore independent of the season, is called an aquifer. When an aquifer breaks the surface, the water that flows from the earth is called a spring (B).

We can also reach the water in the ground through wells: digging a hole until we reach the water table (C), driving a pointed pipe through sand to the water table (D), or drilling through solid rock to an aquifer (E).

Water

Table 3
WATER POLLUTANTS

Problem	Symptom	Correction
Muddy water	cloudy water	sand filter
Acid water	green stains under dripping faucets	neutralizing tank with marble chips or by injecting soda-ash solution
Hard water	difficulty lathering	reverse osmosis unit
Red water (iron) Black water (manganese)	red or black stains on fixtures or clothing	chlorinator followed by carbon filter
Bad odor (sulfur)	smell like rotten eggs	chlorinator followed by carbon filter

WATER PURITY. Table 3 lists the problems that can plague drinking water and what you can do about them. Unless you live on the shore of a large lake in an unpopulated area, a surface pond or lake is a bad bet. Typical pond water contains sediment from streams, microscopic algae, organic compounds from decaying vegetation, and pathogenic bacteria. Yuck!

If you live downwind of a major industrial area, both surface water and groundwater may be acidic. Acid water further dissolves calcium and magnesium from limestone and marble, leading to "hard" water in more than half of the United States (see Illustration 33). Acid water may also dissolve iron — leading to red water stains on your fixtures — and manganese, leading to black water and stains.

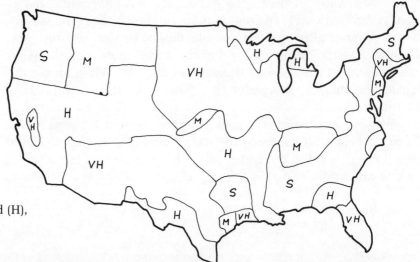

33. Water hardness: very hard (VH), hard (H), moderately hard (M), soft (S)

A bad odor, such as the smell of rotten eggs, is most likely due to decaying organic matter but may also be caused by sulfur in the ground or by industrial pollution.

Though we think of soil as dirty, the earth itself tends to purify water. As water slowly sinks through the fine soil, solids are filtered out, anaerobic bacteria are killed by the oxygen in the unsaturated soil, and then aerobic bacteria are killed by lack of oxygen at deeper levels. Finally, in an aquifer in which the water may rest for hundreds or thousands of years, even viruses expire. So we have opposing forces: The earth is adding dissolved pollutants at the same time it is removing pathogenic ones.

CITY WATER. Cities obtain their water from the same sources I mentioned earlier, although on a grander scale. Some cities have wonderful water. New York City gets its water from reservoirs in the mountains, and its tap water compares favorably with bottled water. Other cities and towns have disgusting if not dangerous water that has been filtered and chemically treated after being taken from polluted rivers and lakes. Since your street is served by the water main, you have a choice to make, John.

Unless you do a lot of lawn and garden watering, town water will probably be the least expensive option. If your water has a distinct chlorine taste, it can be removed by installing an inexpensive activated charcoal filter in the cold-water line to your kitchen sink.

But before you decide, check around the neighborhood to see what kinds of wells existed before the water main was installed and whether the well water is better or worse than town water. As a final check, have samples of both well water and town water tested by the State Department of Health. In case you decide to go with your own well, here are your three basic options.

WELLS

DRIVEN-POINT WELL. In areas of deep sand and a reasonably shallow water table, driven-point wells are inexpensive options. Sears sells all the necessary equipment, so you know it's a common solution and relatively easy to do. A sharp point with very fine slots (smaller than sand grains) is driven to beyond the level of the water table by pounding on the end of coupled lengths of galvanized pipe. Provided the water table is within 25 feet of the surface and there are no boulders lurking down there, it's a reasonable job for a handyman. Otherwise, in any area where driven wells are common, professional well-driving companies will be found.

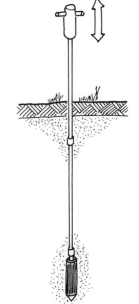

34A.   DRIVEN-POINT WELL

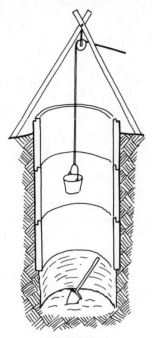

34B.   DUG WELL

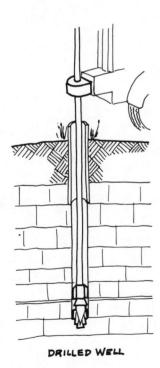

34C.   DRILLED WELL

DUG WELL. The oldest method of all is the hand-dug well. It's not as backward as it may seem. Just make sure the water table is within striking range! The illustration shows a well being dug by hand (it's lunch break in the picture). One person digs and fills the bucket; another operates the bucket. As the bottom worker digs, he evenly undercuts the bottom edge of the 4-foot-diameter concrete well tile, causing the tile to "follow" the worker down the well and act as a shield against cave-ins. When the top of the tile pile reaches ground level, another tile is rolled into place.

An even more common method used when the water table is within 15 feet of the surface is excavation and setting of the tiles with a backhoe. In this case, a very large hole is excavated to the maximum reach of the hoe. Provided the hole fills with water, crushed stone is spread on the bottom, the well tiles placed, the hole backfilled with clean sand, and the area around the well covered with an impervious material, such as clay or concrete, to divert dog pee.

DRILLED WELL. The most common well, and the one usually proving most satisfactory, is the drilled well. A 4- or 6-inch hole is drilled through solid rock in search of a water vein or aquifer below the water table. It's an expensive and risky business. The farther one drills, the less likely it is that water will be found, but the more likely it is that the water will be good.

Arguments rage over which is better for drilling: the old-fashioned "pounder," which literally pulverizes the rock by repeatedly dropping the heavy drill rod, or the modern rotary hammer. Common sense says that the pounder is more likely to open up water veins, but the rotary hammer is much faster and potentially less expensive per foot. I've had good luck with both.

But some haven't. Many a 500-foot dry hole litters the countryside. At $5 to $8 per foot, some water seekers are driven to consult dowsers, who claim to be able to divine the location, depth, and flow rate of aquifers. However much my romantic soul might like to believe in such arcane abilities, it simply cannot. I tried mightily once, but the old geezer let me down. I had struck a deal with a straight driller for 1 gallon per minute for a fixed price. I then called a local dowser much acclaimed for his ability to find missing relatives as well as water. He also happened to drill wells as a sideline.

On the appointed day, the old fellow cut an alder branch, assumed the well-known position, and tacked back and forth across my site. After a half-dozen passes he proclaimed a water vein at

90 feet that would undoubtedly produce 10 gallons per minute. Interestingly enough, the vein he traced passed directly over the spot where the other driller proposed to drill. Intrigued by the coincidence, I asked if I might try the rod. Furthermore, in the interest of science, might I be blindfolded? So blindfolded and guided by the dowser's directions, I too crisscrossed the site. And damned if the rod didn't seem to pull downward at the same spot!

Needless to say, my whole M.I.T.-instilled scientific frame of reference seemed in jeopardy. However, at this moment a certain thriftiness passed on by my maternal grandfather prevailed.

"How certain are you of this vein?" I asked.

"Never missed one yet!" (An impressive answer considering the age of the old coot.)

"Well, then, you ought to be willing to guarantee the well for a fixed price, oughtn't you? After all, everyone has his price."

"Never guarantee anything. Against principles."

My advice? Wait until the dead of winter when all the well drillers are sitting around wondering how they're going to make the next payment on that $250,000 rig in the yard. Tell them all you're going for the lowest fixed-price bid and wait for the calls.

HOW MUCH WATER IS ENOUGH? Everyone I tell about my half-gallon-per-minute well feels sorry for me. They don't say anything; they just shuffle their feet and look down at the ground. They're probably picturing me in the shower with the water dribbling on my head. Well, multiply ½ gallon per minute by 60 min-

35. Don't panic — one-half gallon per minute is a lot of water!

utes and then by 24 hours and you'll find (Illustration 35) that my well gives me 720 gallons per day. Furthermore, my 6-foot-diameter well stores 1½ gallons per foot, or 150 gallons above the submersible pump. So there!

FREEZE PROOFING YOUR PIPES. Nearly everyone with a well has experienced frozen pipes at least once. I'm somewhat of an expert on the subject, having suffered every possible variation.

There is one foolproof way to avoid frozen pipes. That is to make sure every inch of pipe is either beneath the depth of maximum frost or inside a house whose temperature never drops below freezing. Illustration 36 shows the maximum depth of frost, in feet, across the United States. What the map doesn't show is that the soil beneath driveways will freeze as much as 2 feet deeper because of the lack of an insulating snow cover and the higher conductivity of the compacted soil.

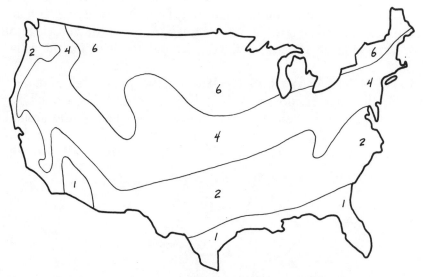

36. Maximum depth of frost, in feet (add 2 feet under driveway)

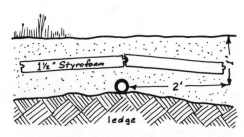

37. Insulating over a pipe is equivalent to burying the pipe deeper

But if you can't bury your pipes as deep as the map suggests you should, there are technological solutions. Illustration 37 shows a water pipe running close to the ground over a shallow ledge. Above it is a layer of extruded polystyrene (blue Styrofoam). This rugged and waterproof foam acts like deep snow cover in preventing the stored heat in the deep earth from escaping upward. Each horizontal foot of the foam sheet has about the same effect as a foot of burial, so the installation shown provides the same protection as burying the pipe 3 feet deep.

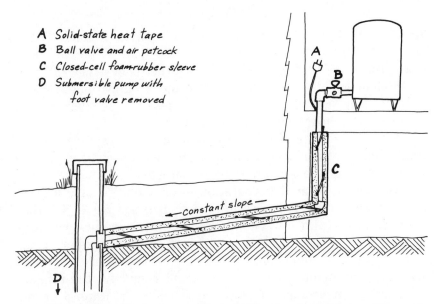

A Solid-state heat tape
B Ball valve and air petcock
C Closed-cell foam-rubber sleeve
D Submersible pump with
   foot valve removed

—constant slope—

38. Foolproof freeze proofing

Illustration 38 shows another trick we use in Maine. The poly-ethylene pipe is wound with a solid-state heat tape (A). The heat tape, which has no thermostat, draws no power at 70 degrees Fahrenheit but begins to draw increasing power as the temperature drops. Unlike heat tapes with thermostats, it can't overheat and fail. Power is conserved by the 1-inch-thick foam-rubber jacket around the pipe (C), which slopes continuously from the tank in the house back to the well. The foot valve has been removed from the submersible pump at the bottom of the well (D), so when the owners expect to be away for an extended period, they merely turn off the power and open the petcock (B) to admit air into the pipe. This allows all of the water in the pipe to drain back into the well. Now that's what I call freeze proofing!

An alternative is to run the polyethylene supply pipe right over the surface of the ground with no heat tape at all. An automatic petcock keeps the pipe empty at all times except when the pump is actually running (just a few minutes each day). The only disadvantage is a hissing sound each time the incoming water displaces the air in the pipe.

Sewage

Did you know there are twenty-two million individual sewage-treatment plants in the United States, and that three hundred thousand more are being added every year? You can tell I'm setting you up for something, right? But it's not to go into business pumping septic tanks. I'm going to try to convince you to put in your own sewage system rather than adding to the load of the municipal treatment plant.

WHAT IS SEWAGE? Only 0.1 percent of sewage is solid. That's right — 99.9 percent of sewage is water. About 40 percent of it comes from the 5 gallons we flush down the toilet every time we pull the handle. The other 60 percent comes from bathing, clothes washing, dishwashing, and cooking. Altogether, the average person uses 100 gallons per day around the home.

We usually think of this incredible volume of water as a pollutant. But it's a pollutant only if we mismanage it, if we fail to safely dispose of the small number of pathogens.

We can perform this operation — or should I say, we can have friendly little bacteria perform this operation for us — either on a grand scale at a sewage-treatment plant or in our own backyards. The operation at the municipal treatment plant is so massive that the effluent has to be dumped into a lake or river. Since the treatment is never 100 percent complete, the remaining chemicals necessarily pollute these bodies of water to some extent.

Municipal treatment plants must speed up the natural processes involved in sewage breakdown; otherwise the treatment plant would cover a considerable percentage of the town. They actively heat, stir, and introduce oxygen into the sewage. The sewage-disposal system in your own backyard operates on exactly the same principles, except it is completely passive.

All that is required to eliminate your sewage bill and contribute to the cleanup of America's lakes and rivers is a large enough area of acceptable soil and a permit from your local plumbing inspector.

THE SYSTEM. The system I'm describing is simply that much-maligned septic tank / drain field combination. I know you used to write a lot about compost toilets, and I agree that they are the greatest thing ever invented . . . in theory. But I know a lot of people who invested in those things — even built special rooms for them — who later traded them in for flush toilets. I even tried a passive solar outhouse one year. It was glorious that first summer. It had a south-facing skylight, a wide pumpkin pine seat, a built-in magazine rack, and an odor-eating vent pipe of proprietary design. But it was hell on wheels in winter. Even preheating the toilet seat by the wood stove and finally using a flannel slipcover didn't work. By mid-December my body had adopted a perverted circadian rhythm, urging me to the outhouse only at solar noon on clear winter days.

Don't get me wrong. I still love outhouses, but at a summer

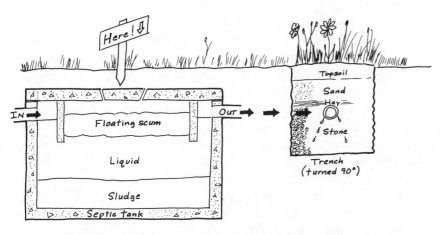

39. Cross section of a typical individual sewage-treatment system (septic system)

cottage where I don't have running water. Wherever one has plenty of water to return to the earth and plenty of soil in which to recycle it, I believe the septic tank / drain field is the perfect solution.

Illustration 39 shows how this marvelous system works. The raw sewage (a terrible thing to call what is actually 99.9 percent water) enters the septic tank from the left. Grease and whatever else is lighter than water floats at the top as scum. The heavier solids settle to the bottom. The tank is sized so that the water stays in the tank on the average of at least a day, allowing plenty of time for the solids to either float to the surface or sink to the bottom.

The septic (from the Greek *septikos*, meaning rotted) tank is filled with anaerobic (in the absence of oxygen) bacteria, which eat sewage the way kids eat Big Macs. What is left after the feast is a clear liquid (effluent) and solids (sludge). The minimal sludge remains in the bottom of the tank to be removed every few years, and the effluent flows out of the tank at the right to the drain field.

In the drain field (here shown as a trench), the liquid effluent is distributed along the length of a level pipe with holes in the bottom. As the effluent percolates downward through the bed of stones, any pathogens not killed by the anaerobic bacteria are again set upon by aerobic (in the presence of oxygen) bacteria, altogether achieving a rather complete slaughter. The liquid is further filtered and purified as it travels downward through the soil toward the water table and upward to be evaporated by the plants to the atmosphere.

Maintenance. Obviously the rate at which the tank fills with sludge is proportional to the rate at which solids are flushed down the drain. I know Jean composts all of your garbage for her garden, but ask her if she knows that by so doing she is doubling the time between septic-tank clean-outs.

Once the sludge accumulates to the bottom of the outflow pipe, you are in big trouble. From that point on, all solids flow right on through the tank and out to the drain field, where they clog the trench, requiring expensive replacement of the entire drain field. You and your neighbors will know this has happened immediately, since the untreated liquid rises to the surface of the ground. It's wise to check the sludge level every two years through the access hatch in the top of the tank.

That little sign with the arrow on top of the hatch is no joke. I once spent the better part of a day poking my lawn with a crowbar in search of my septic tank. Someday I'll find that map I sketched showing its location. I stored it in a place I was sure I'd never forget.

With periodic pumping of the sludge, a good septic system should last fifty years. The sandy, well-drained soil on your site is perfect, so I'm sure the whole system will cost less than $1,500. The way town sewage rates keep climbing, your system will pay for itself in only ten years.

Your friend,
Charlie

LETTER
12

Dear Charlie,

It's been a while. You probably thought I'd been devoured by my creditors, or that Jean had won the lottery and we'd taken off for Tobago.

Neither of the above. The real work began after we received yours of some weeks ago, the letter that tried to answer each of my questions about site services. Which is not to say the answers weren't there — they were, but you included options in almost every case.

It was deciding on which of the options might be best for us and our site that has taken this long. The good news is: We have made our decisions. We have lift-off and are about to go into our house-building orbit, the goal we have been moving toward ever since we began.

What I never realized was the number of preliminary steps that have to be taken. Perhaps if I had listened to Jean I would have realized. After all, essentials like a driveway and utilities are part of every home that's built from the ground up.

As you will see — and with a smile on your face, I hope — in the enclosed sketch of the site plan, we have responded in one way or another to each of your suggestions.

Fortunately, the soil on our lot turns out to be well-drained sandy loam, a break for us. Preparation for the driveway will be minimal, according to the contractor who has visited the site, tested the soil, and taken a preliminary swipe with his dozer blade. In this case, the absence of trees on the former pasture (I learned from a neighbor that the land had been a grazing spot for a farmer's beef creatures for years) means there isn't any heavy cutting

40. John and Jean's plot plan showing location of site services

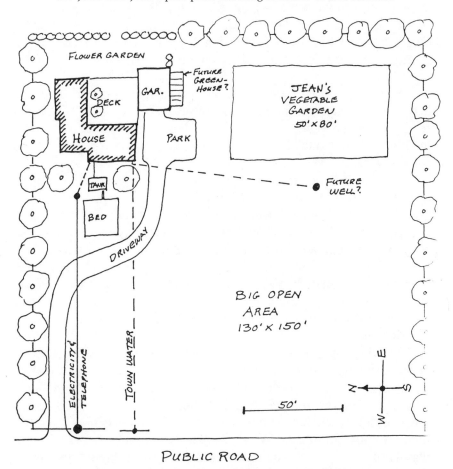

or uprooting to do. And the sandy, well-drained soil will hold up once the trucked-in gravel has a chance to settle.

The curve in our road is another of your options; this one cost just a bit more. But for the money we get a more interesting driveway, more privacy, and — most important — an area for the septic tank that isn't right in the middle of the meadow or the space Jean will most likely use for a vegetable garden.

This brings me to the next option, the one that was the toughest to decide about. Your warnings about the cost of town sewage disposal are correct, Charlie, as are your estimates of what a septic tank and drainage bed should cost, provided the soil and topography are suitable.

You estimated we could have our own waste-disposal system for about $1,500, and we came in about on the nose. It's your argument that we'll be paid back for the system in ten years or less, if we calculate that payback on what it would cost to hook up with the town sewage lines and what we would have to pay the local sewer district each quarter for the next decade. That's true enough, Charlie, as far as it goes. And if the district raises its rates, as it indicates it will surely do, the payback time will be even less.

But suppose we took the $1,500 we're spending and invested it conservatively, say in a certificate of deposit at 8 or 9 percent. In less than ten years, barring any withdrawals, that $1,500 would double, which would be more than enough to cover the cost of town services.

But we are not good savers. That's one reason we chose to install our own system. And our soil and site are perfect for the system. That's another. But perhaps the most compelling reason is that if we take care of our own wastes, properly and hygienically, we are not adding to the growing burden the town system has to bear. The sewer district's treatment plant is already close to being overworked; neither Jean nor I want to be responsible, even in a small way, for adding to the Androscoggin River's heavy burden. So, economics aside, we opted for our own on-site sewage disposal.

We did not, however, drill our own well. Your stories about how costly that can be, and the ready availability of town water, made it easy for us to decide to postpone any well drilling for a while, dowser or no dowser. (I believe in them, by the way.) I'm not worried about how the water tastes. When it comes to drinking the stuff, I emulate W. C. Fields, who had this to say about water: "I never touch the stuff. Fish fuck in it." Washing, watering the garden, and hosing down the family car every now and then are the primary uses we make of water. So it matters little if it's chlorinated; the stuff seldom touches my lips. Besides, as you pointed out, an in-line charcoal filter is simple to install. I saw one down at Sears for $29.

Would that the decisions about our phone and power lines had been so easy. For a while we opted for running our lines underground, and damn the extra cost. But when we analyzed the view and saw how little the overhead wires would impose on our daily vistas, we shifted gears and went for the standard (in Maine) overhead lines. It seemed easier and less expensive. And it surely seemed to please the Central Maine Power Company. We are close enough to existing lines, by the way, to avoid paying any extra fees or installation charges. That's another good reason for living closer to town, in a compact house on a compact lot. Snug and secure.

You'll note I got a bit carried away with the enclosed drawing. After we bulled our way through each of the site-preparation decisions, I was so cheerful that I included a flower garden, a greenhouse, and Jean's vegetable garden on the sketch, even though they are just figments of our imagination at this stage. I am, however, determined to call it Jean's vegetable garden. That way I'll be able to argue that it's not mine to weed.

Whew! I'm glad this preparation is over. Now we can get down to the real heart of this project: the new home we want so much.

Your friend,
John

P.S. I know I sounded sure of the decision to go ahead with the overhead wires for the utilities, but don't be too surprised to find the lines underground. Jean is lobbying hard to spend the extra money, because she is unwilling to add to littering the landscape with unnecessary poles and wires. She claims the service is as good, if not better, because the squirrels will be unable to commit suicide, birds will be safer, and the approach to the house will be more in keeping with the snug-harbor idea she has of the new place.

5. Materials

Dear Charlie,

Perhaps I'm jumping the gun, but I have a feeling we should start lining up the materials we're going to need for building. Spring, in spite of all that snow on the ground, is not that far away. And now that we have the site-services problems resolved (well, almost resolved — Jean still hasn't given up on her efforts to get the utilities underground), we're starting to get excited about the house itself, the way it's going to look, the way it's going to go together.

And that's what got me started on materials. As I told you, we want the house built almost totally from wood. You may be wondering why I've been so insistent on that score. It's a personal trait, and a strong one at that, with a history that goes back more than thirty years. Unlike foundations, heating systems, and plumbing, about which I know next to nothing, I feel I have a friendship with wood, an understanding of its origins, a recognition of some of its qualities and its beauty. And because there is this acquaintance, I am naturally more inclined to want to use it everywhere it's suitable. Formica, on the other hand, could be a word from a foreign language for all I understand of its genesis and character.

Wood I know about. Not that I always did. Until my thirtieth year I scarcely knew where it came from, much less how to analyze its strengths and recognize its weaknesses. That's what can happen to a fellow who is raised in the city and educated in classrooms.

In that thirtieth year, however, I began my apprenticeship as a commercial fisherman, and wood was what kept us afloat. With scarcely any capital at our disposal, my partners and I had to make do with whatever boats we could acquire at incidental prices or, quite often, merely in return for hauling the wrecks out of a boat yard.

For seven years I restored, repaired, and rebuilt ancient and abused wooden watercraft, and in the course of that education I became acquainted with most of the different kinds of wood, with their vagaries and frustrations as well as strengths and needs. I painted wood, scraped it, sanded it, drilled it, steamed it, caulked it, nailed it, fastened it, and fashioned it into stems, sterns, planks, masts, booms, hatch covers, tables, door frames, tackle boxes, net carriers, engine beds, and clam-rake handles. Everything — mahogany, oak, pine, cedar, spruce, teak, cypress, and ash — suffered under my clumsy hands.

By the time I departed that career, older and wiser but still a zealous fisherman, I had learned a bit about wood. I had learned that oak is stringy, heavy, and strong; that one sands with the grain; that large nails driven near the ends of planks will usually split those planks; that spruce is lighter than ash (and therefore better for oars); that even a bit of rot in a mast will weaken it; that wood and water react in wondrous ways; that even relatively delicate lengths of wood, if properly fashioned, can be incredibly strong and resilient enough to resist the battering of awesome seas.

I also discovered and learned to appreciate the enduring beauty of wood as is, unpainted and unstained.

From those beginnings I developed a love for wood that still grows. I find sensuality in the texture of a well-sanded, well-oiled plank. I am captivated by the aesthetics of knots, grain, and hue. I am inspired by wood's organic immortality; it never dies. With every change in temperature, with every ray of sunshine, drop of rain, breath of salt fog, or splash of ocean spray, wood responds. It swells, shrinks, curls, changes color; it reacts as if the soul of the tree still locked within it has never departed but is there, reaching and responding to the presence of moisture just as the parent tree did every day of its life in the forest.

Wood is never still. Unlike steel, aluminum, plastic, stone, or brick, wood moves. It is alive, it glows, and, if you care for it, wood will shelter you with maintenance-free strength, wood will warm you, wood will please your eye, and wood will wrap you in its immortal strength when you go to your grave. Nature has provided us with no better structural material. Wood needs only to remain dry or be well ventilated if it becomes wet. It's best to keep it dry and ventilated, and to rub it with natural oils now and then to replace those it has lost in the process of separating from the tree.

Let me tell you one wood story.

A few years ago we lost one of the great oak line trees that grew alongside the roadway into our former home. It had been living, green and strong, when we moved in. Then, one spring, no new leaves pushed from its branches; the tree just stood there, its bare gray limbs spread stark against the sky. The road must have come too close. Perhaps the pressure of the passing cars had crushed too many roots. Whatever unseen injury had occurred, it had proven a mortal wound. The great line tree we had worked so hard to save had given up the ghost.

It stood there a year, indomitable, towering, and awesome. I knew it would have to be cut down, but I could not bring myself to swing the axe. One fall on a bright Saturday, impulsively, I took two of the same sons who had helped build the road, and we went to fell the tree. I rationalized that the approaching winter storms could drop it on the road, perhaps blocking the way when it was needed most. Also, the giant held a month's supply of stove wood in its trunk and limbs, wood we needed to help us keep warm.

The two-man saw cut deep. The seasoned wood snapped clean, and the tree came down with a crash that was heard a mile away on that autumn afternoon. The ground shook; the three of us trembled at the shattering consequences of our deed.

On the ground, the oak looked even larger than it had standing. It took a while to walk the distance from the trunk to the tip of the farthest branches. Working like pygmies over an elephant's carcass, the three of us sawed and hacked and pulled and heaved for the rest of that day and most of the next to get the bones of the fallen giant cut into sections small enough for us to move. Then we piled them atop each other like a temple in front of the barn, where they waited to be sawn still more and split, stacked, and carried to the stoves inside the house.

I counted 120 rings on the stump. Ten years before the Civil War, the tree had been taller than most men. It had gotten its start just after the shipbuilders had left this land for the lure of California gold, and it had lived a proud life as the guardian of a pact between neighbors.

How much better are old oaks than old men. Oaks grow stronger and mightier as they grow older. Their years push them toward the sky instead of bending them against their frailties and fading senses. The longer an oak lives, the more lordly it becomes; a man who lives too long can know no pride.

An old man passes with a whisper; he slips away almost silently. The crashing of an oak trembles an entire afternoon. The service an oak performs reaches its peak with every year it lives; centuries only add to the measure of an oak's performance. Men become infants once again, helpless with the weight of their years.

And after death the bones of an oak bring light, warmth, and structure to the world, while the body of a man becomes a matter for disposal.

Yet it is man who brings down the oaks. For that, it seems, we pay a heavy price.

Perhaps my romanticism has obscured my vision a bit. I'm never certain, for example, just what to ask for when I go to a lumberyard. The grades, the numbers they assign are confusing, as are the measurements. What some lumber retailers call a 2 × 4 doesn't measure 2 inches by 4 inches, not by a long shot. And when I'm asked whether I want yellow pine or white pine or hardboard or flakeboard, I'm hard-pressed for an answer. I usually mumble, reluctant as I am to reveal my ignorance, and end up with a piece of wood that may or may not be the best choice for the job it has to do.

Which brings me to my questions, Charlie. (I'm not reluctant to ask you — you already know I'm relatively ignorant.) Just what are the qualities of the new synthetic woods, the hardboard and flakeboard and the other stuff I see at the building-supply places that was obviously not cut straight from the tree? What should I ask for when we begin ordering the wood we should have for our new home?

What it boils down to, Charlie, is that as much as I know I like wood, and as much as I like to think I know something about it, I still have a great deal to learn. Anyone who has ever seen me at a lumberyard can tell you that. But if you tell me everything you know about wood, I'll have what I need to become an expert, for which I thank you in advance.

Your friend,
John

Dear John,

Does it make you nervous every time I begin with "Dear John" because this is getting to be a lot of work? Don't worry, I'm enjoying the correspondence. It's giving me an excuse to practice my new skills of drawing and word processing. Besides, I've never had more attentive or appreciative students than you and Jean.

I never knew you had such poetic feelings about wood! Me, too. I think the ambience of wood should be added to the architectural patterns I described in Letter 6. For years now I've been trying to sort out my feelings about vinyl and aluminum sidings. From purely practical and economic regards, both are superior to wood clapboards or shingles. They cost less to install, align more perfectly, and eliminate painting. But why do you suppose the manufacturers try to make them look like real wood? The most expensive versions even have a wood grain molded in or painted on so that you almost have to feel them to tell the difference.

I have nothing against vinyl or aluminum per se. I love my vinyl boat cushions, and I'd rather fry an egg in an aluminum skillet than one handcrafted from wood. But damn it, there's something strange about vinyl siding. I think I know what it is; it's the same thing that bothers me about nondairy coffee lighteners and "genuine vinyl leather." It's dishonest; it erodes the distinction between natural and artificial. Ultimately, I fear, it may contribute to a confusion between right and wrong, at least in an environmental sense.

How Trees Grow

First I'm going to give you a short explanation of tree biology. Look at Illustration 41. Starting at the outside of the tree:

The bark is a thick layer of dead cells, similar to the outer layers of human skin, that protects the living parts of the tree from insects and fire. A tree is very resistant to insects as long as its bark forms a complete barrier.

The phloem is the inner bark, consisting of live cells that transmit nutrients, as do the cells of the sapwood.

The cambium is a single layer of cells where, remarkably, all tree growth occurs. The cells of the cambium continually divide, first adding a cell to the phloem outside and then a cell to the sapwood inside. Except for the first shoot, all growth is therefore radial. As a result, a tree limb that first appears at a height of 5 feet above the ground will remain 5 feet high forever, even though the tree grows taller.

The sapwood consists of the most recently formed layers of wood and, as its name implies, it carries sap up and down the tree. When the rate of growth varies throughout the year, or even ceases during cold winters, the sapwood shows annual growth rings. Wide rings are due to rapid growth in wet summers; narrow rings indicate dry summers. These ring patterns form fingerprints in time that allow the dating of historic buildings! One of the first to study this subject, dendrochronology, was my hero, Thoreau.

Over time the sapwood cells die and become **heartwood.** Chemicals and minerals are deposited in and between the heartwood cells, making the wood more dense, strong, dark, and resistant to decay than the sapwood.

The pith, at the very center of the tree, is the remnant of the original shoot.

Rays are at right angles to the circular rings. Not defects or cracks in the wood, as they may at first appear, rays are bundles of cells that transport and store food across the annual rings.

The illustration also shows how this tree recovered from **damage** to its bark (perhaps from fire) by eventually enclosing the unprotected wound with new sapwood.

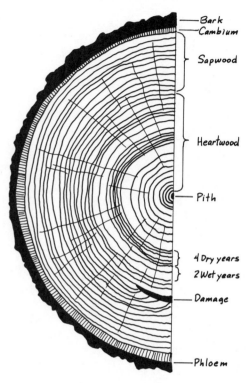

41. Cross section of a tree

Variations in Properties

Wood species are lumped into one of two categories: hardwood or softwood. After you spend some time nailing the "hardwood" poplar and the "softwood" southern pine, I think you will agree these two categories were a very bad idea. Better classifications are deciduous (dropping their leaves) and evergreen (retaining their leaves or needles all year). The two different types have radically different cell structures which, coupled with variations in the thickness of the cell walls and the relative proportions of the molecular building blocks cellulose and lignin, accounts for most of the differences in their properties.

There are several correlations that generally hold true, however. Heavier or more dense species are harder, stronger, and stiffer, and hold nails better. Generalities beyond these are unreliable.

Table 4
WOODS COMPARED

GROUP	SPECIES	Strength in Bending	Stiffness	Hardness	Nail Holding	Warping	Workability	Decay Resistance	Pitch Content	Paint Holding
1	Douglas Fir–Larch	●	●	◐	●	◐	◐	◐	◐	○
1	Southern (Yellow) Pine	●	●	◐	●	◐	◐	◐	○	○
1	Rock Maple	●	●	●	●	◐	●	○	●	◐
2	Hemlock–White Fir	◐	●	◐	◐	○	◐	◐	●	○
3	Eastern Spruce	◐	◐	○	◐	◐	◐	◐	●	◐
3	Redwood	◐	◐	◐	◐	●	◐	●	●	●
3	Soft Pines	○	○	○	◐	●	●	○	◐	●
4	Western Red Cedar	○	○	○	○	●	◐	●	●	●

I know you consult *Consumer Reports* when you buy things for your home, so I've come up with a *CR*-style report (Table 4) on species of wood that you might consider for your new home. Because I don't have a blue pen, my code is a little different from theirs: My solid black dots mean best and empty circles mean worst. Of course, it is foolish to spend money for a quality that is not needed. For example, don't spend extra money for the paint-holding ability of redwood attic rafters.

Strength in bending is the limiting factor for roof rafters: You care whether the roof collapses under a snow load but not how much it bounces when you walk on it (stiffness).

Stiffness is most often the limiting factor for floor joists. You'll give up trying to play records while dancing long before you have to worry about your floor collapsing.

Hardness is important wherever a lot of traffic is expected. Few woods make a prettier floor than soft white pine, but white pine is so soft that finishes crack when the wood dents under pressure. At the other extreme is the very hard rock maple, a favorite for bowling alleys and gymnasium floors. I'm not telling you not to use pine for flooring; just don't use it in the kitchen or entrance hall or you'll be very sorry.

Nail holding is important wherever varying stresses work to move a wood joint. Examples are corner braces in a wall, joints and splices in a roof truss, and stair treads. Generally, a wood low in nail-holding ability is also unlikely to split when nailed. Therefore, low nail-holding ability can be overcome by more nails.

Warping can be unattractive in the rafters of an exposed cathedral ceiling. It can also be dangerous in a heavily loaded slender post. But I once used it to my advantage: I bought every severely warped 2 × 6 in the local lumberyard for half-price and nailed the bastards down as a deck.

Workability relates most to how often and how sincerely your carpenters swear as they pull splinters from their palms and thumbs.

Decay resistance is extremely important for wood exposed to standing water or constantly moist conditions. Although I saved a lot initially by using warped 2 × 6's in my deck, I'll never build another deck of plain spruce 2 × 6's. Better to invest in warped redwood or pressure-treated southern pine at twice or even quadruple the material cost!

Pitch content. Other than an annoying stickiness while building (which turpentine will remove), the chief problem with pitch is its tendency — hell, its insistence on bleeding through paint. This, too, can be reasonably overcome by first sealing with a white shellac sealer/primer.

Paint holding is obviously important only if you plan to paint, and then only if it's to be outside. Wood that ranks low in paint-holding ability can be treated with a penetrating stain or preservative.

Lumber

Lumber — which includes the more specific categories of boards, joists, planks, rafters, posts, etcetera — is all made by sawing tree trunks lengthwise. The most skilled job at the sawmill is that of the sawyer, who turns a log into the optimum mix of lumber. The sawyer must make an instant judgment at each pass of the blade, weighing the defects uncovered by the latest pass against the orders of the mill customers and the relative value of each lumber category. Each time the sawyer can either repeat the last pass, change the thickness, or rotate the log by 90 degrees.

Illustration 42 shows how a small log might be sawn into two 1 × 10 boards, four 2 × 6 floor joists or rafters, three 2 × 4 studs, and four edge-grained 1 × 6 boards suitable for resawing into clapboards. But the log I drew was small; it's not uncommon to get fifty or more pieces from a large redwood or Douglas fir log.

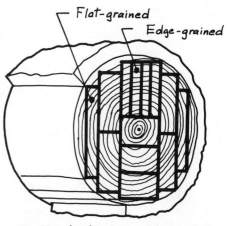

42. How lumber is sawn from a tree

Table 5

**LUMBER DIMENSIONS
(IN INCHES)**

Rough or Nominal	Surfaced, Dry 19% Moisture Content
1	¾
2	1½
4	3½
6	5½
8	7¼
10	9¼
12	11¼

LUMBER SIZES. With the exception of specialty items, most lumber is sawn in increments of 1 inch. That is, if you were to measure a "green," or undried, piece, it would measure exactly x inches by y inches. Two further things will usually happen to lumber before it gets nailed into your home: It will be dried to a stable moisture content, and it will be surfaced smooth (planed) to a smaller dimension. Sometimes the order of operations is reversed: surfacing, then drying. In either case the desired result is the same — lumber of specified dimension that will neither swell nor shrink appreciably from its installed dimensions. Table 5 compares rough-sawn dimensions and surfaced-dry dimensions.

Nothing is lost in the length of the piece, however, since the ends are not planed and wood shrinks negligibly in drying. Thus a 10-foot S4S (surfaced on four sides) 2×8 floor joist actually measures 120 inches $\times$ 1½ inches $\times$ 7¼ inches.

Obviously, working with smooth lumber of predictable dimensions is easier for the carpenter. It results, in addition, in a more finished appearance. But something is also lost in the process. As a rule of thumb, surfacing rough lumber decreases its bending strength by one size; i.e., a rough 2×6 has the same strength as a surfaced 2×8. In fact, merely sawing a round log into its equivalent square section reduces its bending strength by 50 percent!

DRYING AND SHRINKAGE. When a tree is first cut, the wood is referred to as green. The moisture content (MC) of wood is defined as the ratio of the weight of water contained to the weight of the wood when it is oven-dry, or contains absolutely no water. For example, if a 2×6 weighs 14 pounds before and 10 pounds after drying in an oven, then the original MC was 40 percent ($14 - 10 \div 10$). As wood dries, water evaporates first from inside the cells. Only after the cells are empty does the water held in the between-cell spaces evaporate. The MC at this transition point is usually between 25 and 30 percent. Lumber is considered dry by the lumber industry when its MC is 19 percent or less.

In drying, lumber shrinks. For a reason unknown to me, it shrinks about twice as much along the rings (tangential to the circular rings) as across the rings (along the radius of the circular rings). Comparatively, it doesn't shrink at all in the direction of the grain. Table 6 shows, for ten different species of wood, the percent shrinkage from just-cut (green) to perfectly dry (oven-dry). A third column shows the ratios of the shrinkages in the two directions.

Table 6
SHRINKAGE FROM GREEN TO OVEN-DRY

Wood Species	Perpendicular to Rings	Tangential to Rings	Distortion Ratio
White ash	4.9%	7.8%	1.6
White birch	6.3%	8.6%	1.4
Sugar maple	4.8%	9.9%	2.1
White oak	5.6%	10.5%	1.9
White cedar	2.2%	4.9%	2.2
Douglas fir	4.8%	7.6%	1.6
Eastern hemlock	3.0%	6.8%	2.3
Eastern white pine	2.1%	6.1%	2.9
Southern (yellow) pine	4.8%	7.0%	1.5
Eastern spruce	4.0%	7.0%	1.8

Now, there are two problems with wood shrinkage. The most obvious is that the wood gets smaller overall, like a pair of un-Sanforized jeans the first time you wash them. This results in cracks between adjacent pieces, as in a floor, or nail heads popping through drywall as the framing shrinks away from the embedded nails.

The second problem is a distortion of the lumber cross section due to the differential shrinkage in the two different directions. The greater the ratio of shrinkage, the greater the distortion. Illustration 43 shows the distortions to expect as lumber cut from a green log dries.

I've pointed out that lumber can arrive at its final dry and surfaced condition by either of two routes: (A) dried, then surfaced; or (B) surfaced, then dried. If you think about it for a minute, you'll see that the order makes a hell of a difference. I call Route A lumber Sanforized lumber; it's preshrunk and should remain pretty much as you bought it. Route B lumber, however, is guaranteed to change in both size and shape as it dries to its final moisture content. Make sure that you or your contractor use lumber that has been surfaced dry rather than surfaced green for any application where appearance counts.

Even so, your lumber is likely to dry even more after you move into the house. Your nose and throat prove that a warm house in winter is a lot drier than either the outdoors or the inside of the same house in summer. The almost unavoidable cupping that results has led to this finish carpenter's rule:

"Heart side up; heart side out."

Illustration 43 shows that following this rule results in more rounded visible surfaces and minimizes visible cracks.

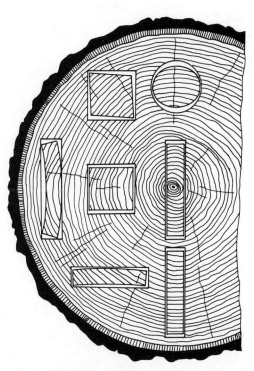

43. Shrinkage patterns in lumber sawn from green (still-wet) log

I don't know whether it's obvious from my drawing, but the thinner the board, the more severe the cupping. Therefore, observe a second rule:

"The width should not exceed eight times the thickness."

A board sawed more or less parallel to the rings is called flat-grained. A board sawed perpendicular to the rings is called edge-grained. As Illustrations 42 and 43 show, edge-grained boards are much less subject to cupping. For this reason they command a higher price. Should you choose to side your house this way, I would insist that clapboards be sawn from edge-grained boards.

AIR DRYING. In wooded rural areas, there are generally a lot of small sawmills (more than four hundred exist in Maine alone). Their owners don't have the capital to invest in lumber-drying kilns or large inventories of boards drying in the air. The name of the game for the small mill is selling rough, green lumber as quickly as it comes off the saw. If you plan to use the lumber unsurfaced, and if you have the time and the space required for air drying the boards yourself, you can save a lot of money by going to such a mill.

Illustration 44 shows how to "sticker" boards the way they do in a sawmill. The result of the operation is a pile of boards dried to an MC of less than 19 percent, flat and straight, uniform in color, and without checks, splits, or rot. Considering all that you're trying to do, the operation is simple:

Step 1. Find a cheerful helper. This may be the most difficult step. It may depend on what you're serving for refreshments.

Step 2. Clear a reasonably flat area of all vegetation. Your neighbor's tennis court would serve nicely.

Step 3. Place three straight, dry timbers on the ground in an east-west direction, all in the same plane, and of sufficient thickness that the lumber will clear the ground by at least 2 inches.

Step 4. Ask the mill where you bought your rough lumber for a dry "sticker" (the 1-inch-thick edges trimmed from the boards during sawing) for each board purchased. It's important that the stickers be dry to prevent sticker burn where sticker and board make contact.

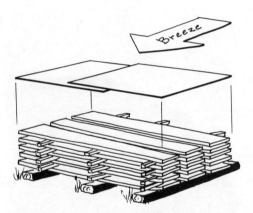

44. A sticker pile for air drying lumber

Step 5. With your cheerful helper on the other end, place the first layer of boards on top of the timbers and perpendicular to them, with a minimum of 1 inch between edges.

Step 6. Place the first three stickers on the boards directly above the three timbers on the ground.

Step 7. Repeat Steps 5 and 6 until the pile is as high as you can reach. As you add layers, place each sticker about 1 inch to the south of the sticker below so that the south ends of the boards have a built-in sunshade.

Step 8. Cover the whole pile with anything that will shed rain, but don't cover the ends or sides. Several pieces of plywood are usually perfect. Tie the cover down by passing ropes over the cover and tying them to the ends of the stickers near the bottom.

If you follow these instructions, you will create a gigantic lumber press that forces the lumber to dry flat, allows drying breezes to pass through unhindered, prevents fungus stains and dry rot, and keeps the ends of the boards from drying too quickly, which would cause checking of the ends. If you really care about the appearance of the boards, redo the whole pile several times during the six- to eight-week process, moving the stickers to avoid color banding. Color changes in lumber result from exposure to sunlight. After your lumber is dry, expose it to the full sun. Don't lay the boards directly on the ground, however, since they'll probably mold. As they reach the desired shade, remove and store in shade. Tan takes just a few weeks. A pure silver or gray requires several months.

LUMBER DEFECTS. Even with the best of care, your lumber will still have a variety of defects. Some are cosmetic; others may be serious, depending on the application. Illustration 45 shows what the defects look like, both in cross section and on the face of the lumber.

Check is the lumber version of a stretch mark, a cosmetic crack caused by the surface of a timber shrinking more rapidly than the interior. This can be very dramatic and unsightly in a post-and-beam frame that has dried rapidly in a warm house the first winter. Solutions include air drying the timbers a full year before using in building or treating the surfaced timbers with linseed oil to retard the drying process.

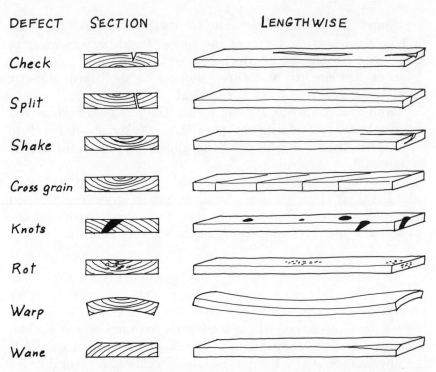

DEFECT	SECTION	LENGTHWISE
Check		
Split		
Shake		
Cross grain		
Knots		
Rot		
Warp		
Wane		

45. Categories of defects in lumber

Splits pass clear through the wood and are sometimes due to rough handling. They constitute a serious structural weakness. Timbers with splits should not be used in bending (floor joists, roof rafters) or as posts in compression. The solution is using the piece as blocking or as kindling.

Shake is a separation of growth rings. Lumber with visible shake should not be used to support bending loads, since the zone of weakness probably extends the length of the piece. Use such wood in nonbending applications.

Cross grain occurs when a board is sawn from a crooked log. Since wood is ten times stronger along its grain than across, a cross-grain angle of more than one part in ten seriously weakens the wood in bending. The solution is, again, cutting up for blocking and other nonstressful applications.

Knots are the high-density "roots" of the limbs. They may actually add to the beauty of a board, but one has to be careful in structural applications. Knots are very tough but not well connected to the surrounding wood. The rules for use in joists and rafters are: (1) Tight knots are okay in the top third, (2) loose or even missing knots are allowed in the middle third, and (3) no knots at all over 1 inch in diameter are allowed in the bottom third. The solution is sometimes as simple as reversing top and bottom by turning the piece over.

Rot is rot: holes, spongy areas, missing material. This is obviously structurally forbidden. However, such boards look just dandy as paneling. Just make sure the bug motel has been vacated.

Warp is cosmetic in a board and can sometimes be overcome by lots of nails. It can be serious in framing, however, if it causes an irregularity in spacing or a bulge in the plane of a floor, wall, or roof. Sometimes two warped framing members can be saved by nailing them together back to back. Otherwise, cut the offending piece into shorter pieces so that the warp will be less noticeable.

Wane results from a miscalculation on the part of the sawyer. There simply wasn't enough tree to complete that board. The only real problem, in the case of a joist or rafter, is the lack of a full-width nailing surface. Placing the bottom side down or making sure no plywood edges or board ends meet at the wane are good salvations. As a last resort, finish the sawyer's job on your own table saw.

DEALING WITH THE SMALL MILL. If you have the time and can design into your home a sufficient percentage of rough lumber, you can save money and have a hell of a good time to boot by dealing with a small local sawmill. The people who own and operate these mills live close to the earth and with constant danger. As with commercial fishing, the result is a no-nonsense view of life that most of us could beneficially incorporate into our own philosophies.

The foundation of my life philosophy began with my first experience with just such a mill. I had ordered all of the lumber for my first house from a one-man operation, Carl Bickford (Inc.) in Lisbon Falls, Maine. Unfortunately, I had also contracted for the services of two college students and their live-in girlfriends and assorted pets. The "help" arrived, bag and baggage, and promptly moved into my house. But the lumber didn't. A week went by, and I called Mr. Bickford to inquire about the projected delivery date.

"I'm doing the best I can," was the reply.

"Thanks," I said. "Do the best you can."

Another week passed. "Hello, Mr. Bickford? How are you doing on my lumber order? I've got a lot of people in my house waiting to build."

"I'm doing the best I can."

"Gee, that's too bad. Well, do the best you can."

Mr. Bickford did the best he could for the next six weeks — while I felt increasingly sorry for the poor fellow. I know you're anxious to receive these letters and get on with your house, John, but believe me, I'm doing the best I can.

If you plan to begin construction in June, place your lumber order in January, allowing two months to get in line, two months for unforeseen delays, and two months for at least partial air drying in dry, warm weather.

If there is more than one mill in your area, shop around. The quality and dimensional accuracy is likely to vary considerably. I waited for Mr. Bickford to do his best because it was *so* good. Most of the delay experienced was due to his penchant for adjusting the old mill nearly every time he sawed a board. A 1-inch board from some mills may measure 1⅛ inches at one end and ⅞ inch at the other, but Mr. Bickford's could have served as the 1-inch model at the National Bureau of Standards. And I've bought worse so-called finish pine at some retail lumberyards than Mr. Bickford's run-of-the-mill product.

EXTERIOR SIDINGS. As far as I'm concerned, there is only one way to protect the walls of a house from water — the same way God protects ducks. Two types of wood siding operate in the same way as duck feathers, shedding the most driving rain but breathing naturally and lasting for generations. These are clapboards and shingles. Clapboards have two advantages: They go on faster, and they can be nailed through insulating foam sheathings directly to wall framing, eliminating the need for an additional nail-base sheathing. Disadvantages include a higher price for top quality and the necessity to either paint or stain. Illustration 46 shows schematically how a proper clapboard is made. Being thin, it must be resawn from a dry, surfaced, knot-free, edge-grained board. Otherwise you'll quickly be faced with curled, split, and holey siding.

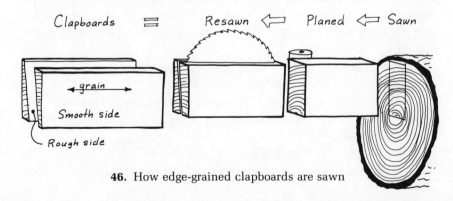

46. How edge-grained clapboards are sawn

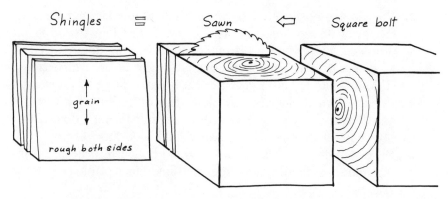

47. How shingles are sawn

Cedar shingles are less expensive and require only an initial staining, if any. But you could spend all summer putting them up. I don't mind, because I'd rather shingle, basking in the fall sun with classical music on my Walkman, than be indoors watching someone else play football.

Illustration 47 shows how clear cedar shingles are sawn from a bolt of knot-free cedar. After shingling four houses, I recommend you spend the extra money for the clearest (most knot-free) shingles you can find. A very expensive version of shingle is the hand-split shake. People who pay twice as much for the same degree of protection must think they look better.

Really Big Pieces of Wood

I know how you and Jean feel about synthetic materials. It's clear from your present house, your furnishings, your clothes, and all the other things in your lives that you and Jean have a love affair with nature as well as each other. But let me also point out that your natural wood furniture is held together with synthetic glue, your prized fishing rod is laminated from fiberglass and resin, and the chessboard in your living room contains inlaid veneers of exotic woods.

Okay, here it comes. I think you should sheath your floors, exterior walls, and roof with plywood or one of its modern equivalents. Plywood and the other large panels I recommend are simply rearranged pieces of wood held together with glue. For places where the wood won't be seen, I can't think of a single reason not to use plywood. The advantages over boards are:

1. Mr. Bickford doesn't make them, so they are available at a moment's notice.
2. They measure 48 × 96 inches, so large areas of 16- and 24-inch on-center framing can be covered rapidly with little waste.

3. Boards are easily split because of their low strength across the grain (even I can karate-chop a board like that guy on television) but plywood is made of alternating layers at right angles and so is almost uniformly strong in both directions. (I'd sure like to see Mr. Kung Fu break a piece of plywood!)
4. Because wood doesn't shrink in the direction of its grain, and because plywood has grain running in both directions, plywood shrinks no more than ⅛ inch in either direction.
5. Plywood on the walls is like a whole bunch of braces. Nothing makes a building stronger and less susceptible to plaster cracks.

Plywood is made by alternating thin veneers of wood peeled from a log by a giant lathe. The ⅛-inch-thick veneers are glued and pressed together to form a gigantic (relative to a board) sheet of wood, 48 × 96 inches. With the development of better glues, it has become possible to produce panels with many of the same qualities as plywood from wood shavings and sawdust. Since the only previous uses for wood shavings were as chicken litter, paper, and fuel, it is obvious that these new panel products are more economical.

The properties of panels made in different ways vary a bit. Recognizing that the carpenter is most interested in how a panel performs its expected function, the plywood industry has begun to refer to all panels as performance-rated structural wood panel products. While I still prefer good old plywood as long as I can afford it or someone else is paying the bill, you should be aware of these cost-saving products. Most particularly, you need to know how to decode the identifying labels.

If you read newspaper ads directed at the weekend do-it-yourselfer by the Handyman Heaven Cut-Rate Chain, you'll soon notice that there are two types of certification or guarantee. "Agency certified" means guaranteed by a nationally recognized association of manufacturers, such as the American Plywood Association (APA), to perform as promised by the label or your money back. The other, less expensive type — "mill certified" — means that the place that made the product certifies the panel. My experience has been that they must be guaranteeing self-destruction in the first encounter with water. I think you would be wise to stick with the more expensive agency-certified products unless you are building shelves inside.

Illustration 48 is a guide to the most common types of APA grade stamp that you will find on the faces of structural panels and on the edges of panels intended for appearance. For the top example, the codes can be translated as follows:

LINE 1 The APA certification.

LINE 2 Rated for use as roof, wall, and subfloor sheathing.

LINE 3 Allowed roof-rafter and wall-stud spacing of 32 inches and floor-joist spacing of 16 inches. Panel thickness ½ inch.

LINE 4 Panel is slightly smaller than 48 × 96 inches (generally ⅛ inch) to allow for recommended ⅛-inch installation gap.

LINE 5 In order of decreasing resistance to water: exterior (permanent exposure to water), exposure 1 (long construction delays), exposure 2 (very short delays). Exposure 1 is your best buy for house building.

LINE 6 Manufactured at Mill 123 (in case you want to call Oregon and complain).

LINE 7 U.S. Product Standard PS 1-74/ANSI A199.1. (Don't ask!) The two face veneers (because this panel is plywood) are C grade (small knots and plugs) and D grade (big ugly holes and knots). The core is of a wood species suitable for interior use, but the glue is exterior, or waterproof.

LINE 8 Recognized by the National Research Board (sponsored by the three major building codes) as doing what it promises.

The second label is similar but stamped on a nonplywood panel intended for use as the only floor under carpeting or linoleum. The panel has a thickness of ²³⁄₃₂ inch and can be used over floor joists spaced up to 24 inches apart.

The third label is an edge stamp for APA-certified interior plywood made of Group 1 wood (the strongest), with A (smooth and paintable) and B (solid surface with minor splits) face veneers. Conforms to PS1-74 (see Line 7) and is manufactured by Mill 123.

I know you must still have a million questions about wood. For example, I still haven't told you how to frame a house. But first things first; let's start from the ground up. We should look at foundations next.

Your friend,
Charlie

APA
RATED SHEATHING
32/16 1/2 INCH
SIZED FOR SPACING
EXPOSURE 1
123
PS 1-74 C-D INT/EXT GLUE
NRB-108

APA
RATED STURD-I-FLOOR
24 OC 23/32 INCH
SIZED FOR SPACING
T&G NET WIDTH 47-1/2
EXPOSURE 1
123
INT/EXT GLUE
NRB-108 FHA-UM-66

A-B · G-1 · INT-APA · PS1-74 · 123

48. Typical APA grade stamps for ½-inch C-D plywood (top), ¾-inch nonplywood structural panel (center), and A-B interior plywood (bottom)

6. Foundations

LETTER
15

Dear Charlie,

I'm tickled you said we should postpone more discussion about wood for a while. Your treatise on the nature, quality, cost, grading, and nomenclature of wood is so thorough it tells me more than I want to know. I'm hesitant about showing it to Jean, because for years I've been saying (in so many words) that I have an understanding of wood, an understanding — as I tell the story — learned the hard way during those romantic and adventurous years in the commercial fishing trade.

And now you've gone and spoiled all that with your exhaustive case studies about wood, what makes it do what it does, and how and where to buy it, or not to, as the case may be. Well, I may still make pronouncements every now and then like "That's a nice piece of oak," but the old zip won't be there.

Now, foundations are a topic I do know something about, mostly because I've spent so many traumatic and terrifying times in basements, crawl spaces, and every other sort of dark cavity there is under structures of all sorts, including homes I have lived in, some I've visited, and barns I have tried to keep from collapsing.

To paraphrase Will Rogers, I've never met an underspace I liked, not in any of our own places, anyway. I have, on one occasion, visited an underspace that overwhelmed me with its difference. By that I mean it was so different from any others I'd ever seen that I came away wondering what sort of magic had been perpetrated.

Case in point: I was sent as a boy to pick up a chair my father had had re-caned at the workshop of an old (I would have said very old in those days) carpenter who seemed to make a living restoring and repairing furniture at his home. I say "seemed to," because I never really inquired into his finances, but judging from the masses of furniture waiting to be fixed, the piles of desks, chairs, tables, commodes, and bookcases that bulged from his barn, I'd say that if the fellow wasn't making a good living, it was because he didn't charge enough.

Well, I don't mean to wander, but the fellow made a vivid impression on me, and part of it had to do with the piles of furniture in his barn. The other part, which I haven't forgotten for more than fifty years, had to do with his basement.

That was where he did all his work, and it was where I had to visit on those times when I stopped by to see if my father's chair was ready. First, I remember how easy the basement was to get down to. That may not seem like much, but then you haven't been in many basements like Mr. Fithian's. The door that opened on the basement stairs was a wide one that swung easily and quietly on its hinges. The stairs were wide, well lit, and even welcoming. Indeed, they were the only welcoming cellar stairs I have seen in what is now becoming an increasingly long life of descending cellar steps or ladders, or just plain dropping through trapdoors.

Mr. Fithian's cellar was never dark. I don't know if the door was linked to a light, but I never once opened it and found myself confronted by a black hole from which came an occasional moan, squeak, scrape, scattering of clawed feet on a littered floor, or the smell of musk and the wafting of cobwebs across my brow. That's what happens when every other cellar door I ever opened is pushed ajar; but it never happened at Mr. Fithian's.

There I would be greeted by the sweet smell of wood and glue, the warmth of a coal stove, and a flood of reassuring golden light from which the cellar's proprietor would eventually emerge like one of the benevolent magicians of my childhood bedtime stories: absolutely unthreatening, welcoming, and somehow possessed of certain enchantments that a boy would be privileged to share.

Mr. Fithian was a kind and gentle fellow, slight, disarming, and soft-spoken; he had warm eyes that looked over his rimless glasses. But it was the quality of his cellar that gave him his magic. It was the warmest, the most golden, the most snug, reassuring place I had ever been. There were no shadowed corners, no spiderwebs, no puddles on the floor, no trashy piles that stirred with lives of their own, no threatening machines humming, no exposed electrical wires, no moldy fungi, no wispy trails of droppings marking the perambulations of some rodent, be it mouse, rat, or mole. Nor were there signals of more awesome presences:

groandles, slimes, slipperies, and rustles . . . my half-imagined terrors of the dark that everyone knew lived in cellars and underspaces, the black holes where none of us ever went or wanted to go.

How Mr. Fithian had managed such a stunning reversal I never knew. I was a boy then, not a home planner. I never checked the details of his cellar's construction, never tried to find the secret of its friendliness, its security, its dryness, its benevolent lighting, its freedom from damp, rodents, demons, and dark.

Of course, I have never seen another cellar like it. Nor, I'm certain, has anyone. By last count, I have lived in some twenty-nine other structures, and repaired or rebuilt dozens more, and I have never seen such a cellar, not even one that comes close. Neither, I'll bet, have you.

But what I learned from Mr. Fithian is a lesson I have never forgotten: Such cellars are possible. And that is the sort of cellar I want in our new home. However, I'm pretty sure it's not going to be what we'll get. I've seen too many other underspaces to believe that.

Should I tell you about one from my childhood? This underspace projected such an image of horror that it is still hanging there with other unforgettable portraits in the gallery of my memories. It had to have been a sort of dug cellar; its walls and floors, in my memory, were earthen. Surely some of them were, because they were holed with rat tunnels.

The house was a large, rambling, old country place. At one end, probably the most recent addition, there was a coal furnace, the central heating system that struggled to keep the place warm. That small space wasn't so bad, but it opened onto the earthen tomb that stretched under the rest of the house. It was space almost tall enough to allow my brother and me to stand; we were about nine and ten, so it must have been tough going for an adult along the dark passage we sometimes traversed, where we often played hide-and-seek with our sister.

That was when we would run underground from one end of the house to the other, and that was when we would see the rats, their pointed, whiskered brown noses pushing from the entrances to their black-holed tunnels, their darting forms scuttling ahead of us and vanishing into the dark as we approached.

Had enough? It's true, every word. That was the underspace of my childhood, my formative years. But don't jump to any hasty Freudian conclusions. It is not the only reason underspaces have always been such an awesome presence in my consciousness.

After the old house in the country, we moved to an old house in Manhattan — comparative luxury, to be sure, but only for those who never descended the cellar steps. They were narrow, rickety, and dark, accessible from a small door in a corner of the kitchen. They led to a grimy space under a mountain of coal, coal that thundered through a chute poked through the cellar's only window, which was opened once each fall when the coal truck arrived to deliver its black avalanche.

The coal was fed to a furnace, and those two presences — coal and furnace — dominated that underspace. The rest of it was filled with dusty trunks, huge cobwebs, and dark corners where God only knows what lurked. My brother and I never played down there, not even when we most wanted to terrorize our sister.

Well, I could go on, but I think it's better to skip some of the other underspaces of my formative years, like the crawl space under another house in the country. The only times I recall having to creep in there were when I had to pull out some animal or other who had chosen to die under our dining room.

Skip all that; skip thirty years and arrive in Maine, at the underspace of an otherwise lovely house built in the 1890s by some of the finest shipbuilders in the nation. Upstairs, the woodwork sang of their shipfitting skills. In the cellar, we were reminded of how much these shipwrights must have missed the open water. Earthen-floored and sided with fieldstone, loosely cemented — if, indeed, that muddy mortar could be called cement — that underspace was habitable enough about nine months of the year. I mean, there were few rodents that I ever saw; a full-size person could stand up; and there were enough lights that worked so every dark corner vanished at the flick of a switch. But in the spring, when the ground began to thaw and the snows to melt, water sprang from the cellar's rock walls as if each stone had been struck by the rod of Moses. If it hadn't been for our sump pump, running off-on, off-on, off-on twenty-four hours a day, that basement would have taken just a day or so to become an indoor swimming pool.

And when the electrical power was cut off, as it frequently was in the ice and wind of March, the boys and I would have to line up in a familial bucket brigade, a human chain that was also a human sump pump. Without us, the oil burner, the fuse boxes, the washer and dryer, and the stored paraphernalia of a family of nine would have been submerged in an icy lake. I caught my own case of the flu from one of those stretches on the bucket brigade, and I vowed that the next place would never require such damp sacrifices.

Well, you know what happened at that next place. You and I and Jean, and all the kids, had met by then. With some of your advice (perhaps not quite enough), we built that passive solar house that had such a lovely and spacious soul. Framed as it was with century-old barn beams, open as it was to a glorious southern exposure that overlooked the full, free expanse of Middle Bay, it was a dramatic and happy "postindustrial" home for us all.

Provided we didn't spend too much time in the underspace. Perhaps you don't remember the first problem we ran into at the site (although I mentioned it in an earlier letter). The very qualities that made that point so spectacular — its view, its height above the bay, and its impressive rocky shores — were also the root cause of our foundation problems.

The point was what's known in Maine as a whaleback, a hump of solid granite scraped clean by the glaciers some ten thousand years ago and covered since then with a few feet of alluvial marine clay and a few inches of agonizingly accumulated topsoil. All else is, was, and always has been rock.

To put a stand-up cellar in that place would have meant blasting I-don't-know-how-many tons of granite; the cost would have meant we couldn't build the place we wanted. So we settled for a crawl space under the entire 104′ × 28′ structure, a crawl space among some fifty-two concrete posts protected from freezing by a skirt that enclosed the whole, kept the wind out, and allowed us to run our water pipes the length of the building. Even at a windy 25 degrees below zero outside that skirt of wood and insulation, those pipes never froze, so that part of the design worked.

But the total underspace was not a fun place to be. It was dark down there. Cobwebs reached for you as you crawled along to replace a filter in the oil burner or check a drippy connection under the boys' shower. And we had more than our share of resident field mice and chipmunks who moved in after the first frost, hauling a half-ton of acorns along to get them through the winter.

We avoided water problems, however, by what I thought of as a unique system. With rock and clay, we could have had a repeat of the pool we'd come so close to at our other place. So at the new house, we made a place for the water to gather on one side of the house — in a catch basin that drained a considerable area — and then we piped it right under the house, through a cistern that acted as an emergency water supply, and from there out and over the bank into the bay it had been trying to reach from the beginning. No more bucket brigades or sump pumps, and was I happy about that. I guess you could call it progress of a sort.

But it wasn't Mr. Fithian's cellar, and that's what I want, Charlie, that's what I've always wanted, ever since I was a boy.

Now here we are, Jean and I, about to build our own place, a place that will be the beneficiary of everything you and I and Jean have learned about houses and underspaces. And, as you have just realized, that includes my experiences with a variety of answers to the question, What goes under the house?

Well, now I'm asking you. And I want you to keep Mr. Fithian very much in mind as you run down the list of choices. Remember, Charlie: warm, dry, golden, secure, clean, drip-free, rat- and monster-free, and sump pump–free . . . and full of those glorious memories of that wonderful place I visited when my father sent me to get our re-caned chair.

Can we have a cellar like that, Charlie? Can we?

Hopefully,
John

Dear John,

Yes, a basement such as Mr. Fithian's is possible. The key requirements are: dryness, light, ventilation, heat, and regular use. To achieve the full impact that you describe, however, I think we would have to throw in Mr. Fithian himself and let the whole mixture age a few decades.

You've certainly done your research, John. Clearly you've spent more than a few sleepless nights worrying about what was going on down there. Still, the full basement lecture would probably clear up some of your slight misconceptions.

I'm a thorough person. I'm bothered by partial solutions, inventions that solve one problem brilliantly while ignoring one or more fundamental requirements. The geodesic dome is an example. It encloses the maximum volume of space using a minimum amount of material. But have you ever been in a dome? The space enclosed is spherical, so every partition, every cabinet, every window has to be custom-fitted, as in a yacht. And it's impossible to find acoustic privacy, since the dome shape focuses sound waves. And what do you cover it with, roofing or siding?

(Which reminds me of a story I just have to repeat, since you love stories so much. Seems a contractor was building a bunch of wood structures shaped like Quonset huts — those things that look like halves of gigantic culverts. He was using union labor, and an argument erupted between the roofers and the siders over whether the structures were all roof or all wall. The contractor's Solomon-like solution: Let the roofers begin and the siders take over at the point where the roofers fall off.)

Anyway, because I'm such a nut on complete solutions, I begin every design project with a list of requirements. That way I can judge the success of my brilliant solutions against the list. It keeps me honest.

The fundamental requirements for a foundation are to:

- Bear the load or weight of the house
- Anchor the house against wind
- Prevent vertical motion due to frost
- Isolate the house from the damp ground

Less universal, but sometimes very important, are to:

- Protect against termites
- Prevent winter heat loss
- Store heat in the winter
- Absorb heat in the summer
- Provide storage, working, or living space
- Contain heating, wiring, and plumbing

BEARING THE LOAD. Living in Maine, we are surrounded by examples of a wide range of soil-bearing capacities, the ability of the ground to support a load. I'm always amazed by the properties of beach sand. Crossing the upper beach is like walking on a pile of ball bearings — your feet sink several inches into the uncompacted sand. But below the high-tide line, where the sand has been gently agitated and settled by the wave motion, the same sand is nearly as hard as concrete.

A country road in summer is as hard as the turnpike, but not in mud season! I'm reminded of another Maine story. It seems a fellow was sitting on his porch waiting for the mail (probably the seed catalogue). He sees the mailman slogging up the road waist-high in mud.

"Hard goin'?" he yells.

"Not too bad," is the reply. "But a lot worse for my horse."

These examples illustrate two of the situations that must be avoided if your foundation is to bear its loads for a lifetime: uncompacted earth and wet soil. A third situation to avoid is soil that contains vegetation.

The soil beneath the frost line has been settling for thousands of years. Good; leave it that way. Soil disturbed during excavation should be carefully removed before placing the foundation. If that proves impossible, then the disturbed soil should be compacted either by vibration or by flooding with water, or it should be mixed with cement and water and allowed to set.

Soil above the water table (the level of constant saturation) can generally be dealt with through proper drainage. Unless your site is worth hundreds of thousands of dollars (like the Back Bay in Boston), however, stay clear of saturated soils and filled areas.

The problem with partially decomposed vegetation in a soil is that the vegetation is likely to continue decomposing, ultimately leaving you with just 1 percent solid matter and 99 percent water or void. Sometimes piers can be placed on a more solid footing below the organic material.

Building codes require that you either have the soil-bearing capacity of your site tested or that you assume the strengths listed in Table 7.

Now you see why the Bible advises one to build on bedrock (assuming it isn't referring only to moral foundations). Actually, as the following example will show, it's very easy to keep building loads smaller than the numbers in the table. In addition, soils loaded to these values are expected to compress a small amount. Since even the smallest amount of nonuniform settling can lead to cracks in rigid concrete foundations and plasterboard walls, I make the following recommendations: distribute the loads evenly, and limit them to about 1,000 pounds per square foot.

Illustration 49 shows the loads you might expect on a 1,000-square-foot (25′ × 40′) single-story house in Brunswick, Maine.

Table 7

ASSUMED SOIL-BEARING CAPACITIES

(in pounds per square foot)

Soft clay	3,000
Medium clay	5,000
Fine sand	4,000
Coarse sand	6,000
Gravel	8,000
Bedrock	30,000

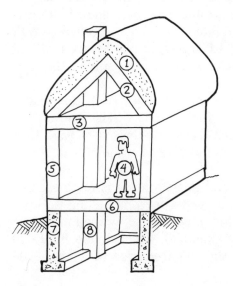

LOADS	PSF	LB
1. Snow	40	40,000
2. Roof	5	5,000
3. Ceiling	5	5,000
4. Live	40	40,000
5. Walls	5	5,000
6. Floor	10	10,000
7. Foundation	1,200	100,000
— Total on footing —		205,000
8. Chimney	2,000	6,000

49. Maximum load (weight) to be distributed by the foundation footing for a 1,000-square-foot house in Brunswick, Maine

1. The snow load is the maximum weight of snow expected once in fifty years. Of course, it might be greater in the mountains and smaller farther south. Every architect in town knows what theirs is, however. Note that the total weight is computed over the floor area rather than the larger area of the pitched roof, since no more snow falls on a roof than on the area of ground beneath it.
2. The weight of the roof itself is about 5 pounds per square foot unless covered with an unusually heavy roofing material, such as slate or clay tile.
3. The ceiling weight is the weight of the ceiling alone and doesn't include any junk stored in the attic. If you plan on finishing the attic for your mother-in-law, add a live load of 30 pounds per square foot.
4. The live load is the load imposed by your living in the house: your furnishings and your rowdy, party-loving friends. The building codes specify 40 pounds per square foot for the first floor. That's equivalent to a water bed or one friend per 4 square feet.
5. Wood walls actually weigh only 2 to 3 pounds per square foot, but the total of exterior and interior wall areas tends to be about twice the floor area, so I always use 5 pounds per square foot spread over the exterior walls. Of course, it would be higher for masonry walls.
6. The weight of a wood floor is around 5 pounds per square foot, but I round it up to 10 pounds per square foot to allow for some areas of heavier tile.
7. The basement wall, if masonry, can weigh as much as the entire rest of the house, including maximum snow and maximum friends. By itself, an 8-foot-high poured concrete wall exceeds the recommended 1,000 pounds per square foot. As shown in Illustration 49, the solution is to spread the load over a wider "footing."
8. Finally, there may be a masonry chimney — in this example, a 24-foot-high two-flue brick chimney. The load of this chimney is even greater than that of the basement wall, thus violating the second rule: uniform distribution of loads.

The solution for excessive and uneven loads is footings: like snowshoes, they provide wider bases to prevent sinking into the earth. First add up all the weights to be carried by the foundation footing (205,000 pounds in our example). Then divide by 1,000 pounds per square foot to get the required area of footing (205 square feet). Next divide this footing area by the perimeter length of the footing (25 feet + 25 feet + 40 feet + 40 feet = 130 feet) to get the required width of the footing (about 1.5 feet, or 18 inches).

Turning next to the chimney, divide its total weight (6,000 pounds) by 1,000 pounds per square foot to get the required area of its own separate footing (6 square feet). So a nice footing for the chimney would be 2 feet by 3 feet. Now wasn't that simple?

ANCHORING AGAINST WIND. Now that we've taken care of holding the building up, let's consider holding the building down. I know it's hard to visualize a flying building, but I have a hard time believing an airplane will fly, too. First of all, we're not talking about a breeze; we're talking about *big* wind, the kind of wind the old-timers talk about from fifty years ago, the kind of wind that makes you walk inclined at 30 degrees, that knocks you off your feet, that uproots ancient oak trees. We're talking about air moving at 80 to 100 miles per hour. In case you still don't get the picture, try sticking your hand out your car window the next time you're speeding on the turnpike.

Second, we're talking about an empty house (deduct live load) with no snow on the roof (deduct snow load) that is possibly disconnected from its foundation (deduct basement walls). Adding all of the remaining weights in the above example, we have a house that weighs only 25,000 pounds.

The maximum force of the wind in an exposed location is usually taken to be 20 pounds per square foot. Our example house exposes a height of about 16 feet from top of foundation to top of roof, and a width of 40 feet. The total exposed billboardlike area is thus 640 square feet. Multiplied by a wind pressure of 20 pounds per square foot, we find that the total sideward thrust of the wind could be as much as 12,800 pounds, which is comparable to the weight of the building.

Illustration 50 shows three things that could conceivably happen in such a wind:

1. The building could slide off its foundation. Much to my chagrin, this happened to my summer cottage. The natives were very amused. One called and said, "You might want to look at your cottage. Had a bit of a blow the other night." The building had moved 12 feet sideways. Not a window was broken, but you should have seen what the chimney did in falling through the roof and two floors!

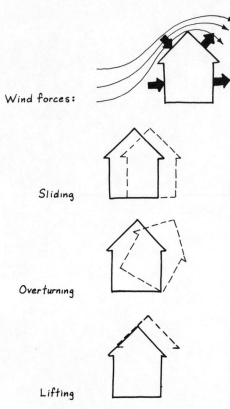

Wind forces:

Sliding

Overturning

Lifting

50. Possible building movements due to extreme wind

Ⓐ

Frost Line

51. Perimeter insulation to prevent frost heaving of a slab

2. If the wind gets under the house (as it might with a pier foundation), it might flip the house over. This way the chimney would spare the floors but take out a wall or two. An overturned house is also more difficult to return to its foundation than is a house that has slid.
3. Unless your house was designed by Eero Saarinen, it's unlikely that it would attempt an actual takeoff. However, it's very common for the leeward roof to depart if poorly connected to the wall and its other half.

It is thus clearly advantageous to include the weight of the foundation in the total weight of the house. This we can do, of course, if we take care to bolt the two together securely. You'll notice that some of the foundations we'll be considering don't weigh very much, but neither does a fence post, and have you ever tried to pull a fence post out of the ground? The ground exerts tremendous lateral pressures on things placed in its embrace, so embedded lightweight foundations work just as well as the more massive versions we are accustomed to.

Accepted practice is to bolt the building sill to masonry foundations with one ½-inch anchor bolt every 6 feet on center, and with two bolts within 1 foot of every corner. Pier foundations require at least one ½-inch bolt per pier. Wood foundations are secured by nailing the sill of the building to the top plate of the wood foundation wall.

PREVENTING FROST HEAVES. Water expands upon freezing. That's all we need to know to predict trouble when the ground freezes under a building. Since, like the milk in the old-fashioned glass bottles, the water-soaked ground has nowhere to expand but up, up goes the building, too. Some of the results are merely annoying, like not finding the front step where you last remembered it. Others can be more serious, like shearing off the incoming water pipe that you safely buried beneath the frost to prevent freezing (Illustration 51A). Mobile homes without foundations are connected to water and sewer through flexible couplings for this reason. There are three ways to prevent frost heaves:

1. Make sure there is no water in the soil to freeze in the first place. Provide drainage around the building by surrounding the foundation with gravel and by lowering the water table to below the footing with drainage pipes.

2. Make sure the building is standing on footings placed beneath the depth of maximum frost (refer back to the map in Illustration 36, page 68).

3. Prevent the cold from penetrating the ground under the building. A layer of waterproof insulation (extruded polystyrene) placed 1 foot below the surface will retard the upward flow of heat from the earth long enough to block the frost. Illustration 51B shows how a layer of 1½-inch rigid blue Styrofoam around the house prevents the incursion of frost and heaving of the house.

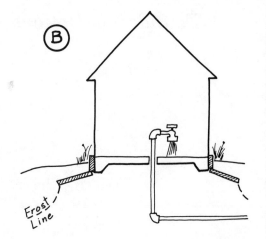

ISOLATING FROM MOISTURE. Water seeks its own level, which is to say that if the ground outside a basement is saturated with water, the water will attempt to flow into the basement until it reaches the same level inside and out. How hard will water try to get into the basement? We have Archimedes (287–212 B.C.) to thank for the answer: with a pressure equal to the weight of the column of water above the basement floor. For example, assume it is spring and the ground around a building is saturated to the surface 6 feet above the basement floor. Thus, the pressure of the water seeking to penetrate the basement floor is the weight of a 6-foot column of water — 6 feet × 62.4 pounds per cubic foot, or about 375 pounds per square foot.

I know you are a great fisherman, John, but the solution is not caulking and painting the basement as if it were a boat. If you by some miracle succeeded, you might also succeed in launching your house like a boat, since the total uplifting force of 375,000 pounds on the 1,000-square-foot basement floor exceeds the total weight of the house and its foundation. More likely you'd simply buckle the basement floor.

Instead, the solution is to purposely lower the water level around the house with perforated drainage pipes. These pipes, seen in each of the basement illustrations, are placed around the outside of the basement wall below the level of the basement floor. They slope and drain away to an even lower point on the site, to the city sewer, or to a sump pump in the basement. The sandy or gravelly backfill around the wall ensures that the water table immediately around the basement is at the level of the drain; in other words, below the basement floor.

There are plenty of high-tech alternative solutions to the dilemma of having built on top of a well, but in my experience none works better than a properly installed drainage system.

Foundation Options

A basement is not a foundation, nor is a foundation a base-ment — necessarily. I wrote that in *From the Ground Up*, and I still believe it. Illustration 52 shows nine options, all of which perform the four basic foundation functions. The following illus-trations (53–61) give the details. Table 8 rates their strengths and weaknesses in eight categories.

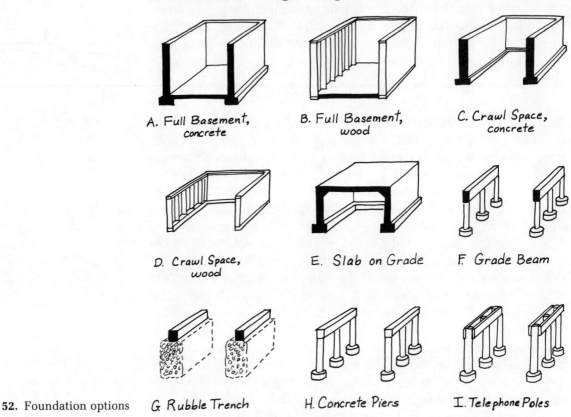

A. Full Basement, concrete

B. Full Basement, wood

C. Crawl Space, concrete

D. Crawl Space, wood

E. Slab on Grade

F. Grade Beam

G. Rubble Trench

H. Concrete Piers

I. Telephone Poles

52. Foundation options

FOUNDATION	Cost, % of Maximum	Living Space	Resale Value	Appearance	Heat Storage	Construction Ease	Utility Ease	Insulation Ease
Full, Concrete	100	◐	●	●	●	○	●	◐
Full, Wood	88	●	◐	◐	◐	●	●	●
Crawl, Concrete	66	○	◐	●	◐	○	●	●
Crawl, Wood	57	○	○	◐	○	●	●	●
Slab on Grade	62	○	◐	●	●	◐	○	◐
Grade Beam on Piers	70	○	◐	◐	◐	○	◐	◐
Grade Beam on Rubble	70	○	◐	◐	◐	○	◐	◐
Concrete Piers	55	○	○	○	○	◐	○	◐
Telephone Poles	55	○	○	○	○	●	○	◐

(Column group heading: Characteristics)

Table 8
FOUNDATIONS COMPARED

This is such a common foundation in northern areas that most northerners don't distinguish between the words *basement* and *foundation*. It provides convenient storage space (if dry), protection against frozen pipes, space for a furnace or boiler, thermal mass for temperature stability both winter and summer, and living space for the uncritical inhabitant. It also is expensive, likely to fail, and the most difficult kind of basement to install.

If you are going to contract any part of your house, this is the project to consider. For the novice builder, the full poured-concrete foundation is the nastiest, most backbreaking, time-consuming, and discouraging job of all — and, because it is the first step in building a home, it may come at a time when the beginner's confidence is low.

Don't attempt this foundation around bedrock. Blasting is very expensive, and allowing bedrock into the basement almost guarantees a water problem.

There are tremendous thermal benefits to be gained from insulating outside a concrete wall with rigid extruded polystyrene. First, counter to intuition, concrete is a lousy insulator. A single inch of foam insulation has the same thermal resistance as 5 feet of concrete! As a result, 15 to 25 percent of the winter heat loss of a typical home occurs through its concrete foundation. Second, large quantities of heat energy can be stored in a concrete wall with small changes in temperature. The thermal mass of the wall acts like a flywheel, holding the building at a constant temperature. As a result, the interior living space of the building becomes less responsive to swings in outside temperature.

PROS. Best resale value, large thermal mass if insulated outside, good access to utilities, low-cost storage space.

CONS. Expensive, often wet; repairs costly and not always effective.

FULL BASEMENT, CONCRETE

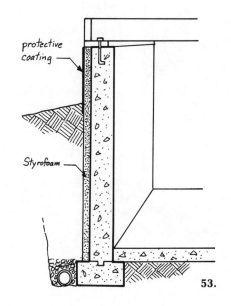

53.

FULL BASEMENT, WOOD

If you're one of those who confuse concrete with foundation, you'll just love this one! Imagine starting your house by building the first-floor wood walls 6 feet below ground. Wow! This one will require heavy marketing.

About twenty-five years ago, a bunch of back-to-basics Canadians (Canadians are like that; they can't afford not to be) asked what would happen if one were to start building a wood house underground instead of on top of concrete, especially if the wood were immune to moisture and rot. They couldn't think of any problems, and indeed there haven't been.

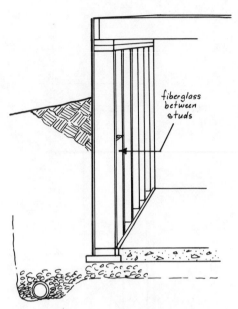

54. Full basement, wood

The all-weather wood foundation (AWWF) has subsequently proven to be faster, less expensive, warmer, easier to insulate, and easier to build than its concrete equivalent. Of course the masonry industry and most lending institutions have been less than enthusiastic. I'm sure you're old enough, John, to remember the initial resistance of plumbers to plastic pipe and of plasterers to gypsum drywall. I can't see why the AWWF won't in time similarly become the common choice, in this case replacing the concrete basement.

Here's how the AWWF works. After the building dimensions are staked out and the batter boards (boards outside each corner of the foundation that serve as a temporary reference) erected, the basement hole is excavated to a depth of 12 to 15 inches below the future basement floor. Drainage can be provided either around the outside perimeter or under the center of the floor. If installed around the perimeter, as shown in Illustration 54, a perforated 4-inch polyvinyl chloride pipe (perforations facing down) is carefully sloped ¼ inch per 12 inches on a bed of crushed stone in a slightly deeper perimeter trench. The loop of pipe connects at a single point to an unperforated pipe, which then drains either to daylight, the city sewer, or a sump pump. A less expensive alternative is a sump pit 3 feet in diameter × 3 feet deep, which serves to collect all groundwater at a central point before similarly draining away. A bed of crushed stone between 6 and 12 inches deep is then carefully leveled over the entire area. Water will never rise above the level of the gravel nor, therefore, of the basement floor provided the drainpipe remains unclogged.

The walls are constructed of water- and termite-proof pressure-treated framing lumber and plywood. It is simplest, especially in bad weather, to construct the walls off-site in 8-foot sections and then bolt them together on site. The wall framing is either 2 × 6 inches or 2 × 8 inches, depending on the depth of the soil backfill. As you'll see when we get into the subject of insulation, I prefer 2″ × 8″ framing because it accommodates R-30 (an insulation measurement) fiberglass batts. The footing member is always one size larger: i.e., 2 × 8 or 2 × 10.

After all wall sections are leveled, squared, and fastened, the gravel is again leveled, a 6-mil polyethylene sheet spread, and a 3- to 4-inch concrete slab poured to the level of a pressure-treated screed board (guide for screeding, or leveling, the slab) nailed to the bottom plate of the wall.

The floor above is constructed before backfilling the trench. The slab below and the floor above resist the pressure of the soil during backfilling. Further protection against incursion of groundwater is provided by a 6-mil polyethylene sheet wrapped around the below-grade area of wall and held in place by a strip of pressure-treated wood at ground level. Finally, painting the plywood gray makes it look like concrete.

The inside of the wall is finished as if it were above ground: wired, plumbed, insulated, vapor-barriered, and drywalled. With sufficient window area, this basement comes close to above-ground space in livability.

The AWWF is much simpler to construct than the concrete basement, but I still steer the novice toward a builder with experience in this specific type of foundation. Critical areas in which experience counts are leveling, squaring, and fastening the foundation to the building.

PROS. Low-cost space, easy to build in all weather, driest of the basements, easy to insulate and finish.

CONS. Negligible thermal mass, low resale value; bankers often reluctant to finance.

CRAWL SPACE, CONCRETE

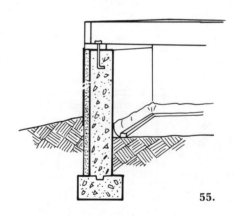

55.

This is what results when you delete the space requirement from the list of functions of a concrete foundation. The wall extends only to frost depth, and no floor slab is necessary. Builders in many areas favor the concrete crawl space because it looks like a full foundation but costs a third less.

Although no slab is required, a perimeter drain and a 6-mil polyethylene ground cover should be installed to prevent excess moisture from rising into the house. Make sure there is also a trapdoor and adequate crawling room down there just in case you want to mess with the furnace, plumbing, or wiring.

Like the full concrete basement, the concrete crawl space can provide thermal benefits. Insulating outside the wall with extruded polystyrene again places the thermal mass of the concrete inside the insulation with the living space. The large heat capacities of the concrete and of the earth floor prevent pipes from freezing in the coldest climates. Insulating outside the wall also allows use of the crawl space as a gigantic plenum or distribution manifold for a warm-air furnace, saving on construction costs. Additional benefits are a warm floor in winter and a cool house in summer.

PROS. Good resale value, easy to insulate, space for utilities, moderate thermal mass.

CONS. Minimal storage space, difficult to construct, expensive considering space gained.

CRAWL SPACE, WOOD

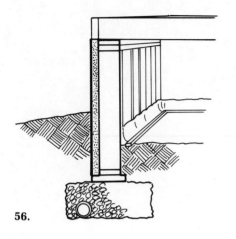

56.

From the three systems above, you should be able to imagine how to build a crawl-space foundation using pressure-treated wood. It's simply a shortened version of the AWWF with the concrete slab replaced by a polyethylene sheet. Recalling the four basic functions of any foundation, however, make sure: (1) that the soil is backfilled against the outside to a depth of at least a foot to provide wind resistance, and (2) that the bottom of the gravel footing is below the maximum depth of frost for your area.

Here I've shown the option of exterior extruded polystyrene insulation. Although more expensive than fiberglass between the framing, the foam insulates deeper and better, and the latex-cement protective coating looks just like concrete. This is such a simple foundation that I don't hesitate to recommend it even to the first-time house builder.

PROS. The most inexpensive way to provide all foundation functions except space and thermal mass, easiest to build, can be built in any weather, easy to insulate, good space for utilities.

CONS. Low wind resistance, low resale value, minimal storage space.

SLAB ON GRADE

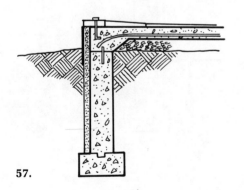

57.

There are several versions of the concrete slab, the variables being what supports the building walls and what supports the slab. The version shown is the most conservative, with both walls and slab supported by a perimeter concrete wall extending below frost depth. If your local building inspector approves, you can save money by pouring the slab on a bed of gravel above ground level (a "floating" slab) and insulating the perimeter against frost to a depth of 1 foot and out horizontally a distance equal to the frost depth. Since the edge of the slab carries the weight of the building plus the snow load, the slab edge should be reinforced in both directions with reinforcing bars ("rebars").

Some builders recommend the slab as the cheapest way to build a floor. That's because they think a concrete slab is a floor. It may be a floor in a cow barn or body shop, but it will never be in my house. By the time you have achieved an acceptably attractive floor by laying tile or slate and then adding area rugs for comfort, you're right up there in cost. And covering the slab with wall-to-wall carpet ruins its most appealing feature — thermal-mass storage.

Another disenchantment is the difficulty of running pipes and wires. Rather than simply running them any which way under the floor to pop up wherever convenient, wiring must be fed through plastic or metal conduit. This is not only expensive; it also requires coordination with the plumber and electrician, and makes future changes extremely difficult.

I recommend the slab in only two instances other than a basement floor: as a garage floor and as the floor of a sun space or greenhouse. But I am keeping my eye on a promising new technique: Masonry contractors are now experimenting with cast-in-place tile floors. They add dark brown, red, or green dye to the concrete mix, press a mold into the still-wet concrete, and finally wax the cured concrete. The result is a "tile" floor at half the cost. Don't get excited about doing a large floor yourself, however. Even the professionals get nervous when the concrete starts setting up faster than they can mold it.

PROS. Excellent thermal mass for passive solar applications, easy to insulate, good resale value, easy to build, reasonable cost.

CONS. Tiring on feet and legs, difficult to keep clean, difficult to run utilities, no additional space.

GRADE BEAM ON PIERS

A grade beam is a concrete beam at grade or ground level supported every 6 to 8 feet by concrete piers extending downward to solid footings below the frost line. Having small cross sections, the concrete piers require footings of at least 24 inches in diameter.

The usual procedure is to auger holes 24 to 30 inches in diameter to below the frost line, pour the concrete footings (using the holes as forms), and insert reinforcing rods while the concrete is still wet. The next day, place and backfill around cylindrical fiberboard forms and again pour concrete to the level of the cut-off forms or to nails driven through the forms at the desired height. On the third day, cut the forms off, level the ground to the top of the piers, build forms for the beams with 2 × 12's, place ½-inch reinforcing rods inside the forms, fill the forms with concrete, and float ½-inch anchor bolts for attachment of the building sill.

If the soil beneath the grade beam contains silt or clay, the ground level should be lowered by several inches. Otherwise frost may push up against the beam and crack it or dislodge the entire foundation. Also, if the space under the building is entirely enclosed, good old 6-mil polyethylene should be spread over the ground to prevent moisture problems.

I don't trust the grade beam in any but well-drained soils because of the potential frost problems. Water expands 9 percent

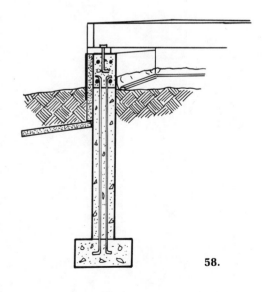

58.

upon freezing. If the soil around the piers is 4 feet deep and contains 30 percent water, then the ground surface could heave 0.09 × 0.30 × 48 inches, or about 1¼ inches. The frost can grab the rough, unyielding, cylindrical piers with a mighty grip. If strong enough, it may lift the piers, footings and all, or it may fracture them. Of course, the piers could be poured in a drained gravel-filled trench, but at added expense.

PROS. Low cost, looks like a full basement.

CONS. Difficult for the novice, no additional space, no thermal mass, no space for utilities.

GRADE BEAM ON RUBBLE

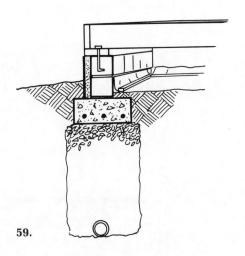

59.

The rubble, or stone-filled, trench makes a lot of sense. Whether it makes a good foundation depends on what you're looking for. As I pointed out earlier, frost heaves occur when water in the soil beneath a foundation freezes. That being the case, there are three ways to prevent the heaves: (1) place the footing below the maximum depth of frost, (2) insulate the ground so that it doesn't freeze, or (3) make sure there is no water in the ground to freeze.

Rubble trenches operate on the third principle. Trenches are dug to below the frost line, and perforated drain tiles are placed at the bottoms of the trenches on a few inches of crushed stone and are sloped at ¼ inch per 12 inches to daylight. Then the trenches are filled with crushed stone or coarse gravel. Water that runs into the trenches immediately drains away, leaving nothing to freeze.

Naturally, it's possible to overwhelm the drainage system, as a friend of mine did. He discovered his trenches were the gathering place for the runoff of his considerable driveway — too late. One winter day, when the ground around the house was frozen (and therefore impermeable), a torrential downpour flooded the trenches. Before all the water could drain away, some of it froze, stopping up the rubble. Every time water ran into the trench, the layer of ice grew thicker and the trench heaved more. To avoid this, slope the ground away from the building and discharge water from gutters and downspouts away from the trenches.

After providing for proper drainage, form and pour a concrete grade beam with reinforcing bars and anchor bolts right on top of the rubble trench. The illustration shows a concrete-block crawl-space wall on top of the grade beam, but a pressure-treated wood sill would work as well.

As usual, place a 6-mil polyethylene sheet on the ground beneath the building. Another polyethylene sheet draped over the grade beam and under the soil backfill will help keep water out of the trench.

PROS. Easy to construct, looks like a concrete wall.

CONS. No additional space, no thermal mass.

CONCRETE PIERS

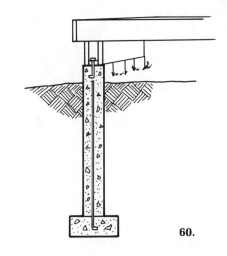

60.

This foundation is exactly the same as the grade beam on piers (Illustration 58) except that the concrete beam is replaced with a pressure-treated wood beam. In the illustration, the wood beam is built up: First a 2 × 4 or 2 × 6 (depending on how accurately you placed the anchor bolts) is bolted to the piers, and then the load-carrying 2 × 8's or 2 × 10's are nailed to the bolted piece. Shingles can be shimmed between the piers and beam for leveling before tightening the anchor bolts.

The reinforcing rods splaying out into the footings are important to the design because: (1) The piers alone have little sideward stability if placed in creeping soils or if projecting far out of the ground, and (2) frost tends to grab the rough cylindrical concrete piers and lift them from their footings.

Due to the potential for frost heaves in poorly drained soils and the lack of protection for pipes under the building, I recommend the concrete-pier foundation only for well-drained soils and for structures containing no plumbing, such as ells, porches, decks, outbuildings, or summer cottages.

PROS. Very low cost, easy to build, easy to insulate (the floor).

CONS. No additional space, likely to heave in poorly drained soils, low resale value, looks cheap, no provision for freeze proofing utilities, no thermal mass.

TELEPHONE POLES

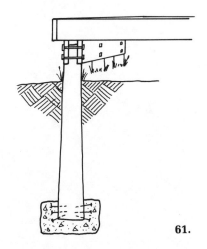

61.

Replacing concrete piers with pressure-treated telephone poles has several advantages: (1) The pole is tapered and slippery so that the frost cannot grip it, (2) poles sticking far out of the ground can be braced diagonally, and (3) mistakes are easily corrected with a saw (to make smaller) or a hammer and nails (to make bigger).

As with concrete piers, cantilevering the floor joists over the sills allows a margin of error of up to a foot in the placement of the piers. This advantage cannot be overestimated in the case of the first-time builder. Knowing that concrete — like vinyl siding — is final leads to quickened pulse, weak knees, indecision, and finally depression.

Unhappily, I speak from experience in relating the major deficiency of the telephone-pole foundation. Although it is technologically superior in many ways, few besides myself believe it is

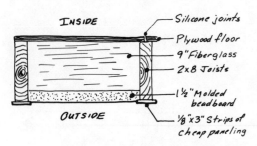

62. Insulating between the floor joists of a building on piers

INSIDE

Silicone joints
Plywood floor
9" Fiberglass
2x8 Joists
1½" Molded beadboard
⅛"x3" Strips of cheap paneling

OUTSIDE

a serious foundation. The assumption that wood poles placed in the ground will quickly rot and crumble must be genetically passed on, for of the hundred potential buyers of my pole-mounted home, only one failed to object to the poles. He worked for the phone company.

However, Illustration 62 shows how to insulate floors over concrete-pier and telephone-pole foundations. The method is simple and results in a floor as well insulated and warm to the touch as the cathedral ceiling it emulates.

Considering resale value only I recommend telephone-pole foundations for outbuildings, porches, decks, and seaside cottages.

PROS. Very low cost, forgiving to build, easy to insulate, frost-proof, easy to fix.

CONS. Doesn't look like a permanent foundation, no additional space, no provision for utilities, no thermal mass.

Your friend,
Charlie

LETTER
17

Dear Charlie,

I always knew you to be a careful, cautious person. Meticulously so, one might say.

And your answers to my foundation/basement (I'm *still* not absolutely certain of the differences) questions are right in character.

You don't tell me directly how we can achieve our dreams, our memories of warm, safe underspace. But you do list every option, with just enough of your own analysis to point us in the correct direction.

Okay. After a week or so of discussion, and after talking with a few concrete contractors and foundation people about cost estimates based on those plans we sent along a month or so ago, Jean and I have made a decision.

Like so many that will be made between now and the time we finish this project, it's a kind of compromise, based on what we most want and what we can reasonably afford. After getting this far with the new home, I've decided that what I've always said about building houses is more true than ever: A building is enclosed space with more decisions than nails holding it together. For every dimension of every design of every space there are dozens of options and thus hundreds of dozens of decisions, because the builder, owner, designer has to choose from combinations of options. And guys like you, with your bushels of detailed information, can sometimes make the process more difficult. After all, think how simple a foundation/basement choice might be if we were ignorant of each alternative.

But, of course, we are not. On the contrary, we have a plethora. And I still have my memories of Mr. Fithian.

Jean has heard that story, and she shares the same hopes, but for a different set of reasons, more physical than metaphysical. She wants a stand-up, warm, dry, and useful space, because she has learned over her years as a mother and chairman of the house-management board that there is no such thing as too much useful storage space.

So we both agree we want what many folks call a full cellar. You call it full basement, concrete, or full basement, wood, which then becomes AWWF for all-weather wood foundation.

We'll take the AWWF. In this case, we're taking it on trust. But then, if we don't trust you, we shouldn't have come this far and certainly couldn't go any further. If the Canadians have been using the technique for twenty-five years, then it must work, considering the severity of their winters and the wetness of their springs. And if it costs less than concrete but gives us the same sense of dryness, utility, snugness, and warmth, then we're going to go for it. You have, after all, been right about these things in the past, Charlie.

But we're only going to put the full cellar, the friendly underspace, beneath the two-story 18' × 24' portion of the house. That's our compromise. Based on the numbers we've collected, it will cost too much to excavate and build a below-ground first story under the entire house. It would mean we'd have to give up on something else further down the line, and, except for my sentimental memories, there really isn't any reason why a compact, cost-conscious home needs a total full cellar. Especially if you keep in mind our commitment to doing this job for $50,000 or thereabouts so we won't be in hock for the rest of our days.

So we'll have an 18 × 24 monument to Mr. Fithian, and then we'll settle for a wood, or AWWF, crawl space under the one-story, rather narrow rectangle (about 35 × 16) that contains the living room, dining room, and kitchen on the building's north side. If, as you said in your latest, this is "the most inexpensive way to provide all foundation functions except space and thermal mass," and we're already committed to the AWWF system for our full cellar, then in our view, we have arrived at a sensible, money-saving compromise that won't really affect the resale value (because we do have the warm, dry, stand-up cellar to show off) and yet does everything you say a foundation should do . . . except give us more storage space and thermal mass.

But then, as I said, this is a compromise, as is every decision when you deal with a budget, when you try to get the most for the least.

I hope you agree with our choice. Well, let's put that another way: You may not fully agree, but let's hope you think what we have decided on is wise and practical, and will work well under the conditions Maine and our budget have set for us.

If I don't hear from you within the week, I'll assume we can proceed, that we are above ground, resting securely and sagaciously on our AWWF that is about half the Fithian ideal and half a practical crawl space — a sensible compromise, it would seem.

Your friend,
John

7. *Framing and Sheathing*

Dear Charlie,

Unless you have sailed away — and it's still early in the season for a cruise, even though it's not too soon to start painting your boat — you must have approved of the all-weather wood foundation mix that we put together. If you hadn't, I'm certain I would have heard a squawk by now.

Hooray! We've gotten above ground level. At least we will once the weather breaks and we can get the holes dug, the insulation put in, and the underground wood panels in place. As important as this may seem to you, I just can't get too excited about it. I mean, I like to be able to see some physical evidence that a structure is taking shape. You know, studs, or whatever the proper term is, where walls will go; and beams, if that's the right word, that define the levels of the place, its floors and ceilings. A hole in the ground just doesn't give me enough to dream on, even though I know we've got to have it if anything else is going to happen.

The word I'm looking for is *framing*. I'll bet you thought I didn't know that. I do. But not because I'm such a great house builder. For me, the word has more to do with what a writer does than what a carpenter does; framing is a kind of outline, even though it's also the basic structural skeleton that sets the shape of all that follows.

When I hear the word, the same image always comes to mind. It was born when I discovered a book about shipbuilding in our local library. Charlie, be patient; I'm not going to wander too far.

But you know where we built our last home, the one I've already mentioned a score of times, the one with the dark crawl space and the sunlit rooms — we built it on a point. Well, that

LETTER
18

point overlooks a cove where the old families of the area, the Pennells, Orrs, and Simpsons, once built some of the finest wooden ships in the world. Made from the great trees of Maine, those ships sailed to China from that small cove beside our point.

When I went to the library, I was looking for more information about those ships. I wanted to learn their names; I wanted to be able to see them in my mind's eye when I stood there at our kitchen corner window and looked out over the cove.

One of the books — actually, more of a collection of sketches — that the librarian found for me was a step-by-step diagram of how a wooden ship went together. The artist had done a superb job of clarifying but not oversimplifying the process of shipbuilding (from the ground up, if you will). In the first sketch, I could see just enough of the memory of a tree in the shape of a keel to understand how it had been hewn. And then, when the ribs were notched, bent, and joined to the keel, I could understand how they would interlock with the planks to make a cross webbing of wood that had strength and resilience enough to withstand open ocean storms.

Once the sketches got past the ribbing and planking, they became much more complex; a fellow would have to have been a shipwright to understand each notation, term, instruction, and footnote that had been penned in the margin. Those details were beyond me, but in the bending, framing, and joining of those graceful wooden designs that began with the great keel, I could comprehend the wonder of wood, the ways it could be manipulated that allowed it to be firm yet flexible, that allowed it to be hewn, sawn, pegged, nailed, and drilled and yet remain sturdy enough to carry a cargo of Kennebec River ice from Casco Bay to the China Sea.

As I often am, I was so taken with my ability to "see" how a wooden ship was built that I came back home and began drawing designs for a home built like a ship. "I want it to look as if one of those old schooners had run aground here," I explained to Jean and the children, "and been remodeled just enough to become our new home."

They were tolerant, as always; they let me happily exhaust my enthusiasm with sketches and drawings that were as impractical as they were imperfect. (Imagine, if you can, the stress problems involved with building a place that looks like a ship's stern hanging out over the bank, over the very bay.) I moved closer to reality from that experience, but I never again moved far away from a love of the structural wonders of wood, wood you can see, wood that is as massive and as obviously functional as those superb ribs rising from the skeletons of those sailing ships. With such wonders as a daily witness in a home of visible wood, I told myself, the place would have a kind of religious integrity as well as structural presence. And it could thus survive every kind of storm, from within or from without.

So there you have it. Once I began to understand the history of this place, of our new home, of the place where our children had been born and raised, I rekindled my romance with wood — with wood I could see, wood that reaffirmed the natural strengths, wood that could be skillfully shaped, steamed, sawn, and sculpted to become its own statement, needing no embellishment, no cover-up, no disguise.

That's the way I want to see wood in our new home, Charlie, as a presence as well as a structural material. I'm sure it's possible; but, like my dreaming over other blueprints and sketches, I wonder if it's practical.

And I don't have the answer. I'm not a physicist or an engineer. I don't know how thick or how wide or how long a piece of wood must be to support X hundred pounds. I don't even know enough about the terms to keep them straight. Just what is the difference between a joist and a beam, or a header and a girder? Charlie, do I have to know these things to go to a lumberyard and buy wood? And where can we find those big beams I want to be able to see, the ones that remind me of the sailing ships that made this nation possible? How can we best design the place to use wood the way it was used by those shipbuilders, for strength and beauty combined?

You're going to have to start working now, Charlie. All I've told you is the way I feel, the way *we* feel, about wood. Now you're going to have to try to convert these feelings to specifics, to framing details. There's a challenge for you, Charlie. And I eagerly await your response. As I said, I get excited when I think that one of these days in the near future, we'll have more to look at than a hole in the ground, even if it is an AWWF hole.

So don't wait too long, Charlie, please.

Your friend,
John

Dear John,

After reading your last letter, I'm afraid you and I are in for some philosophical heavy weather. Your reverence for wood and old ship frames in particular is wonderful, but please don't forget that you and Jean asked me to help you design a compact low-cost house. It's difficult enough to do that rationally. All I ask is that you keep your thoughts and emotions separate, and that you consider what I'm about to present with an open mind. If, after a complete and logical analysis, you decide you still want a timber-framed house, that's okay with me. But your decision will then be based on fact rather than fancy, and my conscience will be clear.

If I seem a little sensitive about this point, it's not due entirely to your letter. My reaction stems from having dealt with the same emotions in a thousand owner-building students before you. As a reaction to the craziness of the world — the pell-mell pace, the shoddiness, the dishonesty — they take comfort in the old ways. It's a sentiment that I share. As you'll recall, that very same feeling called me back to the Maine of my childhood some fourteen years ago. But I also sincerely believe we should keep our eyes open and our heads above the pool of sentimentality, on that off chance that someone, somehow, might after all come up with a better idea.

I ask you the same question I've asked a thousand students before: What do you think Leonardo da Vinci — or the great shipbuilders, for that matter — would have done with plywood or fiberglass?

WHAT DOES THE FRAME OF A BUILDING DO?

Like the bones of an animal, the rigid frame of a house defines its dimensions, its shape. It also supports snow on the roof and parties in the living room, and prevents windows from popping when the wind blows hard.

Have you ever studied a skeleton closely, particularly that of a bird? Evolution has engineered bones to be just sufficient for their applications. They are thickened at points of maximum stress, and precisely in proportion to that stress. (Would thicker bones make a better bird?) And rather than merely supporting flesh, the bones are designed to work in conjunction with muscles and skin membranes for even greater efficiency.

So what about a timber frame? Is more wood better? Do thicker pieces of wood really perform the functions of a house frame better? If one 2 × 4 suffices, are two better? Or, now that we understand structural forces and have new, more predictable materials, should we not be designing optimal structures — houses designed to use no more material than necessary to perform their functions; houses that therefore cost no more than necessary?

"Shoddy," I can hear you muttering. But do you consider a Shaker chair shoddy as compared with a log chair? Of course not. What we find beautiful in Shaker furniture is precisely its graceful optimization.

What are the forces acting on a building frame? First of all, they are called loads in the trade, and they are measured in pounds per square foot, or psf for short. For example, suppose you stage a birthday party for Jean. Now, Jean is very popular, and you have to invite fifty of her friends if you invite one. Unfortunately, not all of Jean's friends are as trim as she; they weigh in at an average of 160 pounds. If they all crowd into your 200-square-foot living room at once, your floor will have to support 50 × 160 pounds, or 8,000 pounds, spread over 200 square feet. That's what we in the trade call a live load of 40 pounds per square foot.

Illustration 63 shows the loads to assume in designing a house:

Dead loads are the weights of the building materials alone. Some constructions, such as unfinished attic floors, weigh as little as 5 pounds per square foot, but tiled floors can weigh 12. Since dead loads are much smaller than the other loads below, it is conventional to assume a conservative 10 pounds per square foot.

Live loads are those weights imposed by occupancy: furnishings, stored materials, and people. Building codes generally specify for residential construction:

Attic, no storage	10 psf
Attic, limited storage	20 psf
Attic, full storage	30 psf
Sleeping quarters	30 psf
Living (awake) spaces	40 psf
Outside decks	40 psf
Stairways	60 psf

Wind load is the pressure the wind exerts against the walls and roof. In Letter 16 I showed how the sideward pressure of the wind necessitates anchoring the house to its foundation. In addition, however, the wind tends to bow in the walls in the same

FORCES ON THE FRAME

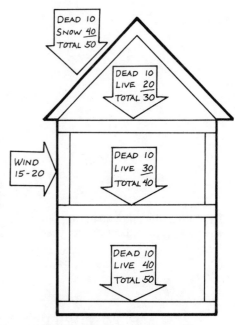

63. Building loads carried by framing members

way Jean's friends tend to cave in your floor. The minimum wind load one should consider is 15 pounds per square foot, but make it 20 for good measure, because I don't want you showing up on my doorstep after the next hurricane. Better yet, check with your building inspector if you live in a windy area. People in the Florida Keys, for example, have to design to 35 pounds per square foot!

Snow load I don't have to tell you about. I saw you up on your roof last February when we got that 6 inches of rain on top of 2 feet of snow. And you call me cheap! You won't have to shovel off your roof if you just spend an extra $50 on bigger rafters! Illustration 64 shows the heaviest snow load in pounds per square foot to expect in fifty years.

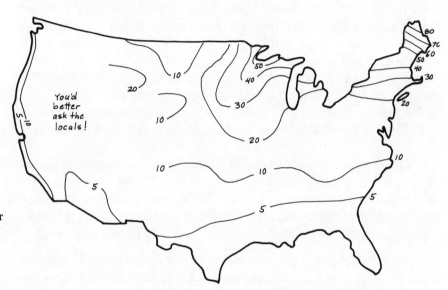

64. Maximum snow load, in pounds per square foot, to expect in fifty years

HOW THE FRAME RESISTS FORCES

There are three principal ways in which external forces act on framing members:

Bending — what you do when you break kindling over your knee. You support the two ends with your hands while pushing down with your knee. Floor joists bend in the same way; the walls hold up the ends, and the dead and live loads push down. Snow bends the rafters of the roof, and wind bends the studs of the wall. Bending is the biggest concern in a house frame. We design to meet two criteria: (1) the member will not actually break under the maximum load, and (2) the member will not deflect excessively (that is, be too bouncy).

Compression — making the wood shorter by pressing together from each end. The wall studs are squeezed between the weight of the building above and the foundation below, so they are subjected to two types of force at once. We rarely concern ourselves with the compressive strength of wall studs, however, since one 2×4 every 8 feet is sufficient to bear the vertical force. But a post supporting the biggest beam in the basement is a different matter.

Tension — making the wood longer by pulling the ends apart. At first one would not think of tension occurring in a building, but what would happen to the rafters in Illustration 65 if it were not for the attic-floor joists forming the bases of triangles? The snow and dead loads would kick the rafter ends outward. Clearly, the attic-floor joist acts like a rope in tension at the same time that it supports the load of the floor in bending. A little thought will make clear that the tension in the joist grows larger as the slope of the roof decreases. The nailed connection between rafter and attic-floor joist is thus one of the most critical in the building.

Illustration 66 shows other triangles at work. In an unbraced building, the rigidity of the nailed joints is all that prevents the building from racking under the sideward thrust of the wind. By introducing diagonal braces, we create triangles within the wall. I'm not sure Pythagoras knew about this bit of magic, but the triangle is the only geometric figure that is perfectly rigid due only to its shape. You can change the shape of a triangle only by changing the length of one or more of its legs. Since wood is extremely strong in both tension and compression, diagonal braces in the building corners are all that is needed to prevent a swaying building. Plywood sheathing accomplishes the same end, since there are plenty of little hidden triangles within the continuous plywood membrane.

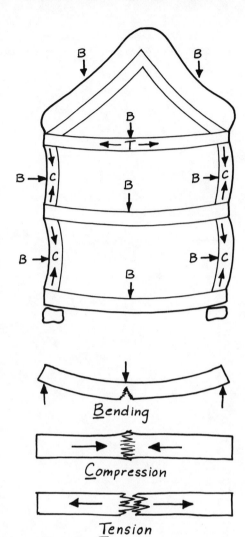

65. Forces exerted on framing members: bending (B), compression (C), tension (T)

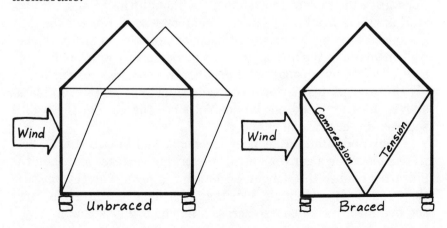

66. Triangular bracing against wind

A TYPICAL FRAME

What do you think of Illustration 67? I'm really getting into this drawing business. Drawing houses sure is a lot easier than building them.

Anyway, Illustration 67 shows how houses have been built for the past twenty years. If you asked a small builder today to build a house, this is pretty much what you would get. I drew it to show what all the pieces are called and what they do. Starting at the roof:

Plywood roof sheathing provides a nailing base for the roofing material, supports the snow load (as well as the temporary load of the roofers), and imparts a torsional, or twisting, rigidity to the building.

Rafters hold up both the roof dead load and the snow load.

Attic joists may or may not support a live load of junk in the attic, but they always support the dead load of the attic floor and the top-story ceiling. They also keep the ends of the rafters from pushing outward. A cathedral ceiling, or ceiling on the sloping rafters above, can be created either by leaving the attic joists exposed or by eliminating the attic joists and supporting the rafters at the top, or peak, with a ridge beam.

Double top plates of the wall serve to tie the top ends of the studs together, connect the rafters to the studs, and provide a nailing surface for inside and outside wall sheathing. Are you wondering why double? You should; merely to facilitate the joining of framing at wall intersections.

Studs carry the vertical weight from above, resist wind pressure from the side, and provide a framework for the interior and exterior wall surfaces. Interior walls have studs, too, although sometimes their sole function is to provide the framework for separating spaces. The multiple studs at corners and wall intersections are called posts (not shown). Although the common 2 × 4 stud is ample from a structural standpoint, 2 × 6 and even 2 × 8 studs are being increasingly used to provide room for thicker wall insulation. We'll examine the question of the proper thickness of walls and insulation later when we consider insulation.

Bottom plates perform the same functions as the top plates above, but they need not be double, since the base of the wall is secured directly to the subfloor.

Plywood subfloor. A floor is usually laid in two stages: first the subfloor for a convenient, flat, working surface, and then the finish floor after the danger of damage is past. The thickness of the subfloor is calculated, like that of a joist or rafter, to carry the live load, but of course across a much smaller span.

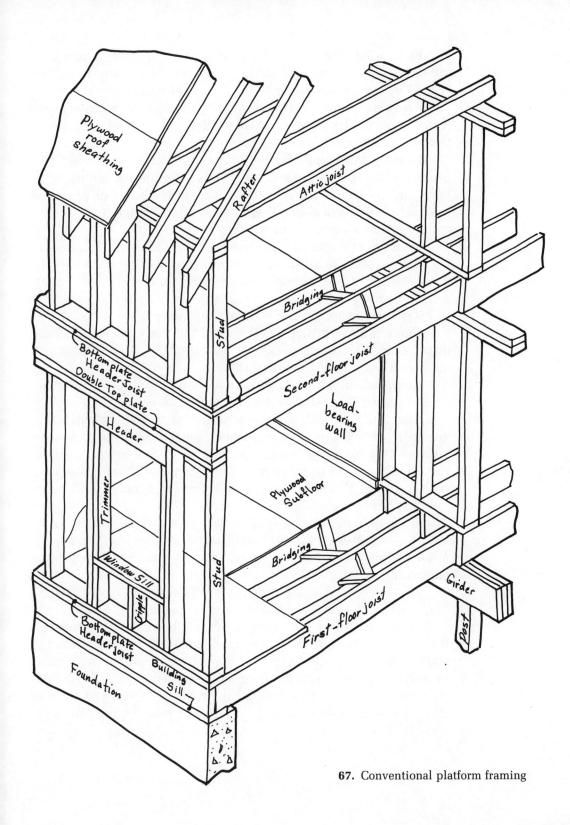

Labels on figure:

Plywood roof sheathing

Rafter

Attic joist

Stud

Bridging

Bottom plate
Header Joist
Double Top Plate

Second-floor joist

Header

Load-bearing wall

Trimmer

Plywood Subfloor

Bridging

Window Sill

Stud

First-floor joist

Cripple

Girder

Bottom plate
Header Joist

Building Sill

Post

Foundation

67. Conventional platform framing

Floor joists carry both the dead load of the flooring and ceiling below and the live load of the occupants. The joists shown are spliced by overlapping over an interior load-bearing wall.

Bridging is supposed to serve two purposes: spread a concentrated load to the joists on either side, and prevent long joists from twisting under load.

Load-bearing walls not only separate interior spaces but also break up the spans of overhead joists so that unreasonably large joists are not required. A wall running in the same direction as the joists is not considered load-bearing even though it may carry the weight of a similar wall above.

Headers are short beams that replace wall studs in supporting loads when the studs have been eliminated by a window or door opening. They are installed as pairs, flush with both the inside and outside of the frame.

Trimmers support the ends of the headers.

The windowsill supports the weight of the window unit, later installed as a complete entity. It also provides a nailing surface for inside and outside wall sheathings.

Cripples often bear no loads but simply maintain the regular frame spacing for installation of insulation and sheathing.

The building sill, although subjected to minimal stresses, generally serves the very important function of tying the wood building to a masonry foundation. Since concrete attracts water, the sill is the wood member most likely to get wet and eventually rot. It should therefore be pressure-treated against both moisture and termites.

Girders break up the span of floor joists wherever the alternative — an interior wall — would serve no other useful purpose. Most houses have built-up wood girders running through the basement.

Posts are used to support girders periodically so that they, too, needn't be excessively large in cross section.

Wall sheathing *(not shown).* A number of sheet products, from plywood to rigid foam, are used to close the wall in from the outside. Structural sheathings, such as plywood, are strong enough to provide the wall-bracing function discussed earlier. With nonstructural wall sheathing, diagonal corner braces in the form of steel straps or let-in (cut-in) 1 × 4 lumber must be used in every corner.

From your lovely home, your reactions to my letter on patterns, and the energy you have thus far put into your design, I can tell that you and Jean have strong feelings about home, about how it should look, feel, and work. I also know Jean is a gourmet cook, and you, John, a wine connoisseur of sorts; but I often see Jean at the discount food store, and I know you drink the same bargain wine I do — you know, the one with the black-and-white label and big letters. From this I surmise that, while you know what you want, you're willing to pay less for the equivalent.

So, in the spirit of the Shakers, let us examine the typical house frame to see if we can't spot some wasted material or effort. Feel free to challenge my analysis if you think you detect the least degree of shoddiness; it is, after all, your house. But please stick to engineering concerns for now. Once the house is finished inside and out, the frame will be invisible except in basement and attic. We can discuss aesthetics later.

I believe you can save between 10 and 15 percent ($5,000 to $7,500) of the total cost with the following engineering optimizations (see Illustration 68):

1. Roof trusses. A truss consists of a bunch of triangles connected in such a way that a lot of the bending stress of the ordinary rafter and joist is converted to tension and compression. Buckminster Fuller's geodesic dome is just a spherical truss, if you will. The result is that the top chord (formerly the rafter) and the "bottom chord" (formerly the ceiling joist) act as rafters and joists over much shorter spans. As an example of the economies that result: to span a 26-foot-wide building with a snow load of 30 pounds per square foot and an attic load of 20 pounds per square foot would require a 2 × 10 rafter and a 2 × 8 joist, but a truss of mere 2 × 4's.

2. Clear-span ceilings. A second benefit of the truss is elimination of the bearing wall formerly required to divide the attic-joist span. Where interior walls are not needed, this represents a tremendous saving. Even if walls are needed for space definition, they can be placed without regard to the attic joists, since they are no longer required to support a load.

3. Single top plates. As pointed out before, the ordinary double top plate serves no useful structural function, and, since the thermal resistance of wood is only one-third that of the insulation in the wall cavity, elimination of the extra top plate results in reduced heat loss through the wall.

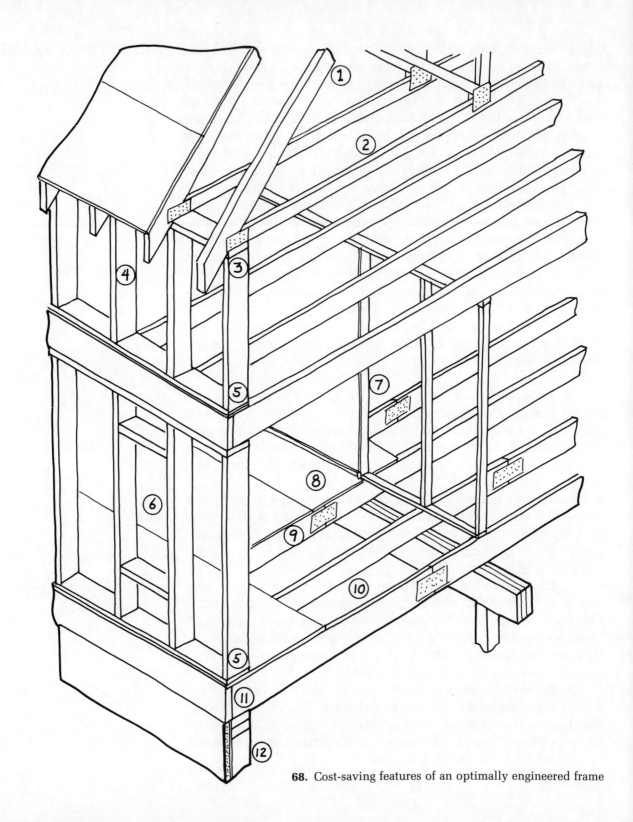

68. Cost-saving features of an optimally engineered frame

4. Uniform 24-inch on-center framing. Rafters, joists, and studs in Illustration 67 were spaced every 16 inches. But plywood sheathing and gypsum drywall are designed to span 24 inches. Switching from 16- to 24-inch framing would require less wood and, as with the top plates above, reduce heat loss or gain. A nice side benefit is that the carpenters can stop thinking in terms of 16, 32, . . . 112 inches, and start thinking 2, 4, . . . 12 feet.

5. One-inch plates. The bottom plate serves only to temporarily hold the stud bottoms together and provide a nailing surface for the interior drywall. A 1-inch-thick bottom plate will do as well at half the cost.

6. Windows sized for framing. If a window fits within the standard 24-inch on-center framing ("rough opening" between studs of 24 inches − 1½ inches = 22½ inches), then no headers, trimmers, or cripples are required. This represents a triple saving of material, labor, and energy. If a wider window is desired, two glazing units can be installed with the stud between acting as a load-bearing window mullion. A third possibility, which I'll raise again when we discuss windows, is the standard and very low-cost 46″ × 76″ patio-door replacement glazing. Fitting perfectly between two stud spaces, it requires only a header of 2 × 8's, fastened to the studs and top plate with plywood sheathing inside and out.

7. Interior walls. Interior walls framed of 2 × 4's occupy, and therefore eliminate from use, about 5 percent of the living space in the average house. First requiring money to build and then occupying space is adding insult to injury. Options: Use 2 × 3's in place of 2 × 4's in walls that are not load-bearing; or drywall only one side of kitchen and closet walls and build shelves between studs, thus recovering some of the lost space.

8. Single-layer floors. The new American Plywood Association Sturd-I-Floor nonplywood panels are engineered to be rigid enough in a single thickness to span 24 inches between joists, and to be smooth and solid enough to serve as a base for carpet and linoleum. Since the panels cost less than plywood, savings are realized both at purchase and in material and labor.

9. Off-center spliced joists. Analysis of the bending stresses in joists shows that joists overhanging a girder can span greater distances than those that end on a girder. Splicing in-line joists together with plywood and alternating the overhangs of adjacent joists leads to greater spans for a given depth of joist, elimination of wasteful joist overlaps, and elimination of the troublesome 1½-

inch joist offset when nailing the edges of the 4' × 8' flooring panels.

10. Bridging. Tests have shown that bridging does not, in fact, improve the performance of a floor. Instead, glueing the floor panels to the joists leads to a stiffer floor and elimination of squeaks and popping nails. Long joists can be prevented from twisting with a single 1 × 3 nailed across the bottom edges of the joists at the middle of the span.

11. Building sill. Since a sill carries no load in bending, its dimensions are not important; a 1 × 6 would function as well as a 2 × 8. With a plywood all-weather wood foundation (see next), a sill isn't even required.

12. All-weather wood foundation. The benefits and savings of this pressure-treated, wood-framed, and plywood-sheathed foundation were discussed in Letter 16.

13. Corner posts (*not shown*). The posts at exterior wall corners and at intersections of interior and exterior walls are conventionally assembled from three separate studs to provide nailing surfaces for all of the interior drywall panels. This is not only wasteful of material, but it leads to increased heat loss through the extra stud and through the narrow and difficult-to-insulate void between the studs. Metal drywall backup clips, available at any lumberyard, perform the same function.

Let me stress the point that the optimized frame is every bit as sufficient as the conventional frame. It has simply been designed, like the frame of an aircraft, to eliminate redundant and therefore excessive material.

Your friend,
Charlie

P.S. I nearly forgot! You'll need tables to determine the sizes of your roof rafters, floor joists, and girders. Let me give you an example of how to use each table. This may be more than you want to know. Skip it if you get bored.

First you must determine the *clear span* of whatever you're selecting (Illustration 69):

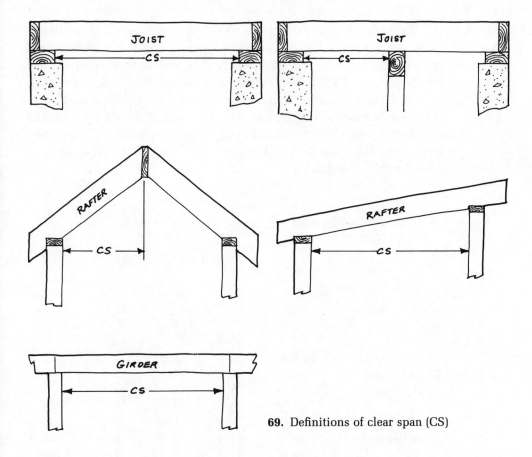

69. Definitions of clear span (CS)

Joists — the distance between supports. For a first floor, the distance between the insides of the sills or, if there is a girder midway, between sill and girder.

Rafters — half of the total span or half of the distance between the insides of the outside walls.

Girders — the distance between supporting posts. I like to divide the length of the building into equal spans of between 8 and 10 feet.

Next, call your local lumberyard to determine the species of framing lumber used by the builders in your area. Builders are no dummies, so they use whatever is currently most economical. I think you'll find in New England that they use hemlock-fir from Canada. Look at the bottom of Table 9 and you'll find that hemlock-fir falls in Lumber Species Group 2.

EXAMPLES   **Table 9.** According to the floor plan you sent, your living room measures 14 by 16 feet. One usually spans the shorter dimension to save on joist size. Therefore, we have to span 14 feet less twice the 8-inch thickness of the foundation wall, 12 feet 8 inches. Looking under "First-Floor Joists, 40 psf live load" and "Lumber Species Group 2," we find that a 2 × 10 (13 feet 1 inch) will do the job. On the other hand, we could install a girder midway to cut the span to 6 feet 4 inches, in which case we could get away with 2 × 6 joists.

Table 9

SPANS FOR S4S DIMENSION LUMBER

	Thickness × Width (in inches)	Lumber Species Group			
		1	2	3	4
Attic-floor joists, 20 psf live load	2 × 6	10' 10"	10' 0"	9' 2"	8' 9"
	2 × 8	14' 3"	13' 3"	12' 1"	11' 5"
	2 × 10	18' 3"	16' 11"	15' 5"	14' 8"
	2 × 12	22' 2"	20' 6"	18' 9"	17' 9"
Second-floor joists, 30 psf live load	2 × 6	9' 5"	8' 8"	7' 11"	7' 7"
	2 × 8	12' 4"	11' 5"	10' 5"	9' 11"
	2 × 10	15' 10"	14' 8"	13' 4"	12' 8"
	2 × 12	19' 2"	17' 9"	16' 3"	15' 5"
First-floor joists, 40 psf live load	2 × 6	8' 5"	7' 9"	7' 1"	6' 9"
	2 × 8	11' 1"	10' 3"	9' 4"	8' 10"
	2 × 10	14' 2"	13' 1"	11' 11"	11' 4"
	2 × 12	17' 2"	15' 11"	14' 6"	13' 9"
Roof rafters, 20 psf snow load	2 × 6	10' 10"	10' 0"	9' 2"	8' 9"
	2 × 8	14' 3"	13' 3"	12' 1"	11' 5"
	2 × 10	18' 3"	16' 11"	15' 5"	14' 8"
	2 × 12	22' 2"	20' 6"	18' 9"	17' 9"
Roof rafters, 40 psf snow load	2 × 6	8' 5"	7' 9"	7' 1"	6' 9"
	2 × 8	11' 1"	10' 3"	9' 4"	8' 10"
	2 × 10	14' 2"	13' 1"	11' 11"	11' 4"
	2 × 12	17' 2"	15' 11"	14' 6"	13' 9"
Roof rafters, 60 psf snow load	2 × 6	7' 1"	6' 7"	6' 0"	5' 8"
	2 × 8	9' 4"	8' 8"	7' 11"	7' 6"
	2 × 10	11' 11"	11' 7"	10' 1"	9' 7"
	2 × 12	14' 6"	13' 5"	12' 3"	11' 8"

All species except oaks: number-2 grade, 2–4" thick, 6" and wider
Group 1: Douglas fir–larch, southern pine, red or white oak
Group 2: Douglas fir south, western hemlock, hemlock-fir
Group 3: Western pine, redwood, eastern spruce, eastern hemlock
Group 4: Eastern white pine, western cedar, balsam fir

Table 10. Let's assume that you have located a Mr. Bickford (remember him?) who can provide low-cost, rough-sawn eastern hemlock from local trees. Assuming his quality is the same as the number-2 eastern hemlock in the table, it belongs in Group 3. Looking in Table 10, we find that we would still have to use 2 × 10's (14 feet 6 inches) full span or 2 × 6's (8 feet 7 inches) with a girder.

Table 10
SPANS FOR ROUGH LUMBER

	Thickness × Width (in inches)	Lumber Species Group			
		1	2	3	4
Attic-floor joists, 20 psf live load	2 × 6	13' 8"	12' 8"	11' 7"	10' 11"
	2 × 8	18' 2"	16' 10"	15' 5"	14' 7"
	2 × 10	22' 9"	21' 1"	19' 3"	18' 3"
	2 × 12	27' 4"	25' 4"	23' 1"	21' 11"
Second-floor joists, 30 psf live load	2 × 6	11' 10"	10' 11"	10' 0"	9' 6"
	2 × 8	15' 9"	14' 7"	13' 4"	12' 8"
	2 × 10	19' 9"	18' 3"	16' 8"	15' 10"
	2 × 12	23' 8"	21' 11"	20' 0"	19' 0"
First-floor joists, 40 psf live load	2 × 6	10' 3"	9' 6"	8' 7"	8' 4"
	2 × 8	13' 8"	12' 10"	11' 8"	11' 3"
	2 × 10	17' 1"	15' 9"	14' 6"	14' 0"
	2 × 12	20' 5"	19' 1"	17' 6"	16' 10"
Roof rafters, 20 psf snow load	2 × 6	13' 8"	12' 8"	11' 7"	10' 11"
	2 × 8	18' 2"	16' 10"	15' 5"	14' 7"
	2 × 10	22' 9"	21' 1"	19' 3"	18' 3"
	2 × 12	27' 4"	25' 4"	23' 1"	21' 11"
Roof rafters, 40 psf snow load	2 × 6	10' 7"	9' 10"	8' 11"	8' 6"
	2 × 8	14' 1"	13' 1"	11' 11"	11' 4"
	2 × 10	17' 8"	16' 4"	14' 11"	14' 2"
	2 × 12	21' 2"	19' 7"	17' 11"	17' 0"
Roof rafters, 60 psf snow load	2 × 6	8' 11"	8' 3"	7' 7"	7' 2"
	2 × 8	11' 11"	11' 0"	10' 1"	9' 7"
	2 × 10	14' 11"	13' 10"	12' 7"	11' 11"
	2 × 12	17' 11"	16' 7"	15' 1"	14' 4"

All lumber equivalent to number-2 grade, 2–4" thick, 6" and wider
Group 1: Douglas fir–larch, southern pine, red or white oak
Group 2: Douglas fir south, western hemlock, hemlock-fir
Group 3: Western pine, redwood, eastern spruce, eastern hemlock
Group 4: Eastern white pine, western cedar, balsam fir

Table 11. Now let's look at that girder. The longer dimension of your living room is 16 feet. I can divide that uniformly into two 8-foot spans. Looking in Table 11 under a beam span of 8 feet and a building width of 14 feet, we find for Group 2 wood a minimum required girder strength S of 28. For Group 3 woods the required strength is 34. To find the actual girder sizes, look at the bottom of the table, where the strength values for various built-up girders are listed. For the S4S (surfaced on four sides) dimension Group 2 hem fir from the lumberyard, we would need a girder of four 2 × 6's (listed as 4/2 × 6 = 30); for the Group 3 rough lumber, three 2 × 6's (listed as 3/2 × 6 = 36).

Table 11
REQUIRED STRENGTH OF GIRDERS, S
ONE-STORY (10 PSF DEAD + 40 PSF LIVE LOAD)

	Building Width (in feet)	Beam Span (in feet)				
		8	10	12	14	16
GROUP 1	14	24	38	54	74	96
	16	27	43	62	84	110
	18	31	48	69	95	123
	20	34	54	77	105	137
	24	41	64	93	126	165
	28	48	75	108	147	192
	32	55	86	123	168	—
GROUP 2	14	28	44	63	86	112
	16	32	50	72	98	128
	18	36	56	81	110	144
	20	40	63	90	123	160
	24	48	75	108	147	192
	28	56	88	126	172	—
	32	64	100	144	196	—
GROUP 3	14	34	53	76	103	134
	16	38	60	86	118	154
	18	43	68	97	132	173
	20	48	75	108	147	192
	24	58	90	130	176	—
	28	67	105	151	—	—
	32	77	120	173	—	—
GROUP 4	14	37	58	84	114	149
	16	43	67	96	131	171
	18	48	75	108	147	192
	20	53	83	120	163	—
	24	64	100	144	196	—
	28	75	117	168	—	—
	32	85	133	192	—	—

Strength of Girders, S

S4S Dimension Lumber

1/2 × 6 = 8	2/2 × 6 = 15	3/2 × 6 = 23	4/2 × 6 = 30
1/2 × 8 = 13	2/2 × 8 = 26	3/2 × 8 = 39	4/2 × 8 = 53
1/2 × 10 = 21	2/2 × 10 = 43	3/2 × 10 = 64	4/2 × 10 = 86
1/2 × 12 = 32	2/2 × 12 = 63	3/2 × 12 = 95	4/2 × 12 = 127

Rough Lumber

1/2 × 6 = 12	2/2 × 6 = 24	3/2 × 6 = 36	4/2 × 6 = 48
1/2 × 8 = 21	2/2 × 8 = 43	3/2 × 8 = 64	4/2 × 8 = 86
1/2 × 10 = 33	2/2 × 10 = 67	3/2 × 10 = 100	4/2 × 10 = 133
1/2 × 12 = 48	2/2 × 12 = 96	3/2 × 12 = 144	4/2 × 12 = 192

Table 12
REQUIRED STRENGTH OF GIRDERS, S
TWO-STORY (20 PSF DEAD + 70 PSF LIVE LOAD)

	Building Width (in feet)	Beam Span (in feet) 8	10	12	14	16
GROUP 1	14	43	68	97	132	173
	16	49	77	111	151	197
	18	56	87	125	170	—
	20	62	96	139	189	—
	24	74	116	167	—	—
	28	86	135	194	—	—
	32	99	154	—	—	—
GROUP 2	14	50	79	113	154	—
	16	58	90	130	176	—
	18	65	101	146	198	—
	20	72	113	162	—	—
	24	86	135	194	—	—
	28	101	157	—	—	—
	32	115	180	—	—	—
GROUP 3	14	60	95	136	185	—
	16	69	108	155	—	—
	18	78	121	175	—	—
	20	86	135	194	—	—
	24	104	162	—	—	—
	28	121	189	—	—	—
	32	138	—	—	—	—
GROUP 4	14	67	105	151	—	—
	16	77	120	173	—	—
	18	87	135	—	—	—
	20	96	150	—	—	—
	24	115	180	—	—	—
	28	134	—	—	—	—
	32	153	—	—	—	—

Strength of Girders, S

S4S Dimension Lumber

1/2×6 = 8	2/2×6 =15	3/2×6 =23	4/2×6 = 30
1/2×8 =13	2/2×8 =26	3/2×8 =39	4/2×8 = 53
1/2×10=21	2/2×10=43	3/2×10=64	4/2×10= 86
1/2×12=32	2/2×12=63	3/2×12=95	4/2×12=127

Rough Lumber

1/2×6 =12	2/2×6 =24	3/2×6 = 36	4/2×6 = 48
1/2×8 =21	2/2×8 =43	3/2×8 = 64	4/2×8 = 86
1/2×10=33	2/2×10=67	3/2×10=100	4/2×10=133
1/2×12=48	2/2×12=96	3/2×12=144	4/2×12=192

TABLE 12. The previous table and example were for girders supporting only a first floor. In your two-story section, you'll be looking for a girder to support not only the first floor but also, by way of the load-bearing wall in the hall, the second story. Table 12 assumes that the full dead and live loads from both floors bear on the girder. Note that your load-bearing wall is off center, spaced 8 feet and 10 feet from the outside walls. This means only that you'll be looking for joists that span 10 feet less 8 inches, or 9 feet 4 inches. The load carried by a girder, however, is always the same, regardless of where it is placed.

Roof trusses are available in several designs and are precisely engineered for span, slope of roof, snow load, and type of lumber. Call the nearest truss manufacturer (look under Roof Structures in the yellow pages, or ask a local builder for his source) to get costs for your application.

We have found a number of alternate solutions: big joists with no girder, small joists with an S4S dimension lumber girder, and small joists with a rough-lumber girder. You'll also face the question of truss versus rafters. How do you decide which is best? All other things being equal (such as Mr. Bickford's delivering on time and the rough lumber being accurately sawn), the best is obviously the lowest cost. Get on the horn to the lumberyards and start figuring your optimums, Cap!

LETTER
20

Dear Charlie,

Cool it. You're right: That's more than we want to know. I mean, we already know that you know more about building design and materials than we do. And we know you understand how to predict snow loads, tension, and stress. But to go through every variety of wood, every dimension, and to predict the sizes that will suffice . . . well, you've left me so far behind I don't know how to respond. Except to say cool it.

Let's get back to the problem at hand. Which is, stated simply, how you can tell us what we should have if we can tell you what we think we want.

That, in my view, does not involve my making complex decisions about plates, cripples, headers, and trimmers. It's handy to have each of these terms described for me, to understand what each does. But, by the same token, it's all but impossible for me to take each of the details and compute every precise dimension, style, and species of every stick of lumber we'll need. Does it really come to that, Charlie? Because if it does, Jean and I are going to have to spend some very long days and some even longer evenings making hundreds of different decisions.

We didn't have those problems with the last place. As you know, most of the material for that home on the point (which now begins to look so pleasingly simple in retrospect) was recycled barn. We literally dismantled two sixty-year-old barns and built our home from the timbers, beams, posts, and planks. It was, as you and other experienced housing specialists would say, overbuilt, in the sense that the actual dimensions of the timbers used were far more than needed; almost the opposite of the bird-skeleton concept you so articulately outlined as a metaphor for framing.

Well, if we had more wood than we needed, more structure than was necessary in terms of stress and tension and load bearing, we also had a relatively low-cost solution to our materials needs. The barns were "free," since we paid only the cost of dismantling them and transporting the materials from Sabattus to Brunswick — about a twenty-five-mile trip. I never did figure the actual cost, per board foot, by adding what we paid the dismantle and transport crew, and then dividing that by the number of timbers and boards we needed for building. In a way, I'm happy I didn't. I know you could have done it in moments with your computer, but then I wouldn't have been able to maintain any illusions. And illusions, as far as I'm concerned, are an integral necessity.

All of that was a bit of a diversion. We aren't using barn timbers in the new place. They aren't easy to come by anymore; they are not inexpensive when they can be had; and they are, by their very nature, too massive, too large, too much of a presence to use in a compact place like the one we're building now. Barn timbers and barn boards are for homes that have a barnlike sense of space, just as that 3,000-square-foot place with its high ceilings had. It was right for the times and for the nine people, including seven teenagers, who lived there.

Now we are building for two. So we are back to your bird, your minimal timber skeleton, and to your incredibly detailed sets of lumber choices and construction techniques. And when I say incredibly detailed, I mean they are so encyclopedic that I become discouraged at the prospect of deciding every possible option and then comparing that final choice with what may or may not be available locally. Do you realize — as you would if you studied each of those detailed tables you put together — that there are options upon options upon options, and several that will do the same job, with only minor differences in aesthetics and price?

I'm a generalist, and I feel great about being able to say that now. Because it means I won't have to pick and choose; you will. I'm going to tell you what we want, in general, and then you can tell us how to achieve it, in particular.

First, let's take what we agree on. We like your use of 24-inch on-center construction. It seems to make more logical sense; it is closer to old-fashioned timber framing; and if "new-fashioned" techniques and materials are making it possible, then why not use it as an overall framing system? And we like the idea of trusses, if we understand you correctly: They provide greater strength for the cost-conscious, and, best of all, they allow us to have an open, airy ceiling overhead.

And that's just what we want. What we like best about your unconventional framing is the ability it has to support fairly wide spans of open space. Because we don't want to give up an echo of the other place, our first owner-designed home. We came to like the feeling of space the high ceiling gave us, and we seemed to get a sense of reassurance from the solid, exposed, "overqualified" beams overhead.

We'd like to do it again, on a small scale. That's what we want. Now you must tell us what we can have. The ideal is an open cathedral ceiling; well, roof, really. Except we'll be looking at it from the inside most of the time. To echo our former home, we hope we'll be able to engineer (or *you'll* be able to engineer) exposed beams. Even if they are not genuine sixty-year-old barn beams, but rough-sawn hemlock from Mr. Bickford's mill, cut to the proper size and delivered on time.

So there is a generalist's response, Charlie, to the cataract of details you flooded me with in your last letter. Yes, we like the wider span, the 24-inch OC, as you house builders say. And we like the use of new, stronger framing techniques, provided they allow us to step back a bit in time and enjoy an open, cathedral ceiling with its beams exposed.

Which is not, I'm thinking, the sort of response you would most like to have. We've mixed two of your framing systems to get the feeling we want our home to express, as opposed to following a system from start to finish just to get every possible advantage, even though it's got little or nothing to do with the way we want our home to look and feel.

So, Charlie, climb down off your computer for a minute and see if it's possible for us to have our hybrid frame. Who knows, it may become standard one of these days and make you famous, like the guy who said everything had to be 16 inches OC. You remember what's-his-name, don't you, Charlie?

Your friend (I hope),
John

Dear John,

Ha! Loved your response. I was just testing to see if you had gone soft in the head, swallowing everything so-called experts endorse. I'll bet you were worried about me, too, but didn't quite dare say so.

You know I'm currently living out my fantasy of spending a year in a little Thoreau cabin in the woods. Of course I'm cheating, but then so did Thoreau. My cheating consists of a refrigerator to keep my beer cold and a computer to record my thoughts. But just last night I was rereading *Walden* by kerosene light and came across this passage, which relates to your thoughts:

> I sometimes dream of a larger and more populous house, standing in a golden age, of enduring materials, and without ginger-bread work, which shall still consist of only one room, a vast, rude, substantial, primitive hall, without ceiling or plastering, with bare rafters and purlins supporting a sort of lower heaven over one's head. . . .
>
> Should not every apartment in which man dwells be lofty enough to create some obscurity over-head, where flickering shadows may play at evening about the rafters? These forms are more agreeable to the fancy and imagination than fresco paintings . . .

I don't wonder that he dreamed of a larger house, his being only 10 × 16 feet. And having lived alone for a year, I can certainly relate to his wish for a "more populous house." But his thoughts about roofs are most relevant to our discussion.

I, too, need to see what holds my roof up. I never walk under a ladder without looking up; how can I be expected to feel secure under an expanse of plaster, held up for all I know by levitation or three horsehairs and a drywall screw? No, in order to sleep soundly I need to know that I'm being protected by a band of stalwart rafters overhead.

I still believe that, for economy, we need to optimize our building techniques. Yet we also need to balance engineering solutions against our psychological shelter needs, those architectural patterns I wrote about in my third letter.

The roof is where I take my stand. I don't generally need to see the floor and wall framing. When I feel a need to see the floor joists, I go down to the basement and check them out; once a month is generally enough. As for the walls, the thickness displayed at every window opening is a constant reminder of their adequacy. But the roof is more significant: It's symbolic, signifying shelter and the heavens overhead. It is — dare I say it? — spiritual. The cathedral builders' response to this need was the cathedral ceiling. So you see, I agree with your idea of a hybrid frame, combining 24-inch on-center floor and wall framing with a timbered cathedral ceiling.

CATHEDRAL-CEILING OPTIONS

The roof truss is a marvel of building technology, but its real forte is in spanning large spaces. Your house is 18 feet at its widest point. At that span, the truss has minimal cost advantage over more standard solutions involving rafters and joists. I've sketched several roof systems that, for me, provide the cathedral-ceiling feeling at a reasonable cost.

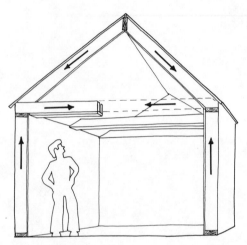

70. Solution One for a cathedral ceiling: alternating ceiling joists

Solution one. The first option (Illustration 70) is a very simple modification of the standard rafter/attic-floor joist system. Joists spaced at the normal 24-inch on-center seem too busy for a cathedral ceiling, so I've deleted every other one. A top plate of at least 2 × 6 cross-section plate will transfer the outward thrust of the 24-inch on-center rafters to those still retaining joists. Next I applied my aesthetic rules of thumb for sizing exposed framing:

1. Width in inches = on-center spacing in feet
2. Depth in inches = 1½ to 2 times the width in inches

Application of these rules dictates either 4 × 6 or 4 × 8 horizontal beams. If constructed of 2 × 6's sandwiching the rafter and covered on the bottom with 1 × 5 pine, you would have beams of actual dimension 4½ × 6¼ inches. The U-shaped channel provides a convenient wiring chase and housing for indirect lighting as well.

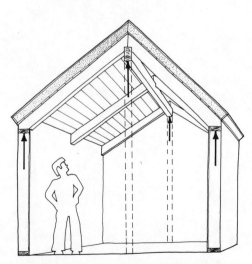

71. Solution Two for a cathedral ceiling: ridge beam

Solution two. A quite different approach is shown in Illustration 71. It is easy to understand if you picture the roof as a tilted floor. Think of the rafters as floor joists, the overhead pine tongue-and-groove roofers as the flooring, the large beam at the peak as a girder, and the dashed posts (posts buried in the end walls) as posts in the basement. With rigid composite foam/plywood insulating panels above, the 1 × 6 tongue-and-groove pine roofers will span 48 inches. The rafters, occurring at twice-normal joist spacing, are okay if of twice-normal joist thickness. And the proper girder is found by interpolating between Tables 11 and 12 for the expected snow load.

For example, let's design a cathedral ceiling of this type for your 14′ × 16′ living room, assuming a snow load of 40 pounds per square foot. First, the clear span of each rafter is 14 feet minus twice the wall thickness (1 foot), divided by two, or 6 feet 6 inches. Looking in Table 9 (page 132) under roof rafters with a snow load of 40 pounds per square foot, we find a solution of 2 × 6's, 24-inch on-center. Therefore 4 × 6's, 48-inch on-center would suffice as well. Next we look in Table 11 (page 134) for the large ridge beam. The 40-pound-per-square-foot snow load is the same as a 40-pound-per-square-foot live load, so we don't have to interpolate. With a building width of 14 feet and a beam span of 16 feet, we need a Group 2 strength value of 112. At the bottom of the table we find a girder of 4/2 × 12 (four 2 × 12's nailed together) S4S dimension lumber will do.

If the snow load had been 50 pounds per square foot rather than 40, then the total load would have been 60 pounds per square foot rather than 50, and we would have multiplied the strength value by the ratio 60/50:

$$112 \times 60/50 = 134.$$

I'll leave it to you to verify the alternate solutions of 4/2 × 12 Group 1 S4S dimension and 4/2 × 12 Group 3 rough.

Other solutions. The two illustrations I've given are extremes. The first is light and airy, showing a minimum of wood but presenting the maximum opportunity for indirect lighting and hanging things like plants from overhead. The second is more rustic and woody but, since pine naturally darkens with age, will seem smaller and darker. Of course, a lot of south-facing windows or a skylight would compensate for the darkness. But the two examples illustrate the basic framing requirements. Feel free to doodle with alternative systems; I'll be glad to check them out so your sky doesn't fall down!

Your friend,
Charlie

8. *Insulation*

Dear Charlie,

One of the best parts of this entire process (the absolute best being the day we're moved into our new home) is when you and I arrive at some sort of agreement. It's such a long process, and half the time I worry that you are going to get fed up with my lack of technical knowledge and my impatience with details, especially numbers. I've had problems with mathematics ever since I was a boy. I can still see my father standing there in all his awesome dimensions, exasperated at my failure to understand, much less learn, what he called the multiplication tables.

I never understood why I had to know them; that was part of the problem. More importantly, I had then and have now no feel for numbers. I can hardly find a reason for them. The human race, I know, would be in tough shape if everyone suffered my deficiency. And especially you, Charlie — who have just the opposite handicap, you for whom numbers are everything — you must be patient with me. Combined we make the perfect couple, each filling the other's vacuums, each with strengths that cancel the other's weakness.

The cathedral-ceiling formula is a fine example. We went at it from different approaches — Jean and I from our psyches and our memories, you from your cost-effective formulas — and yet we arrived at the same place. Each time that happens, it gives me the reassurance I need to press on, to stop thinking of my numberless self as some sort of hopeless ignoramus (no cracks, Charlie).

And, in passing, I might just mention that if my father were still walking this earth, he would be amazed at my skill as a multiplier. I have a Texas Instruments SR-40 on my desk that has multiplication powers even my father might be awed by. I don't know how to use the device to its fullest, but I can sure multiply

3.5 by 48.7 in one hell of a hurry. In the old days, especially with my father hovering, it would have taken at least five minutes, and then someone would have had to check the answer (170.45, according to the SR-40).

One reason I'm pleased at our agreement is that my worries are ended about your objections. I had anticipated the worst, because I believed, and think I'm correct, that a high ceiling wastes heat. And I know what a fanatic you are about that. Anyone who could stop by on the first day of spring and tell me the crocuses at our front stoop were blooming because heat was escaping from under our house has got to be some sort of heat nut. Or perhaps I should say heat-loss nut. You hardly noticed the brave flowers, the colorful blooms announcing an end to our long winter. Instead, you began spouting off about the insulation I should have put down — insulation, by the way, that would have meant the destruction of the crocus bed if it had been installed underground, as you recommended.

Anyone who so casually leads a crocus to the firing squad would take exception to a cathedral ceiling, I thought. I remembered my fisherman friends on Long Island. In the winter months they went cod fishing, using trawls — long lines with a baited hook every six feet or so, set in the open sea from the stern of a small dory. It was rugged work, too rugged for me. But every now and then I would risk a trip, which meant I had to spend most of the previous evening helping to bait up: putting a cold chunk of skimmer clam on every one of those thousands of hooks.

It was not a job that could be done indoors or even in the cellar, not unless you wanted your home to smell like rotten skimmers for the rest of the year. We worked in small, wooden structures called bait shacks. Crudely built, without interior walls, the shacks had ceilings so low that an average-size person could not quite stand up. We worked hunched over the baiting board, and even though we did that unpleasant job on some of the coldest nights of the year, I was never even chilly in a bait shack. That was because each one had a kerosene heater going full blast, and in those confined quarters the shack became a kind of extension of the stove, an oven, if you will, in which I quietly roasted, fighting off sleep but happy to be mutilating ripe skimmers without having to suffer freezing feet at the same time.

The stove's awesome heat, plus the low ceiling and the small space, made that winter warmth possible. Which is why I was worried about a high ceiling in our new home. I expected you to tell me what I'd already learned: Low ceilings are more energy-efficient.

But you didn't, and I think I know the reason. The cathedral ceiling you say you and we both like has wallboard sections nailed to the rafters, even though some beams can still be seen. And behind that wallboard, I'm sure now, you can see insulation, just as you saw it underground at our front stoop, and the crocuses be damned.

I guess because we don't see the insulation we know we have in our current place, we don't think about it much, even when we're in the midst of designing and planning a snug, secure new place, a saving place. I should have thought of insulation before; I can see that now. Because you *have* thought of it and are about to stun me with a mass of detail about it, leaving Jean and me once again sorting through a bushel of options.

One reason I know there will be at least a bushel is because insulation has become a household word. Ever since the so-called oil crisis, just about any home-building, repair, or decorating magazine you pick up has dozens of pages of insulation advertising. And I feel pretty certain that even you have seen the Pink Panther on television telling viewers how much they can save if they unroll some of his insulation in their attics.

If you weren't advising us, Charlie, I'd probably ask the contractor or the fellow at the lumberyard for whatever insulation they think best. And, knowing what I know about the different sorts of insulation (very little, really), I'd probably go along.

And that, I'll bet, would set you to spasming. Which is fine; as I said, we cancel each other's weaknesses. I don't really understand, even though I've heard the expression a hundred times, what R value means. And I know I don't know why one kind of insulation might be better than another. I mean, there's the fiberglass the Pink Panther unrolls; there are solid slabs of what I call compressed foam, the kind of slabs we used in the house on the point; and then there is the blow-in stuff, the rock wool or whatever that is I see being blown into houses every now and then. I can see the trucks in the drive and the long, fat hoses being pushed up against holes drilled right in the side of the house. Insulation means many things: It unrolls, it can be stacked like boards, or it can be piled like sand.

Each system has an R value, each product has a price. How can we decide which is best for the home you have been helping us design? That's your question for today, Charlie. And I expect some preferences, some explanations. Don't come back at me with pages of graphs and tabular matter and tell me to decide for myself. I told you at the start, I never learned multiplication, and I don't know how to ask my SR-40 for decisions about insulation.

By the way, that raises another question. I read about so-called superinsulated places, homes that are so tightly built, with so much insulation in their walls, that the heat from a couple of bodies and a candle will keep their insides warm, even in a New England winter. When I hear about such places, especially when I'm pondering my own fuel bills, I have to remember something else my father told me. "John," he said, "there's no such thing as a free lunch."

If a place is built so tightly and insulated so well that a candle will keep it warm, then the up-front cost must be considerable. A person my age (some punk wanted to give me a senior citizen discount the other day) has to wonder if the "savings" in fuel will ever be paid back if you take the cost of superinsulation and spread it out over a decade or two, or even three (which is about max for me). Suppose I collect firewood or stoke up a coal stove over the same period of time with the money I did not spend for superinsulation. Will I come out ahead?

Now there's another question for you. And, as I said, we want to be told what's best. We don't want to be told there are a number of choices. Got that, Charlie?

Your friend,
John

Dear John,

I'm glad you approve of the cathedral ceiling with drywall and exposed ceiling joists. This is also my favorite, because it's light and airy; classic yet modern; easy to build; and, best of all, inexpensive to insulate, as you'll see in this lesson.

I'm also glad you asked that question, because I enjoy providing the rather amazing — and very long — answer. If you want to skip all the detail, you'll find my recommendations at the end of this letter. But the detail will give you a good idea of how I arrived at my recommendations. Most insulations are really nothing more than materials that stop air from moving. Look closely at any insulation and you'll see millions of tiny air pockets, between fibers, between particles, or within cells. The thermal resistance, or R value, of a fiberglass batt is 3.2 per inch of thickness, whereas the R value of unmoving air is 80 percent higher, at 5.7 per inch!

What Is Insulation?

But unmoving air doesn't exist in ordinary situations; watch pipe smoke as it circulates around a room. To use the insulating property of air, we have to trap it within tiny spaces so that it doesn't travel very far. However, in stopping air movement with even minimal material, we add the higher conductivity of the material to the conductivity of the air. Commercial insulations are thus trade-offs between amounts of material and sizes of air space created.

R-Value Defined

Okay, I know you are turned off by mathematical formulas, John, even though you have an SR-40 calculator. I'm not asking you to do any calculations, but I would like you to look at a couple of formulas. The first is the one for heat loss through a surface such as a wall or roof:

$$H, hr = \frac{A \times \Delta T}{R}$$

where: H, hr = the amount of heat flowing through a surface in one hour, measured in Btu (1 Btu is the amount of heat that raises the temperature of 1 pint of water 1° F)

A = the area of the surface in square feet

ΔT = the difference between inside and outside temperatures

R = the thermal resistance of the surface

This formula should confirm what you have already experienced relative to winter heat loss: (1) the larger the surface (or building), the larger the heat loss; (2) the warmer inside and the colder outside, the greater the loss; and (3) the larger the R value, the smaller the heat loss. Actually, this formula defines what we mean by R value.

For example, the R value of a single-glazed window is approximately 1. By adding a second layer of glazing, we double the thermal resistance of the window to R-2. According to the formula, the heat loss is seen to be cut in half. Similarly, triple glazing results in R-3 and one-third the original heat loss. If you were to stuff 6-inch-thick R-19 fiberglass batts into your windows, the heat loss would be cut to one-nineteenth of the original. (It would also be very dark in your house.)

The second formula predicts the amount of heat a house will lose during a full year.

$$H, yr = \frac{A \times HDD \times 24}{R}$$

where: H, yr = the heat loss through a building surface for the entire year in Btu

A = the area of the surface in square feet

R = the thermal resistance of the surface

HDD = number of local heating-degree days

The first formula gives the heat loss during one hour when the difference in temperature inside and outside is ΔT. The second formula averages and accumulates the ΔTs for all the hours of the year into a single term, heating-degree days. Illustration 11 (page 45) was a map of heating-degree days for different areas of the country. Back then we were interested in finding a warm location for your house. Now that you've picked your spot, we're going to use the heating-degree days for your site to select the proper R values for your insulation.

Insulation Types

There is a bewildering array of insulations on the market, each product promoted by its manufacturer as the best. Each may, in fact, be best for some particular application but certainly not for all. Price and R value are just two of the characteristics with which we should be concerned.

Table 13 lists eleven generic insulation types and my opinion as to their relative strengths and weaknesses. Again, I have used the *Consumer Reports* approach of dots: Solid dots mean great, empty dots mean lousy, and half-dots mean *mezzo-mezzo*. Since

Table 13
INSULATIONS COMPARED

FORM	TYPE	R Value per Inch	Cost, ¢ per Inch	Cost, ¢ per R Value	Ease of D-I-Y Application	Ability to Fill Spaces	Wall Cavity Settling	Fire Characteristics	Physical Strength	Moisture Resistance
Blown	Fiberglass, Long Fiber	2.2	4.8	2.2	○	●	○	●	○	○
	Fiberglass, Short Fiber	4.0	11.0	2.8	○	●	◐	●	○	○
	Mineral Wool	2.1	4.3	2.0	○	●	○	●	○	○
	Cellulose Fiber	3.7	8.2	2.2	○	●	○	◐	○	○
Blanket	Fiberglass	3.2	6.4	2.0	●	◐	●	●	○	○
	Mineral Wool	2.8	3.7	1.3	●	◐	●	●	○	○
Loose	Perlite	2.7	12.5	4.7	●	●	○	●	○	●
	Vermiculite	2.7	12.5	4.7	●	●	○	●	○	●
Foam	Molded Polystyrene	4.0	16.9	4.2	●	○	●	○	◐	◐
	Extruded Polystyrene	5.0	33.7	6.7	●	○	●	○	●	●
	Polyisocyanurate	6.7	45.0	6.7	●	○	●	○	◐	◐

you're hiring a builder, the costs listed include material, labor, overhead, and profit; in other words, what you should expect to pay per square foot for the finished job. An owner-builder may wish to consider material costs only, which he or she can readily obtain from any lumberyard.

Let me write a few words about each product: what it is, how it's made, and what it's best for.

BLOWN FIBERGLASS, LONG FIBER. Fiberglass is essentially silica, or sand, that has been melted and spun into fibers. The fibers are coated after cooling with a colored resin and gathered into blankets of varying density, depending on the desired R value and application. Blown fiberglass is chopped into small clumps with a density of 0.6 pounds per cubic foot. The glass fibers are extraordinarily resilient and resist settling once their settled density has been reached. Therefore, when installed at the proper density, blown fiberglass does not settle in walls and leave empty spots. Although the binding resin is combustible, the amount of it present is small enough for the overall product to be considered noncombustible.

Strong points include cost per R value, inertness, and ability to fill irregular spaces. Its weakest point is low R value per inch. The best application is on an open attic floor.

BLOWN FIBERGLASS, SHORT FIBER. This product differs from long-fiber fiberglass in size and length of fibers and installed density. The fibers and air spaces are smaller, resulting in nearly twice the R value per inch as that of the long-fiber version. More than twice the amount of material is also required, however, leading to a price that is also more than double. Since the cost of material is usually a small component in the life-cycle cost of insulating, I always advise my students to specify short-fiber fiberglass if they can get it. Insul-safe by Certainteed is one such product.

BLOWN MINERAL WOOL. Most people know this material by the name Rockwool. Actually, the generic type includes two products, rock wool and slag wool. Both are manufactured by the same process as that used for fiberglass. The only essential difference is in raw materials: minerals other than silica for rock wool, and molten slag left over from the steel-making process for slag wool. Neither fiber is as resilient as the purer glass fiber. This has two results: The fibers must be manufactured and installed at greater densities to prevent settling; and the impure fibers break easily, making rock and slag wool "dirty" to work with.

Although rock and slag wools are excellent long-term insulations — very low in cost, noncombustible except for resin binder, and unaffected by moisture — they have lost out to fiberglass due to the notion that they are dirty and old-fashioned.

The primary strong point is cost. Recently, a weak point has been unavailability. The best application is on an open attic floor.

BLOWN CELLULOSE FIBER. Cellulosic fiber is a loose, fluffy, fibrous material intended for blowing into cavities. It is generally made by finely shredding old newspapers. (Some claim the finest to be derived from the *New York Times*, although I believe that to be purely a case of elitism, since Charmin toilet tissue has better loft.)

Cellulose is not particularly resilient and must be installed at high density to avoid long-term settling. Settling is not very important in an open attic where R value is roughly proportional to thickness. Due to the thermal short-circuiting effect of air gaps as discussed later on, however, settling in wall cavities leads to great loss of R value.

Strong points are cost, R value per inch, and ability to fill irregular spaces. Weak points are possible settling in walls, susceptibility to damage by water, and possible corrosion of pipes and wiring by fire-proofing chemicals. The best application is, once again, on an open attic floor.

FIBERGLASS BLANKET. Blankets in long rolls and batts in 4-foot lengths are both available in 15- and 23-inch widths, perfect to fit between joists, studs, and rafters with standard 16- and 24-inch on-center spacings. In this bound form, the fiberglass is less likely to settle and so is perfect for insulating regular framing cavities.

The insulation manufacturers have apparently (and unfortunately, to my mind) made a marketing decision to offer the blankets and batts in low-density versions with a rather moderate R value of 3.2 per inch. Paying for and compressing thicker batts into framing cavities is worthwhile: total batt R value goes down, but R value per inch and R value of the fixed-cavity thickness goes up.

Strong points include cost, ease of installation, and wide availability. A weak point is the difficulty of filling irregular spaces. The best applications are between studs and rafters.

MINERAL WOOL BLANKET. This is the rock-wool and slag-wool equivalent of fiberglass blankets. These blankets are less expensive, but they also perform slightly less well and are not nearly as readily available. I see no advantage to using them instead of fiberglass blankets and batts.

LOOSE PERLITE. Perlite is a naturally occurring volcanic mineral containing up to 5 percent water. When the mineral is crushed and then heated rapidly to its melting point, the trapped water turns to steam and blows minute glass bubbles. These highly insulating trapped air cells can be loose-poured, fused into a rigid board, or substituted for sand and gravel in insulating concrete.

Strong points include inertness, noncombustibility, and ability to flow into irregular spaces. Weak points include high cost and wall-cavity settling. The best application is in filling irregular voids between fiberglass batts in attics.

LOOSE VERMICULITE. Vermiculite is a naturally occurring mica with the same quirk as perlite. Between the mica layers are bound water molecules. When the mica is rapidly heated, the water turns to steam before having time to escape, thereby expanding the mica by a factor of ten or more. Like perlite, vermiculite is noncombustible and completely inert. It must, however, be treated with silicone to repel water.

Strong points are pourability and noncombustibility. Weak points are high cost and low R value. The best application is in filling irregular voids and insulating between masonry and flue liner in a chimney.

MOLDED POLYSTYRENE FOAM. Molded polystyrene — or beadboard, as it is appropriately nicknamed — is formed by heating polystyrene plastic beads in a mold until the beads expand and fuse together at their points of contact. In contrast to the extruded, or foamed-in-place, polystyrene discussed next, beadboard is: (1) more easily permeated by water due to minute passages that remain between the beads; (2) physically weaker due to the type of bonding between cells; and (3) more heat-conductive due to larger cell size. All physical properties degrade with decreasing density, and the density of beadboard is exactly half that of extruded polystyrene.

With half the density (and amount of raw chemical) as the extruded version, beadboard sells for about 50 percent less. For this reason, contractors are sometimes tempted to substitute the lower-cost version when dealing with unsuspecting homeowners. In critical applications such as below ground, where physical strength and resistance to moisture are critical, this is false economy.

The single strong point of molded polystyrene is the lowest cost per R value of the foams. Weak points include fragility, the lowest R value per inch of the foams, and the requirement to cover with a fifteen-minute fire-rated material in interior applications. The best application is as the core of large gypsum drywall/foam-sheathing panels, which are used to cover the roofs and walls of post-and-beam structures.

EXTRUDED POLYSTYRENE FOAM. The extruded version of polystyrene is formed by allowing a mixture of polystyrene, solvent, and gas to escape from a pressurized container through a slot into air. As the pressure is released, the gas expands and creates a foam of tiny cells, the walls of which are shared. It is this shared-wall structure that makes the foam so strong and so impermeable to moisture.

In areas other than building, extruded polystyrene is used for flotation of docks and for prevention of frost under highways. In residential construction it has two primary uses: as an exterior foundation insulation, and as a nonstructural insulating sheathing for walls and roofs.

Strong points include high strength (for a foam) and near-perfect impermeability to moisture. Weak points are cost per R value and the requirement to cover with a fifteen-minute fire-rated material inside the building. The best application is as exterior foundation insulation.

POLYISOCYANURATE FOAM. This foam results from spreading a mixture of isocyanurate and alcohol in a thin sheet on a moving conveyor. The chemical reaction produces a very lightweight and fine-celled foam, filled with an inert, low-conductivity gas. The inert gas gives the foam a very high initial R value of up to 9 per inch. But this "manufactured" R value ultimately falls to an "aged" R value of 6.7 per inch as the inert gas and ordinary air are slowly exchanged across the cell walls. Foil and asphalt-paper facings are often applied to retard the aging process, but their effectiveness has not yet been established.

Generally, polyisocyanurate is promoted for the same purposes as extruded polystyrene, but significant differences exist: The former has a higher R value per inch, making it the prime candidate for applications where thickness is a constraint; and the latter retains its original R value better when installed underground.

The single advantage of polyisocyanurate is the highest R value of the foams. Its weak point is high cost. Like all foams, it requires a fire-rated covering over interior applications. The best application is as nonstructural exterior-wall sheathing under vinyl or aluminum siding.

As you'll soon discover, I have my preferences:

1. Between regular 16- or 24-inch on-center framing — fiberglass blanket or batt, because of low cost and ease of installation.
2. In open attics of any joist spacing — blown short-fiber fiberglass, because of high R value per inch and ability to seal small cracks or heat leaks.
3. Over a beamed cathedral ceiling (Solution Two in Letter 21) — composite sheets of polyisocyanurate and waferboard, because of ease of installation and elimination of the roof-venting requirement.
4. As nonstructural exterior sheathing — extruded polystyrene, because of strength and tongue-and-groove form.
5. As below-grade foundation insulation — extruded polystyrene, because of resistance to water and retention of R value.

How Much Insulation Is Enough?

We now come to one of the most fascinating questions in building: How does one determine how much insulation is enough? I love this topic because it's like a game; it exercises, like few other real-life questions, your powers of logic. It also sometimes exercises people's hostilities as their logics diverge. I look forward to your opinions of my analyses of the optimum R values for your house. If you're not in a logical mood, please come back later, because here begins the analysis.

LIFE-CYCLE COST. On average, a house will remain essentially the same as it was built for forty years. Owners may come and go every seven years, a garage or addition may be built, but whatever is in the wall when built is likely to be there forty years from now. Forty years may seem like a long time, but think back; forty years ago was 1946. There are many houses in my neighborhood, built in 1948, for which there are no rehabilitation plans yet. The house we retrofitted in 1983 in the book *HouseWarming* was built in 1902 and first insulated around 1940. Whatever we do to insulate a house today clearly has implications for the next forty years.

What are the economic implications of insulating? I can think of two big ones: Insulation lowers your fuel bill, no matter what your fuel, how big your house, or where you live; and it costs money to insulate, more money for more insulation.

These are opposing effects. If you add more insulation, it will cost you more today, but your fuel will cost less in the future. What we seek is that level of insulation that costs the smallest total amount over the life of the insulation. This combined amount is called the life-cycle cost (LCC) of insulating:

$$\text{LCC} = \text{cost of insulating} + \text{lifetime fuel cost}$$

There's more than meets the eye in each of these terms, so let's look in detail at each one.

LIFETIME FUEL COST. Just a few pages back I gave you the formula for the amount of heat lost through an insulated building surface for an entire year:

$$\text{H, yr} = \frac{A \times HDD \times 24}{R}$$

We can easily modify the formula to express a forty-year fuel cost:

$$\text{Fuel cost, 40 yr} = \frac{A \times HDD \times 24 \times 40 \text{ yr} \times \text{cost/Btu}}{R}$$

$$= \frac{\text{fuel-cost factor}}{R}$$

I have lumped all the numerator terms into one fuel-cost factor, which accounts for: (1) cost per unit of fuel, (2) Btu per unit of fuel, (3) efficiency of the heating system in converting and delivering the Btu, (4) forty years of fuel saving, and (5) heating-degree days. All you have to do to find the lifetime cost of heat lost through your attic, for example, is to divide your fuel-cost factor by the R value of the attic insulation. Let's do that.

Example. What is the cost of the heat lost through John and Jean Cole's attic over the next forty years if they: (1) live in an area with 7,000 heating-degree days, (2) heat with coal costing $150 per ton, and (3) have R-38 attic insulation?

To find the answer, turn to Table 14:

Table 14
FUEL-COST FACTORS

Elec kWh	Oil Gal	Gas CCF	Wood Cord	Coal Ton	Heating-Degree Days				
					2,000	4,000	6,000	8,000	10,000
0.024	0.70	0.49	88	105	13	27	40	54	67
0.027	0.80	0.56	100	120	15	31	46	62	77
0.031	0.90	0.63	113	135	17	34	52	69	86
0.034	1.00	0.70	125	150	19	38	58	77	96
0.038	1.10	0.77	138	165	21	42	64	85	106
0.041	1.20	0.84	150	180	23	46	69	92	115
0.044	1.30	0.91	163	195	25	50	75	100	125
0.048	1.40	0.98	175	210	27	55	82	110	137
0.051	1.50	1.05	188	225	29	58	86	115	144
0.055	1.60	1.12	200	240	31	62	92	123	154
0.058	1.70	1.19	213	255	33	65	98	130	163
0.061	1.80	1.26	225	270	35	69	104	138	173
0.065	1.90	1.33	238	285	36	73	109	146	182
0.068	2.00	1.40	250	300	38	77	115	154	192
0.075	2.20	1.54	275	330	42	84	127	169	211
0.082	2.40	1.68	300	360	46	92	138	184	230
0.089	2.60	1.82	325	390	50	100	150	200	250
0.097	2.80	1.96	350	420	54	108	161	215	269
0.102	3.00	2.10	375	450	58	115	173	230	288
0.109	3.20	2.24	400	480	61	123	184	246	307
0.116	3.40	2.38	425	510	65	130	196	261	326
0.123	3.60	2.52	450	540	69	138	208	277	346
0.130	3.80	2.66	475	570	73	146	219	292	365
0.137	4.00	2.80	500	600	77	154	230	307	384
0.143	4.20	2.94	525	630	81	161	242	322	403
0.150	4.40	3.08	555	660	84	169	253	338	422
0.157	4.60	3.22	575	690	88	177	265	354	442
0.164	4.80	3.36	600	720	92	184	276	368	461
0.171	5.00	3.50	625	750	96	192	288	384	480

Example: Electric Heat $0.075/kWh & 6,000 DD = Factor 127
Assumed Efficiencies: Electric 100%
Oil & Gas 70%
Wood 50%
Coal 60%

1. Follow the column labeled "Coal" down to the current price per ton, $150.
2. Proceed across that row to the appropriate degree-day column or columns. Read the fuel-cost factor or interpolate between factors. In this example, 7,000 degree days is halfway between 6,000 and 8,000, and so the fuel-cost factor is the average of 58 and 77, or 67.5.
3. Divide the fuel-cost factor by R-38: 67.5 ÷ 38 = 1.78.
   Answer: $1.78 per square foot of attic over forty years.

"But what about inflation?" I can hear Jean asking. You're absolutely correct, Jean. Coal will cost more next year, and more the next year, and so on. The fuel cost over forty years will be higher than what we just calculated, but the value of the dollars with which we pay our fuel bills will also be lower. We are comparing money spent presently for insulation with money saved in the future on fuel. Future dollars saved on fuel can be converted to today's dollar by a factor economists call a present-worth factor (PWF):

$$PWF = \frac{(1+F)}{(1+I)}$$

where: F = the rate of increase of fuel price
I = the general inflation rate

For example, suppose the value, or purchasing power, of the dollar declines due to general inflation at 6 percent per year ($I = 0.06$). And suppose coal prices rise at 6 percent per year ($F = 0.06$). Thus, after one year we'll be saving 6 percent more green dollar bills, each of which is worth 6 percent less, so the present-worth factor is 1.0, and the real value of the savings remains the same.

The fuel-cost factors in Table 14 assume that the prices of all fuels will rise at the same rate as general inflation for the next forty years. They therefore account for future fuel prices and, at the same time, equitably compare the value of insulation and fuel expenditures.

COST OF INSULATING. Figuring the true or total cost of insulating is even more fun. What are the costs involved in insulating a wall, for example? Obviously they include the money that you pay the contractor for the material used and the labor involved, but Illustration 72 shows hidden costs you may have overlooked:

Cost = a_1 material and labor for the insulation
+ a_2 material and labor for extra framing to provide space for the insulation
+ a_3 value of potential living space occupied by insulation
− a_4 credit for reducing the required size of the heating and cooling system

Factor a_2 should be included when the framing is increased beyond the minimum required for structural integrity; i.e., 2×4

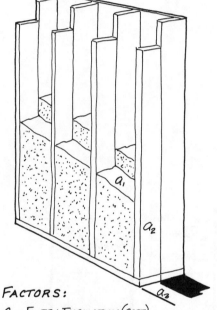

FACTORS:

a_1 EXTRA INSULATION (COST)
a_2 EXTRA FRAMING (COST)
a_3 LOST LIVING SPACE (COST)
a_4 SMALLER HEAT/COOL SYSTEM (GAIN)

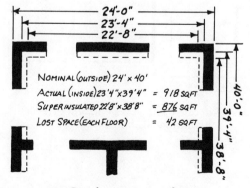

NOMINAL (OUTSIDE) 24' × 40'
ACTUAL (INSIDE) 23'4" × 39'4" = 918 SQ FT
SUPER INSULATED 22'8" × 38'8" = 876 SQ FT
LOST SPACE (EACH FLOOR) = 42 SQ FT

72. Cost factors in insulating

framing for walls, et cetera. This factor therefore applies in a wall but not in an attic.

Factor a_3 is included only when the insulation actually occupies what would otherwise be valuable living space. People often differ as to the value of that space. To say that the value is zero is ludicrous. I have observed that people making that statement also have trouble balancing their checkbooks. On the other hand, to base the value on the full price of a house (concluding that each square foot of a 2,000-square-foot house selling for $100,000 is worth $50) ignores the facts that the house would probably sit on the same piece of land and have identical kitchen, baths, wiring, and plumbing regardless of the thickness of its walls.

Nationally published cost-estimating books for builders break the average costs of houses into component costs. I have calculated the incremental cost (cost of one additional square foot) of floor space by deducting the costs of kitchen, bath, plumbing, wiring, and site from the average-square-foot cost of a medium-quality house. My calculations show Factor a_3 to be $31 per square foot for the average-quality house.

Factor a_4 is a reduction in cost due to the effect of the insulation on the size of the heating equipment. Using the formula for heat loss per hour, one simply computes the maximum rate of heat loss at the lowest temperature of the year for the R value of the uninsulated surface, computes the same rate for the proposed R value of the insulated surface, and then takes the difference. Heating systems are sized in Btu per hour (Btuh) capacity, and so the reduction in required size results in the financial saving Factor a_4. Of course, heating systems come in only a few sizes, so we average the values. From estimating books, I obtained the following factors:

- Oil and gas furnaces and boilers — 0.006 cents per Btuh
- Electric-resistance baseboards — 0.016 cents per Btuh

Illustration 73 shows how all of the factors stack up when I calculate the life-cycle cost of a fiberglass-insulated 2×6 wall for your house. The total cost of insulating is the total of the four a factors; the forty-year cost of fuel is found by dividing your fuel-cost factor of 67.5 by the R value of the wall in question (R-20); and the life-cycle cost is the sum of the two, or $4.46 per square foot of wall.

Illustration 74 shows similarly calculated results for other building surfaces at various levels of insulation:

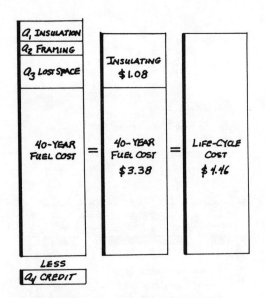

73. Life-cycle cost of a 2×6 wall for John and Jean's house

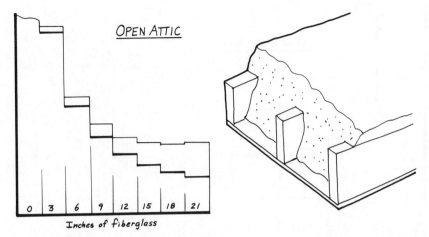

0 3 6 9 12 15 18 21

Inches of fiberglass

74A. Life-cycle cost for loose-fill fiberglass in open attic (optimum 18 inches)

Open attic *(Illustration 74A).* In case you change your minds about having a cathedral ceiling, I calculated the life-cycle cost for a range of thicknesses of fiberglass batt over an open attic floor. This is a perfect example of the utility of this calculation. The optimum thickness of insulation is very high (18 inches or R-57), because the only cost factor in insulating the attic is Factor a_1.

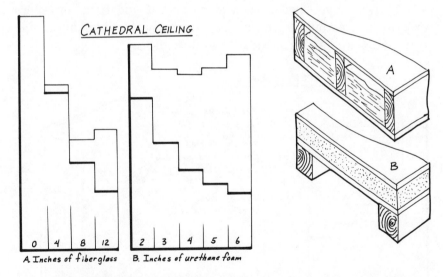

CATHEDRAL CEILING

0 4 8 12   2 3 4 5 6

A. *Inches of fiberglass*   B. *Inches of urethane foam*

74B. Life-cycle cost for cathedral ceilings (optimum 8-inch fiberglass batt)

Cathedral ceiling *(Illustration 74B).* I calculated the life-cycle costs of both the drywall ceiling with collar ties (A) and the exposed-beam ceiling (B). The results show why I was happy to read that you prefer the former. The figures say you should install 8 inches (9 inches compressed to 8 inches) of fiberglass between 2×10 rafters (to allow a roof-venting air space above the insulation).

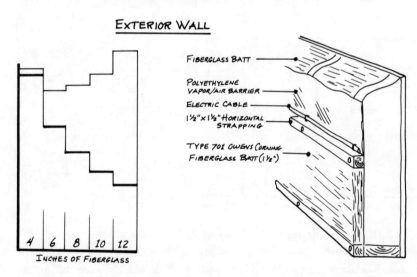

BASEMENT WALL

A. INCHES OF STYROFOAM

0 1 2 3 4

B. INCHES OF FIBERGLASS

4 6 9 12

74C. Life-cycle cost for AWWF basement wall (optimum 9-inch fiberglass batt); optimum for concrete basement wall would be 4-inch exterior Styrofoam

Basement walls *(Illustration 74C)*. You could insulate your all-weather wood foundation in one of two ways: (A) outside the wall with extruded polystyrene, or (B) between the studs with fiberglass. Since the 2×8 stud spaces are already provided for structural reasons, you pay only for the insulation, and B is the less costly. If you had chosen a masonry foundation, however, exterior foam would have proven less costly than building an interior stud wall and insulating with fiberglass.

EXTERIOR WALL

FIBERGLASS BATT

POLYETHYLENE VAPOR/AIR BARRIER

ELECTRIC CABLE

1½"×1½" HORIZONTAL STRAPPING

TYPE 701 OWENS CORNING FIBERGLASS BATT (1½")

INCHES OF FIBERGLASS

4 6 8 10 12

74D. Life-cycle cost for wall with structural sheathing (optimum 6-inch fiberglass batt)

Exterior walls *(Illustrations 74D and 74E)*. Here I looked at two distinct styles of construction: Illustration 74D shows fiberglass only with the wall built inward with horizontal strapping, and Illustration 74E examines fiberglass between studs plus

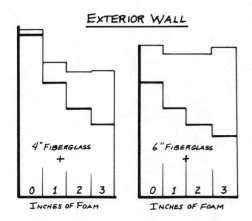

EXTERIOR WALL

4" FIBERGLASS
+

0 | 1 | 2 | 3
INCHES OF FOAM

6" FIBERGLASS
+

0 | 1 | 2 | 3
INCHES OF FOAM

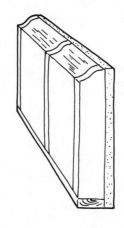

74E. Life-cycle cost for wall with non-structural foam sheathing (optimum 4-inch fiberglass batt with 2-inch foam)

exterior foam sheathing. I found the results surprising: Although the cost per inch of foam is high, the cost of living space is even higher, so the lowest life-cycle cost is for a 4-inch fiberglassed wall with 1-inch exterior insulating sheathing. The results are quite close, so your choice may be determined by the type of siding you plan to install. Wood shingles must be installed over a sound nailing base, such as plywood. Vinyl and aluminum sidings and high-quality wood clapboards tolerate a foam base better.

OTHER FUELS, OTHER CLIMATES. It would be a shame to have to calculate all of those bar graphs every time you built a house. What if friends of yours plan to build a house and wish to benefit from your newly acquired knowledge, but they plan to heat with electricity, or they live in Peoria? I have used the fuel-cost factors from Table 14 (page 154) to create a similar table of optimum R modifiers. To find the new optimum R values, you simply multiply the optimum R values from Illustration 74 by the factor appropriate to their specific fuel price and degree days in Table 15 (page 160).

Example. Your friends plan electric-baseboard heat at 0.102 cents per kilowatt-hour in a climate with 4,000 heating-degree days. From Table 15, their optimum R modifier is 1.3, so their optimum R values are 1.3 times yours:

	Yours	*Theirs*
Exterior wall	R-25	R-32
Attic floor	R-57	R-74
Cathedral ceiling	R-26	R-34

Table 15

OPTIMUM R MODIFIERS

Elec kWh	Oil Gal	Gas CCF	Wood Cord	Coal Ton	Heating-Degree Days				
					2,000	4,000	6,000	8,000	10,000
0.024	0.70	0.49	88	105	0.4	0.6	0.8	0.9	1.0
0.027	0.80	0.56	100	120	0.5	0.7	0.8	1.0	1.1
0.031	0.90	0.63	113	135	0.5	0.7	0.9	1.0	1.1
0.034	1.00	0.70	125	150	0.5	0.8	0.9	1.1	1.2
0.038	1.10	0.77	138	165	0.6	0.8	1.0	1.1	1.3
0.041	1.20	0.84	150	180	0.6	0.8	1.0	1.2	1.3
0.044	1.30	0.91	163	195	0.6	0.9	1.1	1.2	1.4
0.048	1.40	0.98	175	210	0.6	0.9	1.1	1.3	1.4
0.051	1.50	1.05	188	225	0.7	0.9	1.1	1.3	1.5
0.055	1.60	1.12	200	240	0.7	1.0	1.2	1.3	1.5
0.058	1.70	1.19	213	255	0.7	1.0	1.2	1.4	1.6
0.061	1.80	1.26	225	270	0.7	1.0	1.2	1.4	1.6
0.065	1.90	1.33	238	285	0.7	1.0	1.3	1.5	1.6
0.068	2.00	1.40	250	300	0.8	1.1	1.3	1.5	1.7
0.075	2.20	1.54	275	330	0.8	1.1	1.4	1.6	1.7
0.082	2.40	1.68	300	360	0.8	1.2	1.4	1.7	1.8
0.089	2.60	1.82	325	390	0.9	1.2	1.5	1.7	1.9
0.097	2.80	1.96	350	420	0.9	1.3	1.5	1.8	2.0
0.102	3.00	2.10	375	450	0.9	1.3	1.6	1.8	2.1
0.109	3.20	2.24	400	480	1.0	1.3	1.7	1.9	2.1
0.116	3.40	2.38	425	510	1.0	1.4	1.7	2.0	2.2
0.123	3.60	2.52	450	540	1.0	1.4	1.8	2.1	2.3
0.130	3.80	2.66	475	570	1.0	1.5	1.8	2.1	2.3
0.137	4.00	2.80	500	600	1.1	1.5	1.8	2.1	2.4
0.143	4.20	2.94	525	630	1.1	1.5	1.9	2.2	2.4
0.150	4.40	3.08	555	660	1.1	1.6	1.9	2.2	2.5
0.157	4.60	3.22	575	690	1.1	1.6	2.0	2.3	2.6
0.164	4.80	3.36	600	720	1.2	1.7	2.0	2.3	2.6
0.171	5.00	3.50	625	750	1.2	1.7	2.1	2.4	2.7

Example: Electric Heat $0.102/kWh & 4,000 HDD = Multiplier 1.3

Care Is Important — The Effect of Gaps

What would be the effect of insulating 90 percent of your attic to R-49 and leaving the remaining 10 percent in its R-3 uninsulated condition? The average R value would be only 90 percent of 49, or R-45, right? Wrong! It would be R-19, or less than half of its nominal value.

Illustration 75 shows the heat short-circuiting effect of air gaps on the overall performance of insulation. It makes little difference what surface; a small gap in the insulation has a disproportionate effect on the average R value. In fact, the first 1 percent of insulation gap lowers the average R value by 13 percent for R-49, and 5 percent for R-19.

To give you an idea of what 1 percent of an attic looks like, it's the $2' \times 6'$ opening for a foldaway attic staircase in a 1,200-square-foot attic, or a continuous gap of ¼ inch between insulation batts and attic-floor joists at 24-inch on-center framing.

The point here is that the care with which you install insulation is just as important as the amount. Don't be afraid to be there to help when the insulation goes in. In fact, be afraid *not* to be there. It's a job you do just once but live with for the rest of your life.

VAPOR BARRIERS. You know how your bathroom window fogs up when you take a shower in winter? Well, picture that happening inside your walls or attic all winter long. Of course, it doesn't happen that dramatically, if it happens at all. But the principle is the same: Water vapor condenses out of air whenever the air comes into contact with a surface colder than the dew point of the air. In the bathroom, very humid air makes contact with the very cold surface of the window. In your walls, moderately humid air from inside the house may make contact with the fairly cold inside of the exterior-wall sheathing and similarly deposit moisture. In the attic, moisture that has risen from the house below often condenses on the cold underside of the roof sheathing. If enough moisture is deposited, dry-rot fungus may damage the sheathing and adjacent framing.

It is now recognized that the few homes with moisture problems are usually generating excess interior moisture. The amount generated by the normal activities of a single occupant is about a half gallon per day. In studying the reasons for the mildew and dry rot that occur in about one home in a hundred, researchers have discovered the following rather astounding moisture generators:

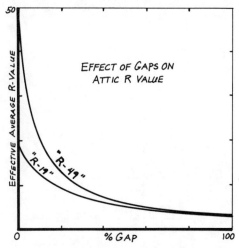

75. Reduction in effective R value due to gaps in insulation (percent of area)

Vapor/Air Barriers

Table 16
SOURCES OF MOISTURE IN THE HOME

Sources of Moisture	Gallons per Day
25 house plants	½
Drying a cord of green wood	1
Framing of new house	1–2
New concrete basement	1½
Dirt crawl space	10
Standing water in basement	40

It was previously believed that water vapor was diffused through the surfaces of walls and ceilings. It is now known that a hundred times as much moisture penetrates cracks and holes in walls and ceilings by convection (moving air) as by diffusion. What is needed to prevent moist interior air from penetrating interior surfaces is not just a vapor barrier but an air barrier as well. In other words, we want to make sure there is no way for air from inside the house to leak through a hole or a crack into the cavity of a wall or ceiling. Imagining your house to be a boat may help you to picture where she needs additional caulking, John. Of course, preventing the passage of air through surfaces of the house serves another equally important function: stopping the heat loss of infiltration.

AIR BARRIERS. Viewed by an uncritical eye, houses seem as tight as boats. Viewed through an infrared scanner or with a smoke stick and a pressurizing fan, however, they are as holey as Swiss cheeses. Wind pushes air into a house on the windward side and sucks air out of the house on the leeward side. Additionally, in winter the relative buoyancy of the warmer indoor air results in a vertical flow: cold air in through low cracks and holes (such as the crack between foundation wall and sill) and warm air out through high paths (such as pipe and lighting penetrations in the ceiling). This combined and complex exchange of air between indoors and outdoors is called infiltration and typically accounts for 40 percent of the annual heating bill. We thus have *two* good reasons to seal our houses: damage from water vapor and the expense of heating.

Illustration 76 and Table 17 catalogue the air leaks found in typical houses by researchers at Princeton University. I was blown away by the sizes of the leaks. For example, one would think from a visit to the local hardware store that caulking and weatherstripping doors and windows and installing foam gaskets on electrical outlets would pretty much seal up a house. But look at the table! Those things are certainly worth doing, but the amount of air that leaks from doors, windows, and outlets pales in comparison to the amounts escaping from a dropped ceiling (item 2), an uncaulked foundation sill (12), an uncaulked band sill (13), a fireplace without a damper (37), and heating or cooling ducts in an unheated space (38). In fact, windows, doors, and electrical outlets all together account for less than 20 percent of infiltration. Table 17 shows that the majority of air leaks can be plugged only during the design and construction stages, never as an afterthought.

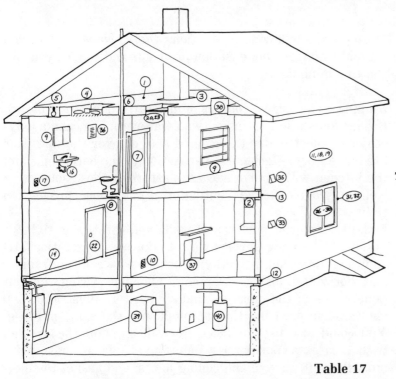

76. Location of common air leaks

Table 17

AIR LEAKAGE OF BUILDING COMPONENTS (AREA OF LEAK IN SQUARE INCHES)

CEILING

1. General per 100 square feet	0.05
2. Dropped ceiling:	
no plastic (per 100 sq ft)	78
plastic vapor barrier (per 100 sq ft)	8
3. Chimney framing: open	12
packed with insulation	1
4. Whole house fan: louvers closed	8
covered with tight box	0.6
5. Lighting fixtures: recessed	4
surface	0.3
6. Pipe or duct: uncaulked	1
caulked at ceiling	0.2

INTERIOR WALLS

7. Pocket door	5
8. Pipe or duct in wall	2
9. Recessed cabinet	0.8
10. Electric box: ungasketed	0.2
gasketed	0.03

EXTERIOR WALLS

11. General per 100 square feet	0.8
12. Sill on masonry: uncaulked	65
caulked	13
13. Band or box sill: uncaulked	65
caulked	13
14. Floor/wall joint:	27
mopboard caulked	7
15. Duct in wall	9
16. Pipe in wall	2
17. Electric box: ungasketed	0.2
gasketed	0.05
18. Polyethylene vapor barrier (deduct)	−30
19. Styrofoam sheathing (deduct)	−15

DOORS

20. Attic fold-down: plain	17
weather-stripped	8
insulated cover	2
21. Patio sliding	16
22. Entrance: plain	8
weather-stripped	6
magnetic seal	4
23. Attic hatch: plain	6
weather-stripped	3
24. Air-lock entry (deduct)	−4
25. Storm door (deduct)	−3

WINDOWS (weather-stripped)

26. Double-hung	0.8
27. Horizontal slider	0.6
28. Awning	0.2
29. Casement	0.2
30. Fixed	0.2

DOOR & WINDOW FRAMES

31. Masonry wall: uncaulked	2
caulked	0.4
32. Wood wall: uncaulked	0.6
caulked	0.1

VENTS

33. Range: damper open	9
damper closed	2
34. Dryer: damper open	4
damper closed	1
35. Bathroom: damper open	3
damper closed	1

FIREPLACE

36. Fireplace: no damper or open	54
average damper	9
tight damper	5
stove insert	2

HEATING SYSTEM

37. Ducts in unheated space: not caulked or taped	56
caulked and taped	28
38. Furnace: with retention head burner	12
with stack damper	12
with retention head and damper	9
39. Boiler or gas/oil water heater	8

Adapted from D. T. Harrje and G. J. Born, "Cataloguing Air Leakage Components in Houses," Princeton University Center for Energy and Environmental Studies, 1984.

By taking the following precautions *during construction*, you should avoid moisture-condensation problems and reduce your infiltration to a minimum.

1. Eliminate the largest sources of moisture shown in Table 16. Proper foundation drainage, wall waterproofing, and a polyethylene sheet under the ground slab or over the dirt floor are mandatory. Mechanical ventilation in the bathrooms and the kitchen will remove excess moisture at those sources as well as provide forced ventilation if the house proves too tight.
2. Make the interior surfaces of walls and ceilings as tight as possible. There are several ways to do this. Illustration 74D shows an unbroken polyethylene sheet between the framing and horizontal inside strapping, allowing wiring without penetration of the moisture and air barrier. Illustration 100 shows surface wiring that accomplishes the same purpose. You could also use foil-faced drywall or paint the drywall with a latex vapor-barrier paint (available at most paint stores), caulk all wall and ceiling joints, and gasket the electrical boxes.
3. Finally, before the start of construction, go over Table 17 with your builder. Ask how he or she plans to eliminate each of the potential leaks. And as your house is being built, use the table as a checklist. As with insulation, it's the care with which the job is done that counts. Be there while it's being done; wade right in and help; be a pain in the ass! After all, it's your house, not the carpenter's.

Your friend,
Charlie

9. *Windows*

LETTER
24

Dear Charlie,

Now that we're done with insulation (at least I hope we are — I've had to learn more than I ever wanted to know), let's move to what I consider the best part of any home: windows.

As I said once before, we want the new house to be generous with its windows, because they mean more to me than just light or ventilation. I like windows because I love the outdoors, because I am a captive of the seasons and watch for every natural signal the way some folks read the Dow Jones averages. I want to know when the first redwing returns in March; I want to be able to see the new moon on something besides our calendar; and even when it's snowing, I want to be able to turn on an outside light at night and watch the flakes spin past.

I am reassured by the steadiness of the sun's movements to its annual equinoctial rhythms: high in the summer, low in the winter. Somehow the notion that we are part of a planetary engine that revolves, tilts, spins, and turns as steadily as the one-cylinder Palmer with the huge flywheel that once powered a great old Nova Scotia fishing boat of mine is a notion that contents me, steadies me with its monumental and perpetual design.

Windows are the way we stay in touch with the natural presences that set the patterns of our lives. We can see flowers, stars, neighbors, clouds, blue jays, and lightning bolts from our windows, so we want plenty of them. Ours was never intended to be a "cave," the sort of dark place with its illusions of security that Frank Lloyd Wright claimed a home should be. We find that our sense of security is keyed to what occurs each of the 24 hours that this earth is turning, and therefore it follows that the place we live should allow 24-hour observation of those occurrences — including being able to check the skies at 3:00 A.M. on a nocturnal visit to the bathroom.

Knowing you, I can sense some squirming as you read. Windows, in your lexicon, I'm certain, are not designed primarily to allow us communication with nature. I can hear you now: Windows, you say, are for light, or ventilation, and for solar heat. They are not able to be used efficiently if they are merely dropped in this wall or that wall or that wall so a nut like myself will always be in a room with an outdoors that's just a glance away.

You are being practical, of course; and practical is what you are supposed to be. But, Charlie, from what I've been reading lately, it looks as if technology may have caught up with my obsessions about windows. The problem is not whether windows lose heat or gain it anymore; the new methods of window manufacture, I'm told, have solved that. What I read, even in the most basic home-building publications, is news of what more than one writer has called a window revolution.

There is one-way glass that lets the solar energy in, but won't let it out. There is double-glazing and triple-glazing, and there is something called a heat mirror, if I recall correctly, that does goodness knows what. I imagine it may take the heat that's generated inside during the winter and reflect it so it stays inside. Or does the term mean the mirrors reflect summer heat away from the home that has them?

I don't really know the answers, Charlie; and besides, I couldn't get away with pretending I do, not with you. But I do get the very real sense that there are window designs that will let home builders do just about anything they want with glass, provided they can afford it.

Which is the point that has brought me up short. Jean and I went to a couple of rather large building-supply places the other day. They have nifty models of windows — windows that slide, windows that crank open, and windows that go up and down just like the ones I grew up with. Every one of the varieties has one thing in common, however: They are expensive. At least they seem so to us. You know I can't do much math, but figuring the square-foot cost of a $3' \times 6'$ window isn't too difficult. Just divide eighteen into the total price. I tried that on my calculator, Charlie, and the bottom line is almost always about $30 a square foot on the high side, $25 on the low.

That's bad news for a guy as much in love with windows as I am. I mean, we are trying to hold to our budget. And I know that no matter what I do, Jean isn't going to let me get too far out of line as far as any costs are concerned.

So I've been thinking. Suppose I can justify the cost of our windows by saying the sunshine they allow will give us enough heat to have the windows pay for themselves after a few years. That's the sort of calculation you and your computers ought to be able to work out in nothing flat. It's also a design possibility that we have already had some experience with, as you know. That place on the point was nothing but a long shed-roofed barn, its entire south side just about solid double-glazed, fixed-glass panels. It was, in the current lingo, a design that maximized solar gain. Although that was never as important to me as what it did for the view over Middle Bay.

I suppose that was a good thing, because there were any number of visitors (you among them) who told me I was losing as much heat *out* those windows at night as I was taking in during the day. Indeed, if I recall, you said there might even be a net loss. The possibility didn't discourage me on those lovely mornings I could see all the way to Whaleboat Island. I just didn't care whether we gained or lost heat; it was the view that had first priority. All else was negotiable.

Suppose we had put in some of the new miracle glass instead of the conventional double glazing. I'll bet that even you would have caved in on your arguments. What are the chances we make that switch, at least for the south-facing windows in the new house, Charlie?

Because I'll tell you: No matter how much pressure is put on me, I'm not going to settle for the so-called efficiency of the small, limited windows I see in some of the designs for those superinsulated houses. That's just not my cup of tea. Nor is the other heat-saving, money-saving (supposedly) system I've also read about: the concrete-block walls, inside, behind the windows. They store a day's heat during the winter and release it during the long night. They may be the solution for some folks, but not for us. I don't want to look at a concrete-block wall; I want to be able to watch the grass turn green in April.

What you have, Charlie, are two clients that like windows of all kinds. Clients that probably can't afford as many windows as they want. And clients who have read just enough about a window revolution to hope that they can, in fact, do better with cost-conscious, energy-gathering, and energy-saving new kinds of glass than they could have a decade ago. Isn't it possible, using the new materials, to allow us a sense of space, the illusion of space, if you will, by having the windows, and glass doors, and glass walls let the outside in so it becomes part of the total environment?

That, after all, will be the key to the place, as far as we are concerned. It's one of the reasons we chose the site we did: It allows us a view from almost every window we decide to install. Which decision we now turn over to you, now that you understand our perception of windows, and our excitement about the window revolution we read about. Having come this far with you, we are certain you can help. And we hope so, too.

Your friend,
John

Dear John and Jean,

You're right, there is a window revolution. With the exception of storm windows, the basic window had changed very little over hundreds of years. But all of a sudden, spurred on by the economics of window heat loss and the chance to make a buck, American glass manufacturers have gone crazy. There's nothing like the opportunity to make a buck to get a manufacturer's creative juices flowing. Just as the gasoline crunch spawned autos that get 50-plus miles per gallon, rising home-heating costs have resulted in Buck Rogers windows that really work: They let the sunshine in, they retard heat loss out, and they do it cost-effectively.

But I know you, John. You're like Toad in *The Wind in the Willows.* You're dazzled by what's new, so impressed with the latest trick that you forget the basics. I'm impressed by the new windows, too, but I'm also mindful of our original concern: the design of a compact low-cost house that works in all ways for you and Jean. Before we get into the new technologies, therefore, we're going to consider all of the things we expect of windows, including the basics.

Our Basic Window Expectations

Windows are generally installed in walls. As with walls, we expect them to *keep out:*

- Wind
- Rain
- Snow
- Bugs
- Intruders

- Noise
- Winter cold
- Summer heat

On the other hand, windows are not walls. We further expect windows to *let in:*

- Outside views
- Natural daylight
- Ventilating air
- Winter solar heat

We'll touch on the first group of functions along the way, but let's concentrate first on the latter group of special functions.

Types of Windows

Illustration 77 shows the eight types of windows sold by major window manufacturers, plus one special type of glazing often installed as a window in the field. For a quick overview I have listed all nine in the ratings format in Table 18. Finally, because windows are so expensive, I have graphed their typical per-square-foot installed costs in Illustration 78 (page 173). I'll be referring to both the table and the illustrations as we discuss each type, so locate them now.

AWNING. The awning window gets its name from being hinged at the top. If hinged at the bottom, the same window would be called, appropriately enough, a hopper window. Some utility or basement windows can be installed either way.

In my opinion, as you can see from Table 18, the awning window has but one strong point: the ability to shed water when left open in a rainstorm. If you are away from home a lot, or forget a lot, the awning may be justified.

Because of its short height, the awning window is often installed over a kitchen sink where the counter height limits the sill height; in a bathroom where you wish to limit the view to above shoulder height; and in combination with fixed windows.

Illustration 78 shows that, though an awning unit may seem reasonable in cost, its cost per square foot of glass is extremely high.

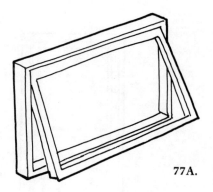

77A.

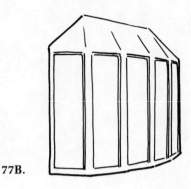

77B.

BOW OR BAY. These consist of grouped windows of the other types. The bow is a segmented outward-projecting arch of five or more units. It usually consists of casements at the ends and three or more fixed units of the same size in the center. The bay window typically contains a single large fixed window in the center and an openable casement or double-hung window at each side.

Everyone wants at least one bow or bay window. Except for the sun space, it is about the most striking exterior architectural feature you can incorporate in your design. On the inside it creates a pleasant, sunny spot for plants and sitting. Since you have a very tight budget, however, carefully consider the things you can do with the replacement patio units discussed later on.

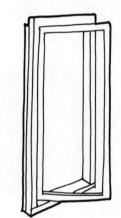

77C.

CASEMENT. The casement window is very similar to the awning, except for being hinged to the side. It is comparable in cost per square foot, but it does a lot of things better.

First, being side-hinged, it can reach out and scoop in the summer breeze like one of those old-fashioned automobile windows. (Remember to consider the direction of the prevailing summer breeze in selecting the hinge side.) Second, it is available in many sizes, from the shortest, for installation over the kitchen sink, to the tallest, reaching nearly to the floor. Third, being tall and narrow, it has a striking appearance. Finally, its narrowness allows cleaning from inside.

Unfortunately, you pay for what you get. Here you get the most and, as shown in Illustration 78, you pay the most per square foot.

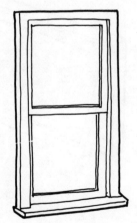

77D.

DOUBLE-HUNG. This is, no doubt, the image that flashes in front of your mind's eye when you hear the word *window*. For some historical architectural styles there is simply no substitute for the old-fashioned multipaned double-hung window.

Perhaps because it is perceived as out of date, or perhaps because there are so many competing manufacturers, the double-hung is the least expensive type of openable window. But price is for once not an indicator of performance: The double-hung looks good, ventilates well, is easy to clean, and comes in many sizes.

PATIO DOOR. The patio door is either an all-glass door or a window large enough to walk through. Either way, because it has become so standardized (most manufacturers offer only three sizes) and because it sells in such great quantities, it is a bargain in cost per square foot.

With a glazed area of 40 to 50 square feet, the patio door has the potential to be either a terrific solar collector on the south side or a terrible heat loss on the north side. Often overlooked is its venting effectiveness. With 20 to 25 square feet of floor-to-ceiling opening, it has the ventilation potential of at least three windows of any other type. Positioning a patio door therefore involves considering much more than traffic pattern alone.

Being of similar size and shape, the patio door works well architecturally with the patio-door replacement glazings I'll be enthusiastically promoting below.

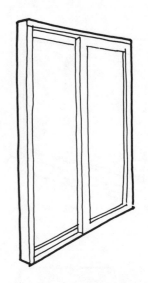

77E.

SLIDING OR GLIDING. The slider is essentially a short version of the patio door. Another way to view it is like a double-hung window lying on its side. I think any window with a width greater than its height is ugly, and this one takes the prize. I forbid you to install a glider, even though they are relatively inexpensive.

77F.

UTILITY OR BASEMENT. I get a big kick out of this window. It's obviously designed to be placed in a masonry foundation wall, but it's also well made and available with a second glazing and screen. Identical to the awning window except for the lack of an exterior trim, it costs half as much. This price/performance paradox is probably explained by the fact that most people would not dream of paying the outrageous awning-window price for a lowly basement window. As the saying goes, a thing is worth what someone will pay for it.

I won't pay awning-window prices either, but I've more than once bought a "basement" window and installed it upstairs!

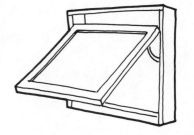

77G.

FIXED OR PICTURE. The next two windows perfectly illustrate a point I like to make to my students: We pay for openable glazings four times — once for the glass, once for the frame that holds the glass, once for the opening hardware, and, finally, once for the glossy four-color ads.

If the window needn't open, do yourself a favor and buy a fixed window at half the price. Better yet, buy just the glass (see patio-door replacement glazing further on) and save even more. Fixed windows are usually available in the same heights as casements and double-hungs, so there is no aesthetic reason why all your windows have to open.

There are good reasons to consider openable windows, however. The first is ventilation, which will be considered later. The second is fire. Fire codes call for two exits from every living, dining, and sleeping room (unless one is a door leading directly outside). One exit can be an "egress window" — any manually openable window with a sill less than 4 feet above floor level, a clear opening of at least 5 square feet, and a minimum opening dimension of 22 inches.

PATIO-DOOR REPLACEMENT GLAZING. As you should have guessed by now, these are my favorites. They are what the glass man brings when a neighborhood kid throws a rock through your patio door. They come in three popular sizes, all glass stores stock them, and wow, are they cheap! The sizes are:

$$28'' \text{ wide} \times 76'' \text{ high}$$
$$34'' \text{ wide} \times 76'' \text{ high}$$
$$46'' \text{ wide} \times 76'' \text{ high}$$

I usually wangle a contractor's price by purchasing several at a time. Including the installation costs, you should end up paying between $12 and $14 per square foot, which, as shown in Illustration 78, is the best window buy around.

They don't ventilate, and you can't use them as exits (except with a sledgehammer), but they are in all other regards superb. I think of them as attractive, cost-effective, airtight solar collectors.

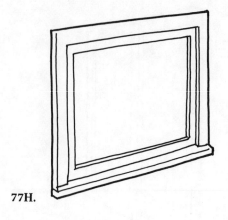

77H.

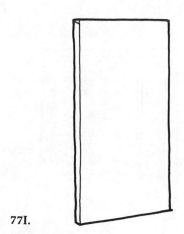

77I.

	Table 18 **WINDOWS COMPARED**	Relative Cost per Sq. Ft.	Venting Effectiveness	Range of Sizes	Appearance	Protection—Open in Rain	Ease of Cleaning	Fire Egress
Openable	Awning	○	◑	◑	○	●	○	○
	Bow or Bay	○	◑	○	●	○	○	○
	Casement	○	●	●	●	○	●	◑
	Double-Hung	◑	●	●	●	○	◑	◑
	Patio Door	◑	●	○	◑	○	●	●
	Sliding or Gliding	◑	◑	●	○	○	◑	◑
	Utility or Basement	●	◑	○	○	●	●	◑
Fixed	Fixed or Picture	◑	○	◑	◑	●	○	○
	Patio-Door Replacement Glazing	●	○	○	●	●	○	○

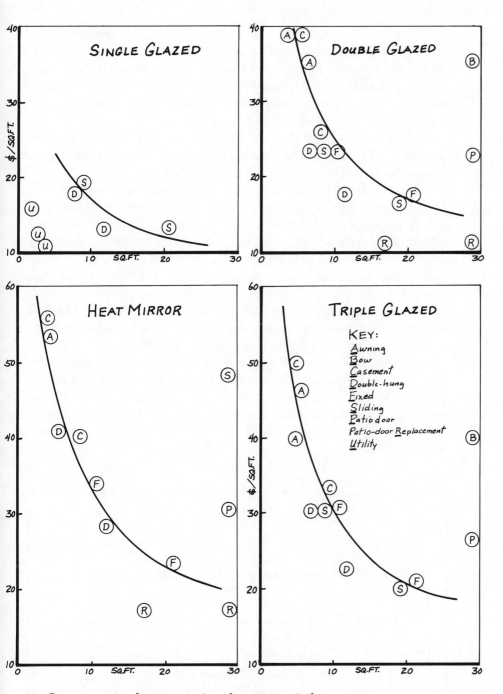

78. Cost per square foot versus size of common window types

The View Through Windows

Now let's consider that window function you consider most important: providing contact with the outside world. You know that I am a strong advocate of energy conservation; in fact, conservation has been my theme for as long as you have known me. But, like you, I cannot understand how anyone can eliminate windows simply in the name of conservation.

In Letter 6 I cited two architectural patterns relating to view: windows with small panes, and low windowsills. Illustration 79 shows the window geometry for these patterns.

First, a large picture window generally frames a view poorly. Like a novice photographer with his first camera, it indiscriminately includes excessive visual information. Breaking the view into smaller scenes with horizontal and vertical muntins creates a lot more interest. Furthermore, these small scenes continually change as the viewer moves around the room. To the extent that there are primary points or lines of interest (such as the horizon), we should space the horizontal muntins so that they miss the line of sight of both a standing person (average eye height 60 inches) and a sitting person (average eye height 36 inches).

Second, events in the foreground are of great interest to the occupants of a building. How many times have you gotten out of your chair and gone to the window to investigate a sound? We can visually connect to the near surroundings even while seated if we place the windowsill at 12 inches rather than the customary 30 to 36 inches.

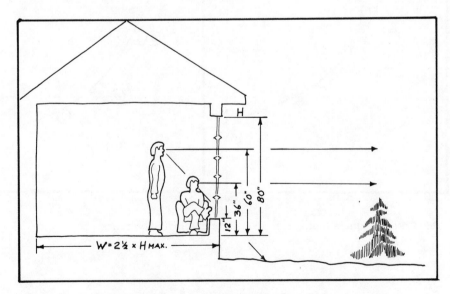

79. Important geometric factors for windows

The third dimension is the standard height of exterior doors and windows, 80 inches. Try to observe this standard with all windows as well as doors; it is key to the appearance of a house. If you doubt it, drive around the neighborhood and note the visual effects that result from violating this rule.

Natural Daylighting

Illustration 79 also serves for a discussion of the second most important function of windows: admitting natural light to the interior. Once again I refer you to a couple of architectural patterns cited in my third letter that have to do with the value of natural daylighting. The first called for a place by a window. I am writing this letter seated in my most comfortable chair, nestled into a window corner framed by two floor-to-ceiling patio-door replacement units — a personal testimony to the pattern.

The second pattern calls for windows on two sides of every room. People and objects illuminated from a single direction appear flat and unnatural. Daylight comes both directly from the sun and indirectly from the whole sky vault, so windows on at least two walls provide more natural lighting.

Illustration 79 specifies one more geometric rule: The width of a room should not exceed 2½ times the height of the window providing the illumination. The standard window height of 80 inches thus limits the proper width of a room to 200 inches, or just over 16 feet. In the case of an open plan with windows on opposite walls, however, the total width can be up to 32 feet.

Depth and distribution of illumination are also improved by painting the ceiling and, to a lesser extent, the walls a light color. Finally, glare — a painful sensation caused by the pupil of the eye responding only to the average light level in spite of extreme differences — is minimized by painting the walls next to windows a light color.

Natural Ventilation

There are two principal reasons to ventilate a house: to cool an overheated house; and to flush out indoor air pollutants such as excess moisture, essence of boiled cabbage, chemical fumes from building products and furnishings, and possibly radon gas from groundwater beneath the house. But before rushing out and buying a whole bunch of openable windows, consider the following facts.

First, with effective shading of summer solar gain through windows and sufficient built-in thermal mass (I'll cover that in my next letter), your highly insulated house should always be cooler inside than outside on a hot summer day. Opening a window would therefore result in admitting hot air. Only at night might window ventilation prove useful, provided the outdoor temperature drops below the interior temperature.

Second, the sources of most indoor air pollution can be pinpointed. Excess moisture can be isolated or eliminated; kitchen and bathroom smells can be eliminated at their source before spreading through the house; chemical sources such as foam rubber and vinyl fabrics can be minimized; and construction materials containing formaldehyde, such as waferboard, can be banished to the other side of the vapor barrier.

After arguing against massive, indiscriminate ventilation, let me now state that efficient, properly placed, and properly directed ventilation is a good thing. Proper ventilation includes:

Point-of-source vents. Install a range hood over the stove and a power vent in each bathroom. Of course, you could install openable windows in the bathrooms if you really believed people would use them, but I have never witnessed anyone opening a bathroom window in winter, regardless of the fog density.

Cross ventilation. In spite of its invisibility, air is a real substance. It cannot enter a space through one opening unless it can concurrently escape by a second opening. The sheltering effectiveness of a lean-to illustrates the point. This is also the reason bathrooms and bedrooms with windows on a single wall do not ventilate well. Remember as you locate ventilating windows and doors that the breeze will enter openings facing the prevailing breeze and then proceed fairly directly to openings facing downwind. Rooms and corners of rooms not *directly* in these paths will *not* be well ventilated.

People ventilation. Remember also that what you are ventilating is not the rafters, nor is it the rugs on the floor — it's people, lying on a bed, sitting at a dining-room table, sitting in front of the television. So in planning, make sure your ventilating windows and doors are placed vertically as well as horizontally to direct air precisely across the people places. I will never forget this principle. I once built a small cabin with a windowless sleeping loft and spent many a sweaty summer night in that stifling, airless loft while, downstairs, cool air swept from front to back door. I finally installed an openable window at the level of my pillow and closed the downstairs door on the same wall. Ah, sweet relief! As the breeze now proceeded from the loft window to the back door, it had no choice but to run smack into my face!

Vertical ventilation. What if it's really hot inside and there is no breeze? Obviously we could use one or more window fans to force ventilation. But we could also take advantage of something we learned as children: Hot air rises. A hot house is like a hot-air balloon, and like the balloon, the house will lose its hot air out the top if we merely cut a hole in the roof. A single open skylight at the top of the stairs can vent several volumes of house air per hour, inducing a breeze through downstairs windows and doors at the same time.

As a final ventilation exercise, I suggest you mark on your floor plan those places where you expect to be sitting or lying on hot summer nights, and then draw arrows from the windows and doors on the wall facing the prevailing summer breeze to the windows and doors on the downwind side. The exercise will show you which of your windows need to be openable (expensive) in order to ventilate the people places and, by elimination, which can be fixed (low cost).

I hope you take all of the above on view, natural lighting, and ventilation seriously. A lot of solar designers (myself included) have in the past ignored these more timeless aspects of windows in our enthusiasm for solar energy. With these lessons firmly in place, we can now safely turn our attention to the energy aspects of windows.

THE SUN'S PATH. I'm sure you know all about the motion of the sun, but my sense of orderliness forbids me from starting without a few words about it. Illustrations 80 and 81 trace the paths of the sun at 42 degrees north latitude on December 22 and June 22. These are the approximate dates of the winter and summer solstices, the times when the sun "stands still."

On December 22 the sun rises to the south of east, climbs to a due-south maximum elevation of 24½ degrees, and then sets

Windows and Energy

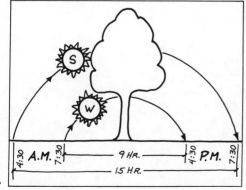

80.

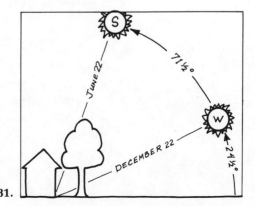

81.

symmetrically to the south of west. (It rises due east and sets due west on the equinoxes, or "equal nights," March 22 and September 22.) The winter day is extremely short; with sunrise at approximately 7:30 A.M. and sunset at 4:30 P.M., its duration is only nine hours. Because of the great amount of atmospheric absorption and scattering at low sun angles, nearly all solar radiation is received between the hours of 9:00 A.M. and 3:00 P.M.

The longest day of the year is June 22. There are probably people who have yet to witness the sun rising at the summer solstice because it does so at the ungodly hour of 4:30 A.M. If they did, they would likely be amazed at how far to the north of east it rises. It reaches east at 8:00 A.M., south and nearly overhead at noon, and west at 4:00 P.M. It finally sets well to the north of west. Whereas there are only nine hours of day and fifteen hours of night in winter, at the summer solstice there are fifteen hours of day and nine hours of night.

ORIENTATION. My solar-path review is not entirely without purpose. I want you to come away with two firmly entrenched ideas:

1. Nearly all winter solar-heat gain occurs between the hours of 9:00 A.M. and 3:00 P.M. If you are serious about solar heating, you must not let *anything* shade your windows significantly during those hours.
2. Most undesirable summer solar-heat gain occurs not at midday when the sun beats fruitlessly on the roof, but at midmorning from the east and at midafternoon from the west. So if you are serious about not having an air conditioner, you must shade not only south but east and west windows as well during those times.

Illustration 82 quantifies these points. It shows the average Btus per square foot per day of solar gain through ordinary single-

82. Average solar radiation (Btu per square foot per day) through single-glazed windows in Boston on June 22 and December 22

glazed windows facing north, south, east, and west on June 22 and December 22 in Boston.

SHADING. With what should we shade? Naturally, there are dozens of devices on the market to shade windows: reflective glass, absorbing glass, reflective films, absorbing films, reflective screens, louvered blinds, awnings, shutters, and so on. But it pleases me that not one human invention is as clever or effective as a deciduous shade tree. A maple tree conforms to my ideal of excellence in design: effective, permanent, aesthetically pleasing, and maintenance-free. It begins shading just as the sun becomes too strong; it drops its sun-blocking leaves upon instruction from the first frosts; it gives us an amazing color show in the process; and it never requires painting or repair. It's even free, if you're not too lazy to transplant one from the forest. Whoever designed the maple deserves recognition!

So plant several maples due south of your house and one each to the east and the west. If you are lucky enough to have mature trees already on your site, make sure the contractor understands that his life is in danger if so much as the bark is bruised. (Contractors tend to think of trees as obstructions and free sources of firewood.)

Of the artificial shading devices, the only ones that conform to my stringent design specifications are roof overhangs and arbors. Overhangs protect siding and windows from weather as well as from sun, but they are fully effective at shading the sun only on the south. Arbors planted with perennial vines function like deciduous trees, with the advantage that they begin providing shade within just a few years. Of course, a house with arbors over all of its windows would look silly, so we may have to settle for some lesser temporary device for some of our windows. As you'll see as you read on, movable window insulation installed for winter heat savings can also be used to block summer heat gain, provided the window opens to release the heat that collects between the insulation and the glazing.

Solar Gain versus Heat Loss

The solar gains to be had through single-glazed windows at the summer and winter solstices are instructive in a gross sense, but let's get down to the nitty-gritty. After you've taken care of the lighting, ventilation, and view requirements, is it worth installing more windows just for the extra solar gain? In other words, does the lifetime reduction in fuel bill equal or exceed the extra cost of the windows?

This is a complex question. Beyond the uncertainty of future fuel prices, there are the complexities of weather and the dynamic thermal behavior of the building and its occupants. Here are just a few of the factors that can render a simple analysis meaningless:

1. The amount of solar radiation that actually gets into a building involves the number of glazings and their transmissibility; the shade cast by overhangs, other buildings, and trees; the precise orientation of each window; the reflectivity of the ground in front of the windows; and the percentage of the radiation reflected to the outside by light-colored interior surfaces.
2. Of the radiation received, how much is usable in maintaining the desired minimum interior temperature and how much simply raises the temperature above the minimum or, worse yet, requires venting? Factors here include the amount of heat generated internally by people, lights, and appliances, and the thermal mass, or ability of the building to soak up and later release solar heat.

Calculation methods have evolved that account for these complexities, but detailed hand calculations for even a small house such as yours require several hours. Fortunately, I have access to a program called PASSIVE SOLAR DESIGN (John Wiley), which runs on the IBM Personal Computer. It predicts, month by month, the fuel bill of a house with up to five passive solar systems (the program recognizes 94 different solar variations) in any of 219 cities — and all in a few minutes. So I asked the computer for the nitty-gritty. I asked it, Of all the different types of windows available today, which is the best for John's house? That is, considering both the extra *cost* of windows and the solar *fuel savings* they would produce over the next thirty years, which type would produce the greatest net savings?

I fed the computer the areas and R values of your basement, exterior walls, cathedral ceilings, and doors, as well as all of the environmental and life-style factors mentioned previously. Then I ran the program eight times, once for each of the following eight types of glazing, assuming 100 square feet of window facing south:

1. **DG** — *double-glazed* window, such as ordinary replacement patio units
2. **DGLI** — a special *double-glazed low-iron* window with higher transmission of solar energy

3. **TG** — *triple-glazed* ordinary glass
4. **TGLI** — the *low-iron* version of *triple glazing*
5. **QG** — *quadruple glazing* formed by two highly transparent plastic films stretched inside an ordinary double-glazed window
6. **LE** — a double-glazed window with a heat-reflecting *low-emissivity* coating on the glass
7. **HM** — a heat-reflective film *(heat mirror)* stretched inside a double-glazed window
8. **MWI** — *movable window insulation*, such as a shutter or quilted shade, over double glazing

I was trying to determine the best type of solar window for your house. The question I asked the computer had specific givens: your house; Brunswick, Maine; coal heat at $150 per ton; and 100 square feet of unshaded south-facing windows. Illustration 83 shows the results, which are also specific.

The heights of the columns beneath the break-even line show the extra costs per square foot of the different windows over the wall sections they replace. The columns above the break-even line show the thirty-year fuel savings per square foot of window. The solid black portions show the net benefit per square foot — the thirty-year fuel savings minus the extra cost of the windows.

Clearly, the new space-age glazings, heat mirror (HM) and low emissivity (LE), are your best financial alternatives, John. Double-glazed windows with movable window insulation (MWI) place a close third, provided they last the full thirty years. Too bad the quadruple glazing (QG) is so expensive. It saves the most fuel, but its high cost wipes out the savings and places it last.

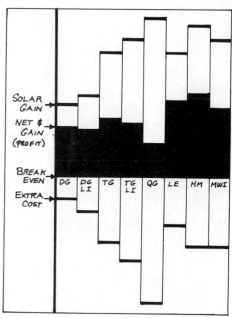

Glazing Type	R Value	% Trans.	$Solar Gain	Extra Cost	Net $ Gain
DG	1.9	77	9.30	3.00	6.30
DG LI	1.9	83	10.60	4.50	6.10
TG	2.8	70	16.20	8.50	7.70
TG LI	2.8	78	18.00	11.00	7.00
QG	3.8	71	20.90	16.50	4.40
LE	3.1	65	16.10	6.00	10.10
HM	4.0	61	19.90	9.00	10.90
MWI	1.9/4.4	77	18.00	9.00	9.00

83. Life-cycle net gain of eight types of south glazing

Recommendations

On the bases of Illustration 83 and the requirements for light, ventilation, and view, I recommend that you and Jean:

1. Install one small openable window at a central point on the north side just so you can see and communicate with whatever is out there. I'd make it an MWI and leave the insulation closed twenty-four hours a day in the winter.
2. On east and west sides I'd install openable windows of the minimum number and size for light and ventilation. You don't yet have adequate shade trees on the hot west side, so I'd install MWI there. The closed insulation would also provide privacy at night. The east-side windows look onto the pri-

vate deck and have partial shading from the existing trees, so HM or LE would work best.

3. On the south side I would put lots and lots of windows. The passive solar computer analysis I plan to run will tell me what total area of south-facing windows to install. I can tell you, however, that you should distinguish between two areas. First, in both upper and lower south bedrooms I'd install fixed patio-door replacement glazings with MWI for privacy and shading. The second area of south window is the wall between the kitchen/dining areas and the deck. There are several special considerations here: We want large areas of glass for plenty of light and heat; the windows should be visually compatible with the patio door to the dining area; Jean will probably hang dozens of plants in front of the windows, making MWI difficult to operate; the windows look out onto the private deck, so privacy is not required; and with such a large expanse of glass, the low R value of simple double glazing would make sitting at the dining-room table on a cold winter night very uncomfortable. I therefore recommend patio-door replacement glazings with HM or LE. You might consider framing them into a spectacular bow or bay!

Installing Patio-Door Replacement Glazings

Okay. Obviously, installing framed, store-bought windows is simple. That's why window manufacturers get away with the prices they charge. But I assure you that installing plain factory-sealed glazings (of patio-door size or any other) can be a simple matter as well. Illustration 84 shows the simplest and most inexpensive method of installation in an exterior wall.

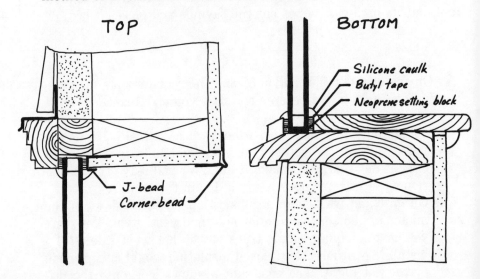

84. Installation of factory-sealed patio-door replacement glazings

Step 1. Cut a windowsill with drip kerf, siding dado, and slope from a knotless 2×10. All of the cuts are easily made on a bench saw. Soak in preservative overnight before installing.

Step 2. Install a preservative-treated pine window stool on the bottom of the opening, set back T (the thickness of the window unit) + ¼ inch from the outside face of the sheathing.

Step 3. Install ⅝-inch galvanized drywall J-bead at the top and sides of the window opening, also recessed T + ¼ inch from the face of the sheathing.

Step 4. Apply butyl glazing tape (obtained from the supplier of the windows) to the edges of the stool and J-bead.

Step 5. Set the window unit on two neoprene setting blocks measuring ¼ inch × T × 3 inches, each placed one-quarter of the width of the window in from the corners. Press the window against the glazing tape.

Step 6. Run more glazing tape around the outer edge of the window; press brick mold (at top and sides) and beveled stop (at bottom) against the tape and nail in place.

Step 7. Prime and paint all woodwork adjacent to the glass.

Step 8. Fill the ⅛-inch gaps between the glass and the inside and outside stops with clear silicone caulk.

Note: With only a ⅝-inch J-bead inner stop, we cannot afford to be sloppy with the framing of the rough opening. The opening should be square, ¼ inch wider, and ⅜ inch + sill thickness higher than the window.

I just have to show you one more detail. I'm sure one of you has spotted the discrepancy between my recommendation of large patio-door replacement units and the architectural pattern of small panes. To solve this problem, window manufacturers offer plastic snap-in muntins. I find these even more degrading and dishonest than fake wood-grain vinyl siding. If you agree with me, here are two honest solutions: either break up the view with hanging plants, or make your own window dividers, as shown in Illustration 85. The shelves are wide enough to hold plants and knickknacks, the whole unit removes for easy washing, it's simple enough for an amateur to build, and it's *honest*.

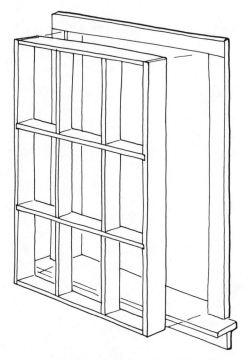

85. An honest, useful, and replaceable window grill

I've shown you which window glazings are the best solar collectors. The ball is in your court. You and Jean now have to select the styles and dimensions of your nonsolar north, east, and west windows, considering not only solar-collection efficiency but also

What's Next?

view, light, ventilation, and appearance. I suggest you obtain window catalogues from the local lumberyards and glass stores. Hurry up, because my next step is to calculate the area of south-facing glass that will minimize your life-cycle cost of heating, and the computer needs to know the areas of all the other windows in the house.

In my next letter I'll also explain how passive solar houses work, the different options available, and how to eliminate your air-conditioning bill at the same time that you lower your heating bill.

Best regards,
Charlie

10. Solar Heat

Dear Charlie,

You have a real knack for coming up with complex answers to my simple questions. I tell you what Jean and I like about windows, and I ask for a few pointers on what's new in the window world, and in response I'm sent (along with other wads of information) a list of eight sorts of window options along with another list of eight sorts of glazing and window coverings. I'm not much at mathematics, as you already know, but I can multiply eight times eight, and it leaves us with at least sixty-four options to choose from, or is it the square of sixty-four? It's too many, that's the answer.

It might have been easier if I'd stayed ignorant. That was not to be, however, and your latest has made me miss the eleven o'clock news two nights in a row. Jean had me bent over the floor plans as she read aloud from your notes on our various window options.

We reached a late-night truce with the following plan:

1. There will be no window on the north side. We went to the site and decided there wasn't much in that direction we wanted to see, not at the cost of giving the winter winds even a small toehold.

2. But on the south side, we went all out. First, because some of the south-facing windows overlook our own deck (a view we can control) and second, because we love the notion of the sun streaming in the kitchen and dining room. Following your suggestion, we've got a bay window *and* a double patio door on the kitchen–dining room south side, and a large casement window on the kitchen's east side, where the view is splendid.

3. Two more south-facing windows look out from one wall of our bedroom. But because these must give us both ventilation

and a certain amount of privacy, we decided on the standard double-hung model, your old reliable, the model you tell us works well, insulates well, and costs less. Knowing this, I'm sure you'll be pleased with the choice.

4. Another double-hung is on the east wall of the entrance hall; and on the bedroom's east wall (because here we can count on privacy) is one of your patio-door slabs of glass, designed to give us a view and some great sun in the morning when we're getting started on our day.

5. The west side of the house gets three double-hung windows, one each for the bedroom, bath, and living room. They'll vary in size a bit, but we believe they are far enough apart so the exterior pattern won't look out of balance. I know these don't coincide with all your recommendations, but they are a fair compromise.

6. As you know, we got all sorts of advice about skylights when we built the other place. "They are nothing but trouble," "They leak," etcetera. It was almost enough to talk me out of installing the small skylight we put in over the entrance hall, a hall that would have been dark without the extra light. What do you know? In ten years that skylight never leaked a drop, never caused trouble of any kind, and did a superior job of lighting the hall. It also gave me the fun of looking straight up at the sky, where I could see the stars at night and tree branches tossing in the wind on stormy days. Given that pleasant and economical experience, we're putting three small skylights above the upstairs apartment: one over the bedroom, one above the bath, and another in my study, which will be where it was first planned. Unlike the one in the other house, these will be screened and openable for ventilation in the summer. Whoever sleeps in that upstairs bed had better get acquainted with the moon. I notice, Charlie, that you don't include skylights on your windows list, but I also recall seeing several in the roof of your home. I assume (a) if you have them, they must be cost-effective; and (b) in your scientific and orderly mind, windows are windows and skylights are skylights, and it does not matter that I see the two performing essentially the same function.

Well, I went crashing ahead anyway, and we'll stay with the plans unless we hear energetic objections from you. You do mention skylights under the heading "Vertical Ventilation," which is, in my opinion, pretty close to what most windows do.

So much for the basic window choices. That job was relatively painless. What's confusing is making decisions about the *kind* of glazing, the amounts and quality of insulation.

We shall follow your basic suggestions about where to install the energy-saving quilted shades that you label "MWI," and take your advice on the location of the heat-mirror glazing. I suppose you have run this through your computer, which makes it easier for you when you look through the catalogues or visit lumber-yards to select the actual window you want for a particular spot. (By the way, I agree with you about the plastic muntins. One thing we know is that we don't want any.) Neither of us is a computer whiz, however, so we'll stick with your fundamentals and select what seems best for your formulas, our budgets, and the house design.

What we look forward to now is your analysis of the break-even line between window and glazing expense and the savings on heating and air-conditioning. Just so much solar energy can be gathered and utilized. How far should we reach for the last possible Btu? Where do we find that ideal compromise between the cost of the window and the heat it helps generate?

I'm sure your computer has the answers to these questions, even if you don't. I'll bet there is one of those Einstein equations for figuring everything out, and I'll bet you've already got a name for it.

But try and explain it without using terms I don't quite understand, can you, Charlie? For example, I hear you and your ilk talking about thermal mass as if it were as easy to comprehend as *door* or *basement*. I'm certain you understand it, but we don't. Okay, a wall of concrete blocks on the south side of a home is a thermal mass, but just what does it do? How does it work, I mean *really* work? Do we have any thermal mass in our new place? If not, why not? Do we need any? Can it be added?

I'm sure already that you find these questions simplistic at best. But believe me, we don't know the answers, and I'll bet a good many would-be home builders are in the same boat.

Like us, they want to know just how large or how small their double-glazed heat-mirror windows should be. Like us, they want to learn about the most cost-effective ways of using solar heat. And I'll bet you a winter day's worth of firewood that everyone building a house would like to come up with a system for predicting the cost of heating the place for a year.

Can you do that? Now that we have chosen the windows we want, now that we have the house oriented, can you and your computer tell us what our heating bill will be the first year we move in? I'm not totally sure I want to know; I like to keep every unpleasant thought at the greatest possible distance. But in this instance, we have some breathing room. If our window decisions are going to cost us an extra cord of wood, tank of heating oil, or ton of coal, then perhaps we should go back to the drawing board and try again. I can miss the eleven o'clock news one more time if it's going to save $150 a year over the next twenty or thirty years.

As I have been from the start, Charlie, I'm certain you can help. I await your next money-saving advisory.

Your friend,
John

LETTER
27

Dear John,

Thanks for the list of windows. (Architects call such a list the window schedule. I once thought they meant when the windows would arrive!)

You and Jean have shown admirable fiscal restraint so far. All along I've been hoping we could achieve a classy low-cost house. Most low-cost houses look like the box a manufactured home might be shipped in, but with Jean's class and our thriftiness, we may be able to do the trick.

Now that the areas and R values of all your house surfaces are known (with the exception of the solar-collecting south windows), we can use the computer to optimize the house for passive solar heating. First, though, let me give you a basic tutorial in passive solar design.

What Is Passive Solar Heating?

Most houses rely on the burning of a fuel to maintain a comfortable winter inside temperature. I have labeled those systems "Fuel Heat" in Illustration 86.

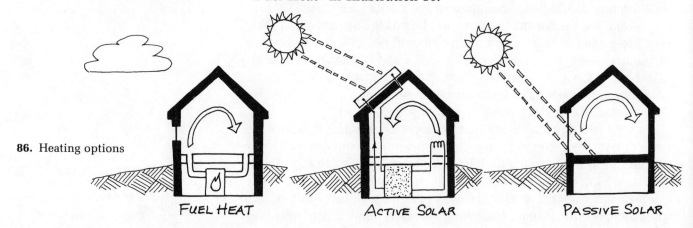

86. Heating options

FUEL HEAT   ACTIVE SOLAR   PASSIVE SOLAR

It is possible, through the application of vast arrays of plumbing and money, to collect, transport, store, and distribute solar heat. The heat is generated in glazed rooftop collectors, transferred in water or air, stored in a basement tank or rock bed, and distributed upon the command of a thermostat. Those systems are called active solar, although auxiliary fuel-heat systems often provide more than half of the heat as well.

Passive solar systems have none of the controls, plumbing, pumps, blowers, or thermostats of an active system, though unless the occupants are solar masochists, they also have auxiliary fuel-heat systems. In a very real sense, passive solar buildings are simply solar collectors in which people live.

Illustration 87 shows the three major types of passive solar systems:

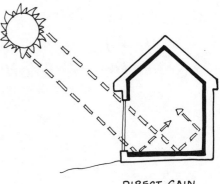

DIRECT GAIN

Direct-gain systems admit sunlight directly into the living space. Most of the sunlight is absorbed by the first surface it strikes, and some of the light is reflected around the room. Ultimately, however, 80 to 90 percent of the sun's energy is absorbed by the surfaces of floors, walls, ceilings, or furnishings and turned into sensible heat.

Lightweight fabrics and furnishings heat rapidly and warm the air around them. The portion of sunlight striking these lightweight surfaces contributes to daytime heating. The portion of sunlight striking massive surfaces, such as masonry floors and walls, is absorbed without great temperature change and later released over a long period. This massive heat storage is usually designed to carry the building through the sunless night, and sometimes through the following day as well.

Indirect-gain, mass-wall systems interpose heat-absorbing mass between the glazing and the living space. Warm air generated in the narrow space between the glazing and the mass wall is vented into the living space for daytime heating, and the remainder of the heat is stored in the mass wall for later release. Heat penetrates concrete mass walls at the rate of only 1 inch per hour, so the peak heat release to the living space from an 8-inch wall occurs about eight hours after the peak solar gain. A quite different version of the mass wall is formed with translucent water containers: Some sunlight passes through the containers for daylighting and immediate heating of the living space, while the remainder is again absorbed for later release.

Isolated-gain, sun-space systems enlarge the space between the glazing and the mass wall and thus create a very pleasant living space with heating characteristics similar to those of the

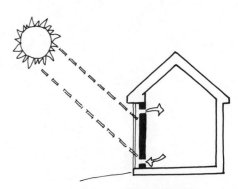

INDIRECT GAIN, MASS WALL

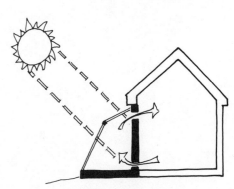

ISOLATED GAIN, SUN SPACE

87. Passive solar types

mass-wall system. If the back wall of the sun space is not a heat-absorbing mass wall, a thermostatically controlled fan may be employed to blow excess daytime heat into the adjacent house, and frost-preventing nighttime heat back into the sun space. The same space can alternatively be used as a greenhouse, but the resulting humidity precludes significant sharing of warm air between the greenhouse and the living space.

How Does Passive Solar Heating Work?

BALANCING LOSSES AND GAINS. Of the three types of heating in Illustration 86, I prefer passive solar; and of the three passive solar systems, I prefer direct gain. The reason is quite simple and consistent with my philosophy: It doesn't cost much! Properly done, a direct-gain passive solar-heating system merely uses ordinary building components to optimize the solar-heating effect. Turn to Illustration 88 to see what I mean.

First we perform an energy-juggling act. Against the three building heat losses — conduction, convection, and radiation — we balance three free heat gains — animal, utility, and solar.

Conduction loss is the heat loss through the solid building surfaces of floor, wall, ceiling, and glazing. Always flowing from warmer to cooler, it is directly proportional to the temperature difference between the opposite sides and inversely proportional to the R value of the heat-loss surface.

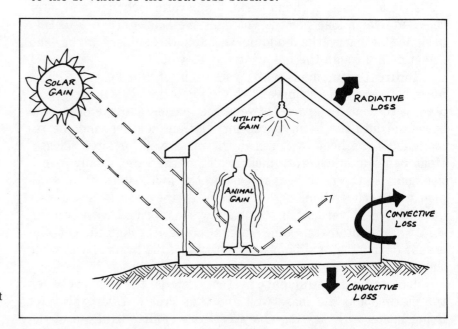

88. Gains and losses of heat energy in a house

Convection loss is the loss of warm air. More commonly called infiltration, it results from cold air entering the building, becoming warmed, and escaping.

Radiation loss is the flow of heat from warmer to cooler bodies in the form of electromagnetic radiation. Frost on a black roof is the result of radiative cooling of the roof toward frigid outer space on a clear night, and the chills we feel when seated next to a patio door on a cold winter night are largely due to the radiative flow of heat from our skin toward the colder glass.

Animal gain is the end product of the assimilation and combustion of food by our bodies — sensible heat. The rate of heat production is proportional to activity, but a rough average is 400 Btu per person per hour. You may find it easier to remember as a little more than the equivalent of a 100-watt light bulb.

Utility gain is the heat given off by lights and appliances. Excepting a vented clothes dryer, nearly 100 percent of the electricity in your monthly electric bill inadvertently heats your home. This free (already-paid-for) heat source averages another 400 Btu per person per hour.

Solar gain is the whole spectrum of electromagnetic radiation that penetrates the windows of a house, most of it turning to sensible heat upon striking the first opaque surface. At noon on a clear winter day, a south-facing window collects about 200 Btu per square foot per hour.

To the extent that we can balance these energy losses and gains, we can maintain a comfortable inside temperature without burning any fuel. Unfortunately, the losses and gains are not constant. The losses depend on the outdoor temperature, and solar gain depends on both season and cloudiness. But if one's only goal is a *zero* heating bill, there are two obvious and distinct paths to pursue:

Superinsulation — reducing the heat losses through vastly increased R values and decreased infiltration to below the steady rates of animal and utility heat production alone.

Supersolar — increasing the solar-gain and heat-storage capacity of the house to beyond the heat losses of the longest cloudy period.

These simple concepts are also simple to implement. But neither, I believe, provides the correct solution. Why not? Because the simple goal of a zero fuel bill is wrong. As we saw in Letter 23, the true cost of superinsulation, which may include the value of lost living space as well as the cost of extra insulation, is unlikely to be recovered in a lifetime of fuel savings. Later in the present lesson I intend to demonstrate that supersolar (100 percent solar heating) likewise costs more than it saves.

Instead, our goal should be a design that minimizes the combined costs of initial construction and subsequent lifetime fuel bill for heating and cooling the house. Toward this goal, we have already determined the optimum R values for basement, wall, and ceiling insulation. In this lesson we will similarly calculate the optimum area of solar glazing.

USING THE BUILDING ITSELF. Insulating to optimum R values results in a very small fuel requirement, at least by our accustomed standards. The small potential for solar savings therefore dictates strict cost-consciousness in our design approach. This is where direct-gain solar systems really shine.

Most houses already have a uniformly distributed window area equal to about 15 percent of their floor area. In your house this would amount to $0.15 \times 1,200$ square feet, or 180 square feet. Redistributing the glazings creates extra south-facing solar glazing at no extra cost.

| | Square Feet of Windows Facing | | | |
	North	East	South	West
Standard house	45	45	45	45
Solar house	0	30	120	30

Beyond the standard areas of window, which are justified on the bases of view, light, and ventilation alone, we should use the most cost-effective types of solar glazing. In Letter 25 we determined those to be patio-door replacement glazings with heat mirror (HM) and with movable window insulation (MWI).

The second cost-effective trick is to keep thermal mass in mind as we select the surfaces of our floors, walls, and ceilings. The thermal mass of a building (its ability to store heat) determines its daytime temperature rise and overnight temperature drop, and therefore the comfort level and need for supplemental overnight heating. The most cost-effective option is usually a concrete-slab floor exposed to direct sunlight. Depending on the nature of the floor finish, this could also be the most inexpensive floor option and could therefore cost nothing in solar terms.

Another cost-effective building technique is double drywalling. Gypsum drywall, or Sheetrock, is the most common finish for residential walls and ceilings. A second layer, at an additional cost of only 30 cents per square foot of wall and ceiling, doubles the heat-storage capacity, doubles resistance to damage, and halves the transmission of sound through walls and ceilings.

Finally, an open floor plan allows heat to distribute itself uniformly throughout the house by the natural and noiseless processes of convection and radiation. In this way, all of the thermal mass of the building is used in storing and discharging solar energy, and at no additional cost.

The Importance of Insulation and Mass

So far I have extolled the virtues of insulation and thermal mass but have demonstrated no evidence of their importance. To illustrate their effects on the thermal behavior of a building, I've developed a program for my computer that I call T-SWING. I feed it the R values and thermal masses of the building, the daily high and low outdoor temperatures, the number of building occupants, and the amount of sunshine received, and it calculates all of the heat losses and gains shown in Illustration 88 and prints the hour-by-hour indoor and outdoor temperatures.

I used the program to demonstrate, for both summer and winter, the effects of insulation and mass on a building identical to yours (except for having windows on all sides). Illustration 89 shows the insulation/mass combinations for the four runs:

1. Light mass / no insulation means the house resembles a summer cottage, with no masonry floor or drywall and no insulation in the walls or ceiling.

2. Heavy mass / no insulation indicates the addition of a double layer of ⅝-inch drywall to all interior and exterior walls and ceilings, plus a 2-inch concrete floor in the kitchen and dining room.

3. Light mass / insulated eliminates the added masses but insulates the basement walls, exterior walls, and ceiling to R-25.

4. Heavy mass / insulated combines both added mass and insulation.

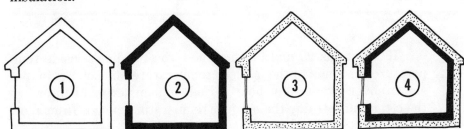

89. Thermal mass / insulation combinations for the thermal envelope

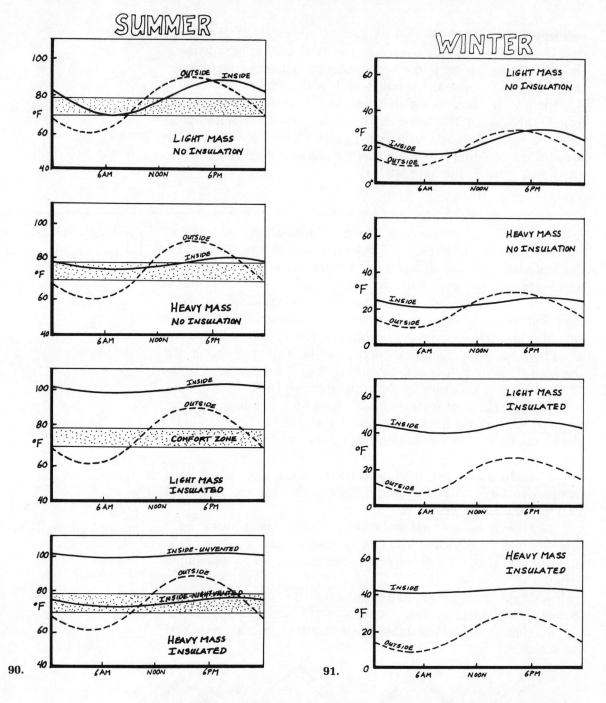

90.

91.

Illustrations 90 and 91 show how the building's inside temperature responds to the outdoor temperature and solar gain (not shown) over twenty-four-hour periods in summer and winter. On the clear summer day the outdoor temperature ranges from a low of 60 degrees Fahrenheit at 4:00 A.M. to a high of 90 degrees at 4:00 P.M. On the clear winter day, the swing is from 10 degrees to 30 degrees.

You can see that the thermal effect of the light mass / no insulation building is practically nil. Heat flows into and out of the building readily, so that the inside temperature virtually tracks the outdoor temperature except for a delay of several hours. This behavior reminds me very much of a summer cottage I once suffered.

The addition of mass to the building — heavy mass / low insulation — does little to the average inside temperature except reduce the peak-to-peak swing to only 7 degrees, both summer and winter. Since average temperatures are much more tolerable than peak temperatures in summer, thermal mass is seen to be very beneficial in hot climates. In the winter, however, such a building is about as comfortable as a concrete parking garage. An adobe building is a version of heavy mass / low insulation construction.

The addition of insulation without mass — light mass / insulated — has more benefit than the addition of mass without insulation. By slowing the flow of heat, the insulation also reduces the temperature swing to 7 degrees in summer and winter, but by retarding the escape of animal, utility, and solar heat, it causes an increase in average internal temperature of 25 degrees. In the winter this temperature boost means that no fuel need be burned until the outside temperature falls below 40 degrees. The zero-energy superinsulated house is the logical extension of this effect. In contrast, the same temperature boost during the summer results in intolerable interior temperatures unless the house is ventilated.

As you might expect, adding both mass and insulation to the building — heavy mass / insulated — results in maximum benefit. The average temperature boost remains 25 degrees, but the peak-to-peak temperature swing is reduced to only 2 degrees. It is important to note that insulation and mass work well together only if the mass is inside the insulated envelope of the building. Otherwise, the heat stored in the mass is free to escape rapidly to the outside.

The heavy mass / insulated building is also very effective in the summer in areas where overnight temperatures drop to comfortable levels. Leaving doors and windows open overnight bypasses the insulation, bringing the temperature of the building down to the early-morning low temperature. In the morning the doors and windows are shut tight, and the mass/insulation combination maintains the interior temperature below the outdoor temperature throughout the day. The line labeled "Inside — Night Vented" shows the very comfortable interior temperatures that may be maintained with this selective ventilation scheme.

The Design   **SOLAR GLAZING.** Having selected (on the bases of view, light, and ventilation) the areas of the north, east, and west windows, we can now use the PASSIVE SOLAR DESIGN program to find the best total area of south-facing solar glazing. As usual, by *best* area I mean the area resulting in the lowest life-cycle cost.

As you'll recall, we determined that patio-door replacement glazings with HM and MWI were two very cost-effective solar-glazing options. With the low-cost installation technique described in Letter 25, each of these systems can be installed for only $13 per square foot. Since the exterior walls cost an average of $7 per square foot, I used $6 per square foot as the additional window cost in the computer analysis. I then instructed the computer to calculate the annual fuel bills of the house assuming south-facing window areas of 0, 100, 200, 300, and 400 square feet (400 square feet is the total area of the south wall).

The results are plotted in Illustration 92. Line A shows the additional cost of the windows at $6 per square foot. Curve B shows the thirty-year fuel bill dropping with increasing areas of glazing. Curve C is the total of the window cost A plus the fuel cost B over the thirty-year life of the windows. As I had expected, Curve C has a minimum. Although poorly defined, it appears that the best area of south glazing is between 100 and 200 square feet, with a thirty-year fuel bill of about $5,000 ($167 per year). Not bad for Maine, eh?

Considering the aesthetic requirement of exterior symmetry in the bedroom south walls and Jean's desire for maximum glazed area in the kitchen and dining room, I propose a total of 170 square feet of south window:

Four 34" × 76" MWI units in the bedrooms = 68 sq ft

Six 34" × 76" HM units in the kitchen and dining room = 102 sq ft

ANNUAL FUEL BILL. In computing the $167 annual fuel bill, the computer also estimated the month-by-month contributions of the three free heat sources — animal, utility, and solar — we discussed in Illustration 88. Illustration 93 shows the relative impor-

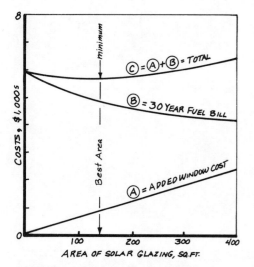

92. Life-cycle cost of solar glazing (optimum window area 140 square feet)

tance of each (in heights of the monthly bars) throughout the heating season, with animal and utility gains combined under the heading "Internal."

First note that, since heat loss equals the total of the heat gains, the total heat loss of the house in a month is the total height of the three bars. The bar graph shows that animal- and utility-heat gains (represented in the dotted bars) are very significant — in fact, larger than the solar contribution. You can see that if we were to cut all our heat losses in half by doubling R values and halving infiltration, the annual fuel bill (the solid black portion) would be virtually zero. This is the simple principle by which superinsulated zero-energy houses work.

The graph also shows that, unlike animal and utility gains, solar gain varies with the month, being minimal in cloudy December and quite high in sunny February. Together, the three free heat sources promise to shorten your heating season from the normal one lasting from September through May to one lasting from November through March. One of the unheralded but priceless aspects of passive solar heating is the psychological benefit of a shorter heating season.

Compared with that of an identical house without the 170 square feet of solar glazing, your fuel bill is 30 percent lower; in solar parlance, your house has a solar-savings fraction (SSF) of 30 percent.

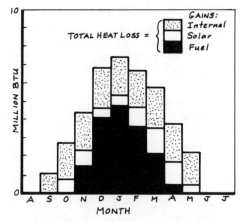

93. Monthly heat budget for John and Jean's house

THERMAL MASS. Illustrations 90 and 91 demonstrated the importance of building thermal mass into a house. There are two consequences of inadequate thermal mass in a passive solar house:

1. Solar heat, with nowhere to go, warms the air of the building to intolerable levels. At night the opposite occurs: Heat loss rapidly depletes the small amount of heat stored in the building furnishings and air, and the temperature plummets.
2. Solar heat not stored during the day cannot make up the nighttime heat loss. Fuel must therefore be burned even after a sunny day, and maximum solar savings cannot be realized.

Thermal mass (TM) is defined as the ability of a material to absorb and release energy when changing temperature. Of all natural materials, water has the greatest such ability: 1 pound (or pint) absorbs 1 Btu in warming 1 degree Fahrenheit and gives back 1 Btu in cooling 1 degree. Table 19 lists the TMs of some

Table 19
THERMAL MASS OF COMMON BUILDING MATERIALS

Material	Thermal Mass (per square foot)
2″ concrete	4.5
4″ concrete	9.0
1″ slate	2.8
2″ brick	4.1
4″ brick	8.4
¾″ softwood	1.3
1″ softwood	1.7
½″ drywall	1.0
1¼″ drywall	2.5

common building materials in Btu per degree per square foot of surface.

RULE OF THUMB FOR MASS. A convenient rule of thumb for thermal mass in a direct-gain passive solar house is to provide, within the same space as the solar glazing, TM = 0.6 × SSF × area of solar glazing.

Your house provides a good example of the application of this rule. Illustration 94 shows the thermal masses I suggest you include in the kitchen/dining area. Winter sunlight, virtually unshaded by the deciduous trees on the deck, shines directly on the floor of 2-inch solid concrete blocks set in mastic and latex grout over the plywood subfloor. The dark brown surface of the concrete absorbs 60 percent of the solar energy immediately. The remainder bounces up to the walls and ceiling of double ⅝-inch drywall (1¼ inches total). The space is thus virtually surrounded by massive surfaces. The ratios of glazed areas to floor areas in the other solar rooms are less than half as great, and so double drywall alone is proposed.

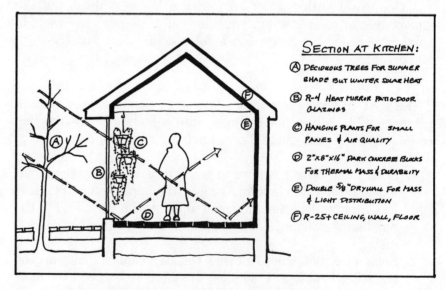

94. Section of Jean's kitchen showing passive solar features

Example: Use the rule of thumb and Table 19 to ensure adequate thermal mass for 170 square feet of solar glazing.

$$\begin{aligned}
\text{Required TM} &= 0.6 \times \text{SSF} \times \text{area of solar glazing} \\
&= 0.6 \times 30 \times 170 \\
&= 3{,}060 \text{ Btu per degree} \\
\text{Supplied TM} &= \text{area of material} \times \text{TM per sq ft} \\
&= 300 \text{ sq ft of } 2'' \text{ concrete} \times 4.5 \\
&\quad + 2{,}400 \text{ sq ft of } 1\tfrac{1}{4}'' \text{ drywall} \times 2.5 \\
&= 7{,}350 \text{ Btu per degree}
\end{aligned}$$

Thus we have more than enough mass to prevent excessive temperature swings on sunny days. I hope you invite me over for brunch some clear January day; that kitchen looks terrific!

I suggest the 2-inch concrete blocks because when they are installed over a wood floor they are not as hard on the legs as a concrete slab on grade, and at 80 cents per square foot installed they are even lower in cost than many cushion-vinyl floorings. They come in green and red as well as brown. I suggest a finish of several heavy coats of polyurethane varnish, but I guess we'd better get Jean's approval of the concept first.

The subject of next week's lesson is wiring. Do you have any experience in wiring, John, or any particular questions you want me to answer?

Your friend,
Charlie

11. Wiring

LETTER
28

Dear Charlie,

So it has come to this: electricity.

It's a stage I've been hoping to avoid ever since the project began, ever since we built our first home, ever since my mother put out every light in the house on Halloween when she tried to hook up an electrified pumpkin to an extension cord that ran from the front door to the downstairs bathroom.

But there our new place is, about to be framed, covered, and studded, and ready for the electrical wiring to go in. And I'm still trying to put off any decisions.

With good reason. I've had my contacts with electricity, and none of them has been friendly. At one point I did consider saving some money and wiring our former home, but in the end I floated another loan and hired a professional to do the critical stuff: the kitchen range, washer and dryer, refrigerator, water pump, and hot-water heaters. Wall plugs, plug molds, and general household lighting were installed by a fairly professional nonprofessional, and that saved us about a month's interest payment on the loan. I ended up not doing a thing electrical except watching the people who did the work and hoping to learn something.

I don't think I learned enough. I just don't have the confidence, Charlie, to begin boring holes through studs so I can run wiring through, or to start picking locations for two-plug outlets or ceiling lights. I know what you're going to say: You'll tell me to smarten up, to get hold of myself, to see wiring for what it is, a basic skill that anyone with common sense can comprehend.

Well, perhaps I'm not anyone with common sense. Perhaps I invented the steam engine in a former life, and electricity has been trying to get even ever since. I have the real feeling that

I'm cursed when it comes to voltages and amps, especially when something larger than a flashlight battery is involved.

I've been given plenty of warnings. Take the water heater in our other house, the first water heater, the one that had to be junked after just a few years even though it was supposed to last a good long time.

I went down into the crawl space that passed for a cellar there to wrap that water heater in a nice, snug blanket of insulation (fiberglass, I think it was). In my patriotism and my stab at Yankee practicality, I was following the advice of folks like you. Conserve, you said, and conservation was my goal. I wanted most of the heater's heat to heat water, not crawl space.

How proud I was when I finished the wrapping. The heater looked like a Christmas present, smothered in insulation held in place with long, silver strips of duct tape. At that point, I would have wired anyone's house.

Three weeks later when I went to the sink for my early-morning shave, I knew I was in trouble. No hot water. I won't say what I said then, this being a letter you might share with your family. But you can guess.

Back down into the crawl space I went to check on the water heater. I had checked the circuit-breaker box, and the switch had flipped. Before I flipped it back, I thought I'd better see if I could locate the cause of the overload.

That job didn't take long. As soon as I began unwrapping the insulation I'd so carefully wrapped just a few weeks before, I could see the blackened places on the white metal of the heater jacket, places where some electrical calamity had arced and sputtered and seared. Lucky the whole place didn't go up in flames, I told myself as I probed further.

As I took off the screw-on cover that hid the lower-unit heating elements, I got the shock of my life. Not an electrical shock but a frightening jolt to my adrenaline. There, coiled in fried glory around the electrodes, was a large black snake. And alongside the now very dead reptile were two very dead field mice. And rising above them was one very dead water heater, its lower-unit electrodes irreparably damaged by the electrocution they had not been designed to perform.

First I had to get rid of the charred corpses, the ones that had been hit with 240 volts when the snake's tail hit a positive connection while its unlucky head touched a negative one: zap! So much for the reptile, so much for the mice, so much for the $200-plus heater I had converted to a winter home for field mice.

Charlie, that's not my idea of conservation.

And electricity is not my idea of fun.

I'm less prepared, however, to turn to the professionals again. I'm about mortgaged out. If you promise you can explain what needs to be done and how it should be done, in clear and simple terms, then I promise I'll consider doing *some* of the wiring. I'm still not ready for the critical stuff, like furnaces, dryers, or stoves.

And certainly not hot-water heaters.

Your friend,
John

LETTER
29

Dear John,

Give me a break! You can't be afraid of everything. I think your problem with electricity is the same one you had with heat: You can't see it and therefore don't believe it. In short, you're just too earthy (get it?). We got through heat flow and insulation just fine, though, so I'm sure I can make you understand the fundamentals of wiring.

But first let me preface the lesson with a statement of objectives. The purpose of wiring is to provide electricity around the home in sufficient quantity, in convenient locations, and in a safe manner.

The way we accomplish these objectives is by following the requirements and recommendations of the NEC (National Electric Code, not Nippon Electric Company). Although local variations exist, there is only one national code; and although a few cities don't allow a person to wire his own home, most do. After reading this lesson and acquiring one of the recommended books on the how-to details, you'll have no excuse for not wiring your new house and saving yourself several thousand dollars.

A WATER ANALOGY. You should have no problem understanding the flow of water in Illustration 95. The pump sucks water up and pressurizes an outlet pipe. If we want water to flow, we turn the faucet on. The resulting flow of water accomplishes a purpose in turning the water wheel. Finally, the discharged water flows back to the pump. Pressure in the pipe is measured in pounds per square inch (psi) and the rate of flow in gallons per minute (gpm).

I maintain that the flow of electricity in a wire is the same. The pump simply becomes a generator, the pipe a wire, water

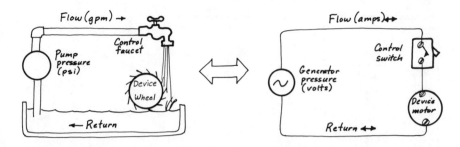

95. A water/electricity analogy for John

molecules electrons, the faucet a switch, and the water wheel a motor or other device. Electrons, like water, are neither created nor destroyed, so every electron that flows out of the generator ultimately returns to it in a circuitous loop. The only difference is that the flow of electrons (the current) flows back and forth. In household wiring, the voltage and current reverse direction sixty times per second, leading to the term 60 hertz (cycles per second) alternating current (AC). The units for electrical pressure and current are volts and amperes, or amps.

CIRCUITS. Now let's make our electrical loop, or circuit, a little more complicated but a lot more useful. Illustration 96 shows that the switched device can be something other than a motor (here it is a light bulb) and that the circuit can be extended to serve more than one device. Just as there is no theoretical limit to the number of plumbing fixtures that can be attached to a water pipe, there is no theoretical limit (though there may be a code limit) to the number of electrical devices that can draw current from a pair of wires.

The receptacle shown in Illustration 96 is not itself a power-consuming device; it is merely a way of temporarily extending the circuit to another device with a cord and plug. Picture the plug connected to the receptacle and you'll see what I mean.

Illustration 97 adds a further element to the circuit concept: the safe distribution of electrical current from a single control center to multiple circuits. Electricity from a generator at the

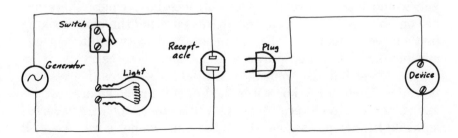

96. Simple electric circuit

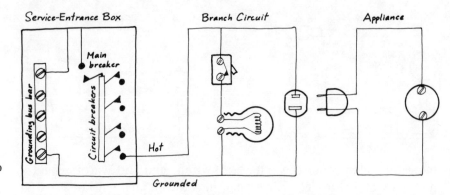

97. Simple circuit connected to service-entrance box

utility power plant enters the house at a point called the service entrance. I showed you the details of the connection from the overhead power-company wires to the service-entrance box in Illustration 31. Go back and review that now (page 61).

One of the wires entering the box in Illustration 97 is bare and is connected physically and electrically to the earth. Relative to the earth or ground, it has a zero voltage and is therefore safe to touch. Electricians call this the grounded wire. Inside the service-entrance box, the incoming grounded wire connects to a large metal bar (the grounding bus bar), which allows connection to the many circuits required to fully service the house.

The other incoming wire in Illustration 97 is hot (carrying voltage and thus dangerous to touch) and is covered with thick, black-rubber insulation. It, too, connects to a heavy metal bar inside the box for distribution of current to the multiple house circuits. Between the main incoming hot wire and the outgoing circuit hot wires are a number of switches called circuit breakers. Circuit breakers serve two purposes: (1) Like any other switch, they allow disconnection of the hot wire so that we can work on a circuit without danger of shock; and (2) they open automatically whenever too many amps flow through the circuit (like when your snake invaded the mouse house) and thus prevent overheating of the wire and a possible fire.

For simplicity I have shown only half the number of wires you would find in a real service-entrance box, where there are not one but two heavy black hot wires entering the box. Looking further, you'd find that they are connected to two different circuit-breaker bars. The purpose is not simply to carry twice as much current but also to introduce different voltages. Here's how it works. Each of the hot wires (and circuit-breaker bars) carries 120 volts AC. You'll recall that the voltage on a hot wire reverses sign sixty times per second. Let's call our two hot wires A and B

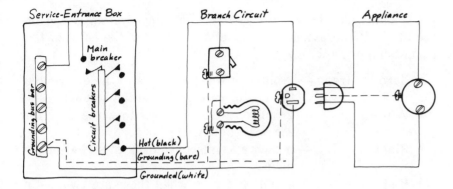

98. Grounding of simple circuit

and the single grounded wire C. When A is at +120 volts, B is at −120 volts, and vice versa. Therefore, if we connect circuits to the pairs of wires A & C, B & C, and A & B, we will get across the wires the following voltage differences:

$$A \ \& \ C = +120 \ v - 0 \ v \quad = +120 \ v$$
$$B \ \& \ C = -120 \ v - 0 \ v \quad = -120 \ v$$
$$A \ \& \ B = +120 \ v - -120 \ v = +240 \ v$$

If you have difficulty understanding the math, ask the paperboy. Anyway, by this neat trick we can have two separate 120-volt circuits for lighting and small appliances and a third 240-volt circuit for large power consumers like ranges and water heaters. And the voltage on any single wire in the house is never more than 120 volts. Clever, eh?

You may have noticed that the plug in Illustration 97 has two prongs, while those in your house have three. Illustration 98 explains this final circuit refinement. Most electrical devices are housed in metal boxes or cases. If something inside the case were to go awry, allowing a hot wire to touch the case, then the case itself would be hot, and anyone touching it might receive a shock. As a safety precaution, the NEC requires a separate grounding wire to run uninterrupted and unswitched from the grounding bus bar in the service-entrance box to all metal cases and boxes containing electrical devices. Although both the grounded (white) and grounding (bare) wires are normally at 0 volts, the grounded wire carries a return current equal to that in the hot wire, while the grounding wire carries current only in case of a defect.

COLOR CODE. Because of the unique roles of the various wires in a circuit, it is important to be able to recognize their identities anywhere they occur. Picture yourself in the attic with three identical wires. You know that two are at 0 volts and one at 120 volts, but which is which? Clearly a labeling system would be useful if not lifesaving. That labeling system is the color of the insulation on the wire:

- **Bare** or **Green** — grounding wire; connects to the device and the box or case with a green screw.
- **White** — grounded wire; connects to white or silver screw on device.
- **Black** — hot wire; connects to darkest screw on the device.
- **Red** — second hot wire when there are two, as in a 240-volt circuit; connects to second dark screw on device.

As an aid to my memory, which has received too many shocks in its brief electrical career, I have developed associations:

- **Bare** or **Green** — "cool," like, all right, man!
- **White** — ditto
- **Black** — "death"
- **Red** — "hot"

"AMPACITY." Just as a larger pipe will carry more gallons of water per minute, a larger wire will carry more amps of electrons. Of course, we can increase the water pressure or the electrical voltage to make the pipe or wire carry more, but in so doing we cause more friction. The friction of electrons flowing through a wire is similar to the friction of two sticks rubbing together: Both produce heat. If enough friction occurs (too much current or electrons for the size of the wire), the heat may melt the insulation on the wires, allowing the wires to touch and thus shorting the circuit and causing a fire. For this reason, the NEC specifies the amps capacity, or "ampacity," of each wire, as shown in Table 20. The code also requires that each circuit be protected by a circuit breaker of the same ampacity.

CABLES. In the old days, circuits were strung with individual wires on insulators. I'm sure you've seen some of those knob-and-tube circuits in an attic or shed. There is nothing wrong with knob-and-tube from a safety standpoint; in fact, the NEC still allows it. But nearly all residential wiring is now done with more convenient plastic cable, in which all of the wires in a circuit are bundled together in a plastic jacket. Four types of cable are most often used, each with a specific purpose and set of limitations:

Table 20

AMPACITY

Wire Size	Amps
NM CABLE	
14	15
12	20
10	30
8	40
6	55
4	70
2	95
SE CABLE	
1/0	150
2/0	175
3/0	200

- **NM** — nonmetallic (plastic) sheathed cable; intended for dry locations out of direct sunlight.
- **NMC** — nonmetallic, corrosive; similar to NM but suitable for wet and corrosive environments except for underground.
- **UF** — underground feeder; embedded in water- and sun-resistant plastic suitable for underground.
- **SE** — service entrance; water- and sun-resistant plastic sheathing over two rubber-insulated conductors spirally wound with bare ground. Intended for service entrance but also allowed for high-amperage appliance circuits.

REQUIRED CIRCUITS. The NEC either requires or recommends (all the same to you) four types of circuits in a residence:

    1. Lighting. The name *lighting circuit* is misleading. The code means lighting plus wall receptacles into which lights, radios, vacuum cleaners, etcetera are plugged. The code suggests a minimum of one 15-amp circuit per 600 square feet of living space. Since it would be extremely unpleasant to have all of the lights in a large area of the house go out with the tripping of a single circuit breaker, I suggest as many circuits as required to have two in every large space.

    The code goes on to require a light controlled by a permanent wall switch in all habitable rooms, hallways, stairways, and attached garages. Such lights may be plugged into switched wall receptacles, but lights in kitchens and baths and at entrance doors must be permanently wired.

    2. Small appliance. Two separate 20-amp 120-volt circuits are required for small appliances such as toasters, blenders, and coffeepots. Both circuits must be present in the kitchen, and one or more in the pantry and dining and family rooms. These circuits may not be used for lighting but may serve the refrigerator and freezer.

    3. Ground fault circuit interrupt (GFCI). This is a circuit protected by a special breaker that trips upon detecting a difference in the currents of the hot wire (black) and the grounded wire (white). It is required outdoors, near a swimming pool, in the garage, in bathrooms, and on construction sites. If the current returning through the grounded wire is less than the current going out on the hot wire, then some of the current must be finding its way home through an improper path. The NEC is worried that the path may be *you*, standing on the ground or floating in the tub or pool.

4. Individual appliance circuits. Some appliances and devices draw enough current to warrant individual circuits. The usual voltages and currents of these circuits are:

Appliance	Volts	Amps
Kitchen range	120/240	50
Dishwasher	120	20
Garbage disposal	240	20
Water heater	240	30
Clothes washer	120	20
Clothes dryer	120/240	30
Oil burner	120	20
Water pump	240	20

Check with your appliance dealer for electrical ratings. For example, a dishwasher may have a built-in booster water heater, requiring a higher rating. The Sears catalogue is once again an excellent reference for planning purposes.

RUNNING THE CABLES. The continuity of a cable is broken when it is connected to a device (anything that either consumes or manipulates electricity). In addition, we sometimes wish to run branch circuits in different directions from the same point. The resulting wire connections are weak points in the system at which the wires may work themselves loose and short out. For this reason, the code requires all devices and splices to be contained in covered boxes.

Illustration 99 shows two typical boxes with cables running to and between them. The lower box (at left) contains a duplex receptacle and is mounted to the side of a wall stud at a height of 12 to 18 inches off the floor. The upper box contains a switch and is mounted on a stud next to a door on the side away from the hinges and at a height of 44 to 48 inches.

Cables between boxes are required to be strapped or stapled every 4½ feet and within 12 inches of boxes. A cable may be run through a hole in the center of a framing member as shown, but it must be protected from stray nails (like picture-hanger nails) with a ¹⁄₁₆-inch-thick steel plate or pipe wherever the hole is less than 1¼ inches from the inside face of the member.

The wall-framing system back in Illustration 74D was designed specifically to get around this requirement. The cables may

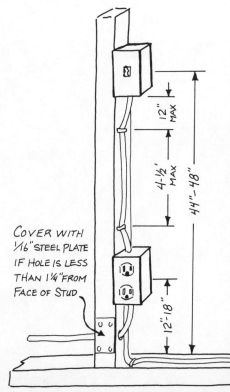

COVER WITH ¹⁄₁₆" STEEL PLATE IF HOLE IS LESS THAN 1¼" FROM FACE OF STUD

12" MAX

4-½' MAX

44"-48"

12"-18"

99. Critical dimensions for wall receptacles and switches

be run on the warm side of the polyethylene vapor barrier, across the faces of the studs, provided the horizontal strapping is at least 1½ inches thick, like a 2 × 4 ripped in half.

Illustration 100 shows a duplex receptacle in greater detail. It exemplifies both the ease and the difficulty of conventional wiring. First the ease. A box of either metal or plastic is first nailed to the side of a stud with its front edge projecting to the plane of the finished wall. Most boxes come with attached nails and depth marks for ⅜-inch, ½-inch, and ⅝-inch drywall finish. Prepunched holes in the box are then knocked out, the cables stripped so that the plastic sheathing extends ½ inch into the box, and the individual wires cut to project about 6 inches beyond the box. At this point, wiring halts while the drywall is installed. Subsequent to drywalling, the black and white wires are stripped of about ½ inch of insulation and pushed into the appropriate holes at the rear of the receptacle, or connected to the dark and light screws at the sides. The bare grounding wires are joined to another short length of bare wire with a wire nut, and the added wire is attached to the metal box. If the box is nonmetallic, then the bare wire goes directly to the green terminal of the receptacle. All of the wires are then folded neatly behind the receptacle, and the receptacle is carefully pushed into the box without loosening the wires.

At this point you may regret either having cut a sloppy hole in the drywall or having removed the four small circular plaster ears from the ends of the receptacle. As the mounting screws pull the receptacle into the box, the plaster ears (if still intact) stop it at the plane of the wall. Finally, a cover plate is attached to the center screw hole of the receptacle.

Now for the difficulty of conventional wiring. The code requires receptacles on every wall of a home, placed so that no lamp or appliance will be more than 6 feet from an outlet. Inside walls pose no problem, but it is clear from Illustrations 99 and 100 that boxes nailed to studs on outside walls violate that polyethylene vapor barrier so meticulously installed on the warm side of the insulation.

I offer three solutions: (1) Frame the wall as in Illustration 74D, running the cable on the warm side of the vapor barrier and fastening the outlet boxes to the drywall with plaster ears; (2) run surface wiring channels concealed as baseboard moldings, as shown in Illustration 101; or (3) seal the interior wall surface with latex vapor-barrier paint and seal the boxes to the wall with foam cover-plate gaskets.

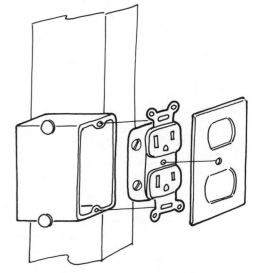

100. Stud-mounted duplex receptacle and box

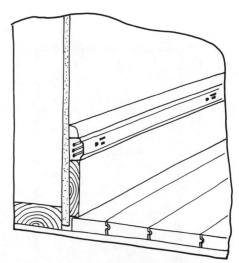

101. Surface wiring (Wiremold) to avoid penetration of vapor barrier

PLANNING FOR CONVENIENCE. The layout of your wiring deserves no less attention than that of your kitchen or bathroom. How many times have you found the only outlet for a lamp hiding just beyond reach behind a 600-pound couch, or groped your way through a dark house searching for a nonexistent wall switch? A complete set of house plans should include an electrical plan, a floor plan that includes the type and location of every fixed electrical device.

Table 21 shows the special symbols used to denote services in an electrical plan. Use them instead of scribbling notes to yourself on the floor plan. After a very short time you'll appreciate their brevity and clarity.

Now, when you see Illustration 102 you'll get excited, John. You're going to think that I've once again done your work for you. I have drawn a wiring plan based on your floor plan but only to demonstrate the use of wiring symbols in typical circuits. I already know that was a big mistake. You'll wire it exactly as shown, and then a year from now you'll complain to Jean that

Table 21

DEVICE SYMBOLS

Receptacle, 120 v	◑
Receptacle, 240 v	◐
Switch, Single	$
Switch, Three-way	$₃
Light, Ceiling	◇
Light, Wall	◯┤
Ventilation Fan	Ⓕ
Telephone Jack	△

102. Wiring plan for John and Jean's house

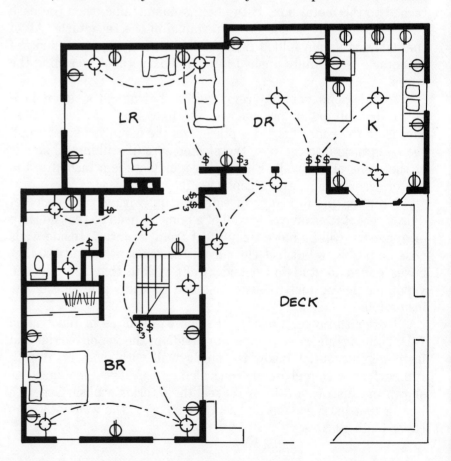

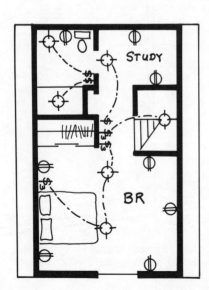

Charlie put the receptacle for the hair dryer on the wrong side of the vanity mirror.

I urge you to review this plan carefully *twice:* right now, with Jean at your side; and after the house is framed and sheathed (just before wiring), when you can better visualize the spaces and furniture placement. Just before actually stringing the cable, walk through the house switching imaginary switches. Plug in your shaver, recline in your easy chair with a book, rush to answer the phone, and walk from one end of the house to the other imagining the switches that control the lights which will illuminate your path. I'm sure you'll discover ten things that aren't just right. Six of them should be the telephone jacks (one for each room) that I omitted.

Now look at Illustration 102 and the checklist below for convenience wiring. Look at every device in the plan and see if and how it conforms to the checklist.

RECEPTACLES	• Kitchen receptacles for every counter space more than 12 inches wide
	• Receptacles for refrigerator and freezer
	• Kitchen-range outlet
	• Separate receptacles for washer and dryer
	• Receptacles on every wall except hall and bath, placed so that no device will be more than 6 feet from an outlet (but don't forget the need to vacuum the hall, either)
	• GFCI receptacle in every bathroom
	• GFCI receptacle outdoors
	• GFCI receptacle in garage
LIGHTING	• At least one light in every habitable space and in every garage, controlled by wall switch near doorway
	• Three-way switch-controlled lights in halls, stairways, and rooms with two entrances
	• Lights at every outside entrance

A FINAL WORD. I've never told anyone this story, John, but I have so much invested in you by now that I may as well pull out all the stops.

Ten years ago I was building my first house and was in the middle of wiring when the family announced it was time for our annual trip to the amusement park at Old Orchard Beach. I love the bumper cars and the gross, greasy, vinegary fries, so I was ready for the break.

This time one of the amusements caught my eye: Sam the weight-guessing man. Five-foot-two-inch Sam challenged every passerby that he could guess their weight within 2 pounds, their age within a year, and their occupation to boot. Now I'm of pretty standard size and weight, and my bald spot is beginning to betray my age; besides, I'm too cheap to bet a nickel. But occupation!

I want to tell you that I felt like a poker player who had just been dealt a royal flush. It just so happened I was then also on the payroll to NASA as a lunar scientist. And this was Old Orchard Beach, Maine, not Cape Canaveral. All that remained was the selection of my prize.

Poor about-to-be-plundered Sam inspected my face and took my hands in his. Then, peering at my palms, he announced without hesitation that I was an *electrician!*

My God, this was too much! I didn't need that teddy bear nearly as much as to discover what Sam had seen. It was simple for Sam: All those cuts and scratches came from wrestling with the cut ends of wire.

I returned home with a new sense of pride. I was a bona fide electrician. See how easy it is?

Your friend,
Charlie

P.S. Next week: plumbing. I've been a closet plumber, too.

12. Plumbing

Dear Charlie,

I know. I know. You'll try to make plumbing look as easy as you thought the electrical wiring might be. Well, let's get a few things straight from the start.

1. Wiring to me is still a challenge, in spite of your analysis, which I'm sure was designed to appeal to your average fourth-grader.

2. If you think electricity is a mystery I'll never solve, you are close to correct. But I will give it a try, with an electrician close at hand.

3. If you think plumbing is a mystery to me, you are wrong. Plumbing is no mystery — it's totally awesome. When I think of what might happen to a plumbing system personally installed by yours truly, I can think of eventualities no householder wants to know about. I keep having this nightmare of a flushed toilet gurgling into the kitchen sink, or our basement silently filling with water during some winter night cold enough to freeze the entire mass into a solid, humongous ice block that will hold us prisoner until May.

Charlie, water uncontrolled *is* a nightmare. And I know it's a bad dream that can come true. How many times have you seen the Three Stooges try to fix a leak, or watched Dagwood attempt to repair a dripping kitchen faucet? Every time they do, they end up with an in-house geyser — water under pressure and out of control, water that dissolves their dignity, the furniture, and eventually the footings that hold the house up.

How much more than the Three Stooges do you think I know about plumbing? (You don't *have* to answer.)

I will: nothing, not a speck.

Any tour of almost any basement has convinced me that lifting up the telephone is better than picking up a wrench anytime I need a plumber. No matter that they are never there when you want them; they arrive eventually, and when they do they make every job look so amazingly easy, and they get it done so relatively quickly, that I'm tempted to think the bill (which always arrives on time) is too high. But then I go back below ground level, under the house where things really matter, and I see copper pipes, plastic pipes, pipes wrapped in white, pipes soldered, and pipes connected to other pipes of different sizes. There are even pipes that go through the roof.

Which reminds me of another plumbing puzzle. Every plumber I've ever known drives a pickup truck or a van that's fully equipped with pipe cutters, pipe vises, blowtorches, soldering irons, and threading devices I've never understood. If we do go ahead and try to plumb the place, or anyone like us decides to do the same, does that mean we have to get a pickup or a van full of plumbing equipment?

Or do the newfangled plastic pipes and connections make all that stuff obsolete? You can tell I don't know much about plumbing just by the questions I ask.

But I know what I like, and Jean does, too.

We like plenty of hot water. There is nothing worse than standing in a shower soaking in the comfort only to have the entire episode end unpleasantly as the water suddenly becomes cold. That we don't like. We don't like running out of hot water. So we're going to get a large hot-water heater or one of the devices that keeps making hot water faster than we can use it.

And another thing I don't like is when I'm steaming in the shower and someone flushes a toilet. Wham! I'm out of the shower like a shot, trying to keep from getting parboiled. There must be a way a good plumber, as opposed to myself, can keep that sort of inconvenience to a minimum.

We like pipes that don't freeze. We have some friends who spend the winter's cold waves in their cellar, massaging their water pipes with hot compresses or the flames from a hand-held blowtorch. Not only do they miss a great deal of sleep on those Maine nights when the temperature drops below zero (and we have quite a few), but somehow they are never quite successful. Some pipes do freeze, and that has always seemed to me to be an aggravating, costly mess. We don't want that.

And we like toilets and sinks that don't clog. I won't go into the definitely unattractive details of the past struggles I've had with balky plumbing, but let me tell you, if I installed a toilet that clogged, I'd sure be angry at myself. There must be a proper technique or an appropriate piece of equipment that prevents this particular indignity. Perhaps if you can just tell me the solution to this single most unpleasant household problem, my faith in your knowledge of plumbing will be vastly enhanced.

Then you can tell me the difference between all those copper and plastic and white and black and cast-iron pipes that I see coiling and writhing along every cellar ceiling and around every cellar bulkhead. If you can make sense out of that linguine, I'll be forever in your debt. (I have the sinking feeling that's already the case.)

And I don't like faucets that drip in the night. There, that's another reason I'm sure I don't want to install our own plumbing. Imagine being awakened every night by the sound of your own mistakes.

Plumbing is a black art, a lost cause, right, Charlie?

Somehow, I know you won't give up and say yes.

Your friend,
John

Dear John,

I can't believe you hate plumbing. Didn't you play with Tinkertoys when you were a child? Plumbing is just a grown-up version.

Right now you're probably thinking there was something wrong with *my* toilet training. I maintain, to the contrary, that those with an irrational fear of plumbing are the ones with the problem. At this point I can't do anything about your childhood, but, as with electricity, I think I can convince you of its simplicity.

The methods and materials of plumbing, like those of electrical wiring, are strictly controlled by code. There is no single national plumbing code, but if your town has an electrical inspector, you can be sure it has one for plumbing as well. A visit to your local lumber or hardware store, however, should convince you that an increasing percentage of homeowners are finding the code no impediment to playing plumber. As I'll stress later, just check your plans with the inspector before investing in nonreturnable materials.

Three Systems for Three Functions

As you suggested, to the eyes of a casual visitor to the basement, crisscrossing pipes of differing size, color, and material make as much sense as a pile of linguine. The visual confusion, however, is due to there being not one but three separate systems with three separate purposes: supply, waste, and venting.

- **Supply system.** The pipes of the smallest diameter supply fresh water to fixtures. A portion of the incoming water is diverted through a water heater so that fixtures can be supplied with both cold and hot water.

- **Waste system.** The term *wastewater* raises interesting philosophical questions that you may want to address, but regardless of its degree of purity, water draining from a fixture is defined by code as waste.

- **Vent system.** As will later be explained in greater detail, it is necessary to maintain air as well as water in waste pipes. The vertical pipes rising above the highest fixtures and occasionally poking through the roof serve to introduce air into the waste-pipe system.

THE SUPPLY SYSTEM. A water-supply system is similar in function to an electrical wiring system in distributing water to fixtures throughout the house. If your house is in the city, your water will arrive through a ¾- or 1-inch copper pipe leading from a larger water main under the street. Those beyond the reach of water mains have to play water district themselves and pump water from wells, as outlined in Letter 11. This lesson deals only with how to handle water after it gets inside the house.

Illustration 103 shows how water is distributed to the individual fixtures. To impress upon you the simplicity of supply systems, I've omitted from the picture redundant fixtures and many of the arms and elbows found in the typical installation. If you can successfully hook up a garden hose, you should be able to follow the flow.

Starting from the point where water first enters the house, a pipe of ¾-inch internal diameter (all pipes are specified by their ID) runs to the vicinity of every fixture requiring water. Because most fixtures consume hot water as well, a ¾-inch branch pipe runs through a water heater before pairing with the cold-water pipe for the run through the house. From these two main supply pipes run smaller branch pipes to individual fixtures.

If you trace the supply pipes of your present home, the odds

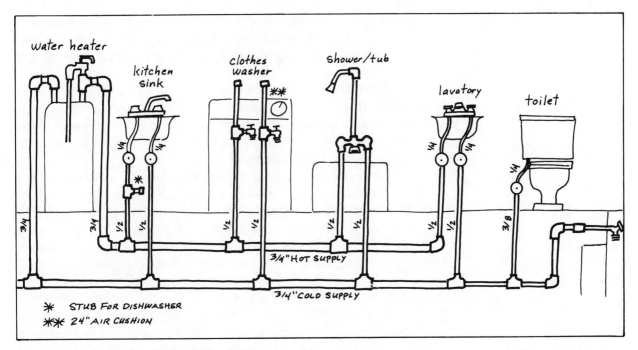

Labels in figure: water heater, kitchen sink, clothes washer, shower/tub, lavatory, toilet

3/4" HOT SUPPLY

3/4" COLD SUPPLY

* STUB FOR DISHWASHER
** 24" AIR CUSHION

103. The supply system

are great that every pipe in the system is of identical size. This is the reason the shower scalds you when someone flushes a toilet. Water flowing through a pipe encounters friction, which limits its maximum flow rate. When a second fixture draws water from the same supply pipe, the two fixtures compete for the same water, and the flow to the first fixture decreases. In the case of the shower, tempered to just the right mix of hot and cold, the sudden reduction in cold water due to the toilet flush results in a higher proportion of hot water and a higher net temperature. Conversely, drawing hot dishwater results in a colder shower. These effects can be minimized if, as shown in Illustration 103, the main supply pipes are larger than the branch pipes to the individual fixtures.

Illustration 103 also shows individual shutoff valves at each fixture. Although there is usually a main shutoff valve where the cold water first enters the building, individual valves are recommended so that a single fixture can be repaired without shutting down the whole house. You'll also wish you had installed individual shutoffs while searching the basement for the main valve as that runaway toilet of your dreams floods the second floor.

The pipes in your present home may be of galvanized iron (really old house), copper (most common), or plastic (really new house or plumbing system). Most supply systems are plumbed in rigid copper, although polyvinyl chloride plastic is increasing in popularity. It is interesting to note the origin of the word *plumbing:* from the Latin *plumbum* (lead) and the Romans' use of lead pipes.

Illustration 104 and the accompanying Table 22 show a more realistic, three-dimensional view of a simple bathroom. Few bathrooms are as linear, but it should be obvious that three fixtures can be arranged in any order and can face any direction with the addition of but a few pipes and elbows.

The real value of the illustration and table, however, is as a dictionary, for plumbingese is as foreign a language as will be found anywhere in eastern Europe. Without the proper terminology you'll find buying your supplies at the local hardware store as difficult as ordering a meal in Budapest. No doubt nonconversants have managed both, but there is a special pleasure in sauntering up to the hardware counter in a baseball cap and ordering a drop ell with threaded outlet.

In an attempt to obtain the typical 20 to 50 percent trade discount, a really daring amateur plumber might open a commercial account at a *real* hardware store. (*Real* hardware stores are

Table 22

SUPPLY SYSTEM FITTINGS

1. Reducing tee, ¾″ to ½″
2. Reducing 90° elbow, ¾″ to ½″
3. 90° elbow, ½″
4. Faucet body
5. Drop ell with threaded outlet
6. Shower arm
7. Threaded nipple
8. Shutoff valve
9. Supply tube
10. Type L tubing, ¾″
11. Type L tubing, ½″
12. Coupling, ¾″

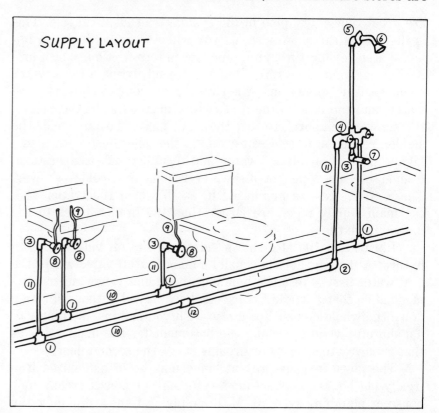

SUPPLY LAYOUT

104.

where *real* plumbers shop and are identified by coarse banter and the absence of blister packs containing three or four screws.) Don't attempt storming such a place if your vocabulary is limited to *pipe*, *faucet*, and *gizmo*.

Plumbing codes require only the bare necessities, but Illustration 105 shows four inexpensive niceties that should be included in a first-class supply system:

- **Draining.** Sooner or later you'll want to abandon your house for a month in winter. To keep the pipes from freezing, you'll then have the choice of heating the whole house and praying that the heating system doesn't quit, or draining the entire supply system. The illustration shows a fitting (a coupling) with a little drain plug that can be installed at every low point in the system for about $1 per shot. Shutoff valves often include drain plugs as well but are rarely located at the low points of the system.

- **Insulating.** Insulating pipes today is as simple as closing Ziploc bags, but the potential benefits are threefold: (1) saving hot-water dollars, (2) preventing damage to ceilings from sweating overhead cold-water pipes in summer, and (3) preventing freezing when installed over heat tapes.

- **Preventing water hammer.** The water in a ½-inch supply pipe can easily reach velocities of 20 miles per hour. When shut off manually with the older type of screw-in valve, the flow is slowed gradually, but the modern washerless valve and the electrically operated clothes-washer valve can be closed almost instantaneously. The result is a hammerlike blow to the pipes when the heavy slug of moving water slams into the valve. This not only causes an irritating noise but can loosen joints in the system as well. Known as water hammer, this occurrence can be prevented by an air column installed near the offending valve. The air in the column absorbs the energy of the moving water like a shock absorber. Water absorbs air over time, so the cushion of air will ultimately disappear unless periodically recharged. The illustration shows a shutoff valve that, when closed, allows draining of the waterlogged column.

105. Low-cost improvements for the plumbing system

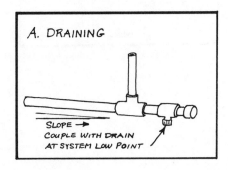

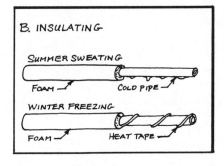

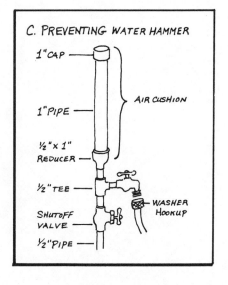

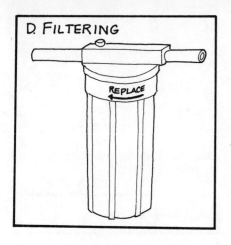

D. FILTERING

REPLACE

- **Filtering.** If you have city water, it probably contains chlorine. Chlorine not only tastes like a swimming pool, but it reacts with biological matter in the water to form compounds suspected of being carcinogenic. Chlorine and its compounds are effectively removed by inexpensive activated charcoal filters. Since the life of the replaceable cartridges depends on the volume and purity of the water processed, and since there's no point in filtering toilet water, I install a filter only in the cold-water branch serving the kitchen sink, where I draw my drinking water.

THE WASTE AND VENT SYSTEMS. Plumbing codes define all water flowing out of a fixture as wastewater, but they distinguish between types of waste:

- Blackwater waste — that which contains human waste; i.e., waste from a toilet or urinal.
- Graywater waste — all other wastewater.

This distinction is important in sizing waste pipes. In the city, combined wastewater flows through a 3-inch house drain and then a 4-inch sewer pipe to a larger sewer pipe under the street and ultimately to the sewage-treatment plant. In the country you supply your own sewage-treatment plant in the form of a septic tank / drain field. (Refer back to Letter 11 for a description of the home septic system.)

Traps and vents. Notice that the pipes between the fixtures and the house drain in Illustration 106 are plugged. The solid black plugs are actually liquid wastewater purposely trapped at low points in the waste system to prevent noxious sewer gas from rising into the house. The illustration shows three code-approved types of traps:

- Drum trap with clean-out plug at the top, often used where the drain from a bathtub or shower stall runs beneath the floor and can be reached only from above.

- P-trap with clean-out plug at the bottom, used under sinks and lavatories.

- Water-closet (toilet) trap, built into the bowl and visible only from beneath.

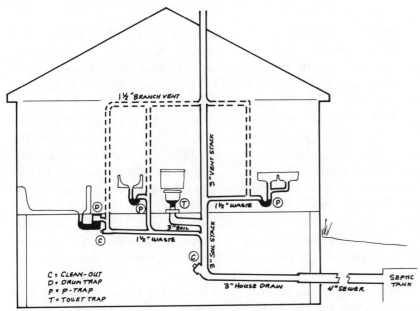

106. The drain, waste, and vent (DWV) systems

C = CLEAN-OUT
D = DRUM TRAP
P = P-TRAP
T = TOILET TRAP

Illustration 107 shows the S-trap found in many older houses but now forbidden by many codes. It also clearly demonstrates the principle of the trap-and-vent system. When water drains from a fixture, the wastewater completely fills the vertical drainpipe and trap. If you have ever siphoned gasoline from an automobile, you'll immediately recognize the potential problem with the S-trap: As soon as the fixture has emptied, the weight of the water in the lower leg of the trap may pull or siphon the water from the upper leg, leaving the bottom of the trap empty. You can tell when this happens by the powerful sucking sound emitted by the trap. Unless the last few dribbles refill the trap, you may be directly and noxiously connected to the inner sanctum of your septic tank or the city sewer pipes.

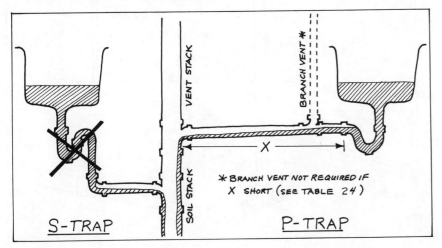

107. How traps work: P-trap (legal), and S-trap (illegal)

The P-trap breaks a wastewater siphon by introducing air at the highest point of the trap outlet. One complication remains, however: Due to friction, wastewater piles up as it flows through the gently sloping waste pipe. If the distance from the outlet of the trap to the inlet of the vertical vent stack (X in the illustration) is too great, the code requires a branch vent closer to the trap. Otherwise the moving slug of drain water may empty the P-trap just as it does the S-trap. Different codes treat the distance X differently. One code simply allows a maximum of 10 feet between trap outlet and stack or branch vent. Another code computes X as the horizontal distance in which the ¼ inch per foot of slope accumulates to the internal diameter of the drainpipe. Because of these restrictions, a two-vent stack system may be your best solution. Flatter the plumbing inspector by asking for his opinion.

Waste and vent layout. Illustration 108 shows the waste and vent systems for the bathroom first shown in Illustration 104. The pipe is all of Schedule 40 (referring to the thickness of the pipe wall), PVC (white or cream color), or ABS (black) plastic. Table 23 lists the terms you should use at the real hardware store. Again, the illustration is intended to demonstrate the principles of waste and vent systems, not to dictate the layout of your bath-

Table 23
WASTE AND VENT FITTINGS

1. Male iron pipe adapter, 1½″
2. P-trap, 1½″
3. Sanitary tee, 1½″
4. Schedule 40 pipe, 1½″
5. Elbow, 1½″
6. Sanitary tee with two 1½″ side inlets, 3″
7. Schedule 40 pipe, 3″
8. Schedule 40 pipe, 4″
9. Adapter to 4″ sewer pipe, 3″
10. Trap adapter, 1½″ to 1¼″
11. Reducing closet flange, 3″ by 4″
12. 90° elbow, 3″
13. 45° elbow, 3″
14. Y branch, 3″
15. Clean-out adapter, 3″
16. Threaded clean-out plug, 3″

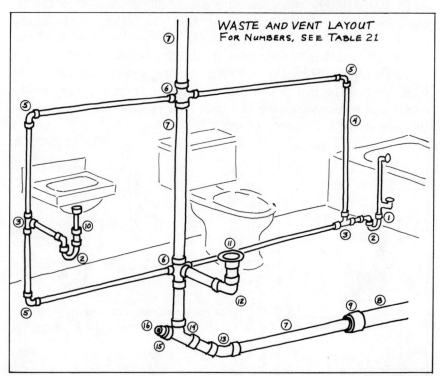

WASTE AND VENT LAYOUT
For Numbers, see Table 21

108.

room. After designing your bathroom(s) and kitchen for convenience, prepare a scale drawing of the proposed waste and vent piping to pass under the nose of the inspector. Be prepared for suggested or required changes, and by no means purchase any materials before obtaining the inspector's blessing.

Roughing in. Both the supply system (Illustration 104) and the waste and vent systems (Illustration 108) require holes in walls and floors. The preliminary hole cutting and running of pipes is called roughing in. Except for tubs and showers, fixtures are usually installed after the paint on the walls dries. Illustration 109 shows the rough-in dimensions of standard bathroom fixtures. Without the actual fixtures on hand, Illustration 109 should prove invaluable, although I'd check with the supplier if Jean orders a metric bidet from France.

Waste-pipe sizes. Getting both liquids and solids to move through traps and pipes under the subtle influence of gravity alone involves both the diameter and the slope of the pipe. Tables 24, 25, and 26 are guides to pipe size. One dictum not specified by the tables but obvious if you think about it is that pipes should never decrease in size in the downstream direction.

Table 24 shows the minimum sizes of drainpipes leading from common household fixtures. It also assigns a number of fixture units (measure of the rate of flow of waste from the fixture) to each.

Table 24
FIXTURE UNITS

Fixture Drained	Pipe ID in Inches	Fixture Units
Toilet	3	6
Lavatory	1½	1
Sink and/or dishwasher	2	2
Shower stall	2	2
Bathtub	1½	2
Washer	2	2
Laundry tub	1½	2

*no toilet
**one toilet only

Table 25
GRAYWASTE PIPE SIZE

Fixture Units	Pipe ID in Inches
1	1¼
1½–8	1½
9–18	2
19–36	2½

Table 26
SOIL-DRAIN, HOUSE-DRAIN, AND SEWER-PIPE SIZE

Fixture Units	Slope ⅛ Inch per Foot	Slope ¼ Inch per Foot
6–12	3*	2*
13–24	4	3**
25–50	5	4

*no toilet
**one toilet only

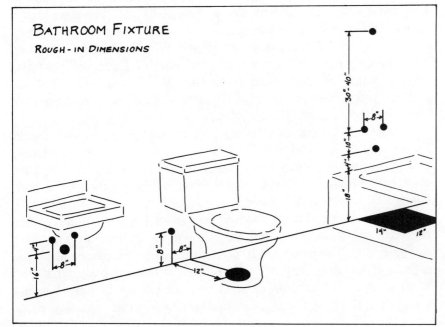

BATHROOM FIXTURE
ROUGH-IN DIMENSIONS

109.

Table 25 specifies the diameter of graywaste (nonhuman waste) pipes according to the total number of fixture units they drain.

Table 26 lists the diameters of soil pipes, house drains, and sewer pipes as functions of both fixture units and slope. Only a very small house with a single toilet or a very large house with more than three toilets would require anything different from 3-inch soil pipes and 4-inch house drain and sewer. Since the vent stack is an extension of the soil stack, it too is most commonly 3 inches, but branch vents can be of the same size as the waste pipes they serve.

Installation Procedures

Table 27 gives short-form instructions for installing the three most common types of pipe and fittings. I list the instructions in this form because you'll be in no position to read a discourse on the subtleties while the PVC cement is setting up or the solder is smoking. So read the subtle points here and now, then keep Table 27 in front of you as you perform your first operation.

PVC AND ABS SCHEDULE 40. These are two different types of plastic, both wonderful in lightness and ease of cutting. Any sharp saw will suffice; I prefer a backsaw, the type used in a miter box. After cutting, you should remove both inside and outside burrs with a file or knife: inside because a burr will catch solids, outside because a burr may scrape away cement as it is inserted into a fitting and thus cause a bad seal.

The single disadvantage of plastic pipe is that you get but one chance. Once the cement sets, no earthly force will part the welded joint. Wisdom dictates cutting and fitting large sections of the system before the final act of fusion. Pencil marks across the joints-to-be make final alignment simpler.

Next, the surfaces of pipes and fittings to be joined should be cleaned of dirt and grease. I don't know where it comes from, but after only five minutes of plumbing my hands are always covered with grease. Cleaning solvents and welding cements are both specific to the type of plastic.

Up to this point you can relax, even take a pie-and-coffee break if you wish. The next step, however, is like jumping off a diving board: There is simply no turning back. So before applying a drop of welding cement, ask yourself if this is really what you want to do. The wisdom of prefitting all parts will here become apparent. If all systems are go, then have at it. Quickly paint

Table 27

PIPE-INSTALLATION PROCEDURES

PVC or ABS SCHEDULE 40 PIPE

1. Cut with backsaw or fine-toothed wood saw.
2. Remove burrs inside and outside with file.
3. Line up fittings and mark with pencil.
4. Paint inside and out with proper cleaner.
5. Paint inside and out with proper solvent.
6. Push in with one-quarter turn and line up marks.
7. Look for bead. If not there, pull out quickly!
8. More solvent; try again.

FLEXIBLE POLYETHYLENE

1. Cut with fine-toothed saw.
2. Remove inside burr with utility knife.
3. If cold, soak pipe end in hot water.
4. Slip on stainless steel hose clamps (double if buried pipe).
5. Insert fitting to shoulder.
6. Tighten clamps well.
7. Use only 45° ells for underground (for ease in thawing frozen pipe).

COPPER TUBE WITH SOLDER FITTINGS

1. Cut with tubing cutter.
2. Remove inside burr.
3. Clean tube and fitting with emery cloth or fine steel wool.
4. Wipe both surfaces with clean rag.
5. Wipe both surfaces with solder flux (paste).
6. Heat tube and fitting evenly with propane torch.
7. Remove flame and test with end of solder to joint.
8. If solder melts, flow into joint; if not, heat more. Length of solder should equal diameter of pipe.
9. Don't move joint for 30 seconds.
10. Don't overheat joint, touch cleaned surfaces, or use too much solder.
11. If the joint fails, drain all water from pipe, heat and disassemble joint, wipe off excess solder, and repeat steps 3 through 9.

---

generous coats of solvent first inside the fitting and then outside the pipe; quickly, I say, because you have no more than fifteen seconds to insert the pipe, rotate about a quarter turn, and finally align the pencil marks. If all is well, a bead of solvent will be squeezed out all around the joint indicating a complete seal; if not, pull like hell, apply more solvent, and try again.

For failure, there is no recourse short of amputating the fitting, installing a coupling and section of pipe, and trying again. Plastic plumbing is like golf: Couplings are strokes, and the lowest score wins.

FLEXIBLE POLYETHYLENE. Black polyethylene pipe is purchased in long coils. Some codes allow its use for cold water within the house, but it is most often used from well to house or from house to lawn or outbuilding. It is available in three thicknesses or pressure ratings: 80, 100, and 140 pounds per square inch. I would use 100 pounds per square inch except down a drilled well, where the pressure increases at approximately ½ pound per foot; there I would use the much more expensive but stronger 140-pounds-per-square-inch version.

Except for removing kinks from the coil, installation of "poly" is simple. First cut the pipe with a saw or utility knife and remove any inner burrs. Slip a stainless steel hose clamp over the end of the pipe. Then slip the ringed end of the fitting into the pipe up to its shoulder. At the time, *slip* may not seem the appropriate term, for the fitting is somewhat larger than the hole for which it is intended. I have actually seen large and mature men reduced to tears in the attempt. Small men such as I, however, have discovered that hot water reduces poly pipe to the consistency of warm tar (hence the ban on its use for hot water). Dipping the end of the pipe in a bucket of hot water makes the insertion job a piece of cake — a perfect illustration of the principle of working smarter, not harder. Tighten the hose clamp well, and if the pipe is to be buried, use two clamps at each end.

Finally, if there is any possibility of the pipe freezing (if possible, it will, of course), design the system to be thawable: (1) install a fitting with an easily removed clean-out plug at an accessible point near the possible freezing point, and (2) avoid all 90-degree elbows between the clean-out and the problem area (use two 45s instead, if necessary). With these precautions, a smaller-diameter flexible plastic tubing can be fed through the frozen pipe to the point of blockage. Warm water pumped through the tubing will rapidly melt its way through the ice blockage. Plumbers use small sump pumps (available from tool-rental stores) immersed in a bucket of hot water.

COPPER TUBE. Soldering copper tube approaches an art form somewhere between welding steel junk and leading stained glass. As with other art forms, it is difficult to explain in words but easy to learn by doing. I strongly recommend soldering your first joints under the tutelage of a practitioner, letting Table 27 serve as a checklist only.

Although five minutes of proper instruction should suffice, beware of amateurs. I once believed the assertion of a young hardware clerk that flux was not necessary in soldering pipe. I soldered 57 joints in my first attempt and, upon christening the new bathroom, discovered that 48 of them leaked like fire sprinklers. Flux paste, I later found out from a real plumber, prevents the newly cleaned copper surface from oxidizing under the high heat and forming an unsolderable copper oxide. I would have pushed the clerk's face in, but he was big and already ugly enough.

Final Words of Wisdom

Plumbing requires understanding, humility, and time:

- If you understand what's going on inside all those pipes and fittings, the code will make perfect sense and help instead of impede your job.

- A little humility will allow you to seek and obtain invaluable advice, not only from the plumbing inspector but from real plumbers as well. Remember: Everyone loves being considered an expert.

- Schedule enough time for failures. They are inevitable. The unscheduled failure is a disaster that ruins your day, but the scheduled failure is a valued lesson.

Your friend,
Charlie

13. Moving In

Dear Charlie,

I know, it's been a while. Almost a month. You probably thought I was so confused by your last essay on plumbing that I went to the mountains to get my head straightened out.

I thought of escape, but Jean wouldn't hear of it. She said we were too close to getting the house finished, and she was absolutely right, as is so often the case. But I must make a confession: I know I could have followed your plumbing instructions (especially the final advisory about being prepared to make a mistake or two), but I just didn't have the pep left to try a solo attempt at pipe fitting. I called in a plumber to help while I did most of the heavy lifting, and he paid attention to the technical details.

It is an arrangement I would recommend to any shelter builders who may be more like me than you. There has to be someone out there, doesn't there, who thinks in terms of the big picture instead of sweating the details the way you do? I'm not the only dreamer who's house building, am I?

Before you answer that, Charlie, I'll tell you the real news. I've been waiting for you to drop by so we could surprise you, but I can't hold back any longer. On the day we called in the plumber to help, Jean made me promise to go all out, to work with her seven days a week at finishing up, running the last lap, getting the place ready to call a home rather than a project.

That's why you haven't heard from me. We had to decide on exterior siding, and I remembered the conversations you and I have had about what goes on the outside of a house. Our opinions haven't changed much over the years. We still don't really like the aluminum and/or vinyl stuff that is supposed to look like clapboards, although it does have the advantage of not needing paint. (And house painting, as you well know, is something I quit years ago.)

Cedar shingles don't need painting either, and they weather to a fine, silvery gray after a few years, especially the ones on the south side, where the sun shines. Shingling is something I have learned how to do, and so has Jean. It's a satisfactory way to spend a day: Progress and accomplishment are defined by the number of bundles converted from raw material to siding. And some of the finest cedar shingles anywhere are made right here in Maine; I can never understand why homes on Nantucket, Cape Cod, and Long Island are shingled in such profusion, while here in Maine, where shingles are born, home builders have been slow to use them.

I grew up with shingles. One of the worst whalings my father ever laid on me was after my brother Chick and I had chased each other across part of our shingled roof, knocking a few loose in the process. By the time my father had put his belt back on and my rear end stopped heating up, I had developed a real respect for the shingling craft. I had even more by the time Jean and I finished this new place. If any of our kids had come along and knocked loose what we had just installed with such loving care, I would have used a baseball bat instead of a belt.

We kept the trim on the windows at a minimum, following your advice again as well as reducing to near zero the amount of painting I'll have to do in the future.

And I know you probably won't believe this, Charlie, but we got into such a finishing frenzy that we would go back to the place for an hour or two after supper and work inside. With the electricity now fully installed and the meter spinning, we had the light we needed to do the final jobs, like rolling paint on the walls and then, that absolute final job that lets everyone know they are approaching the end of the trail: putting down the finish floors.

I remember how thrilled I was when we built that first house on the bay, and we finally got to the point where we hauled over the pine flooring we had stashed in a cellar a year before (a dry, warm cellar where the wood could season). Son Bob installed about every plank of that flooring, and we felt like opening a bottle of champagne when he fit the last one into place and began brushing on the first of three coats of polyurethane gym finish. We knew then we had a home.

We also learned a few years later that pine floors may look lovely but do not perform well in heavy traffic. We had to sand and refinish the floor in our dining area just three years after we moved in, and that's a process Jean and I didn't want to repeat in our next place.

Which is why we took your advice (can you believe it, one more time?) and put concrete toppers in the kitchen/dining area of this new place. When you described them to me, slabs 2 inches thick $\times$ 8 inches $\times$ 16, I never thought I'd like them. But when I saw they came in colors (we chose brick red) and had a fine, smooth surface, and when I looked at our budget and realized how close we were to our limit, I ordered them delivered and was proud to do it. Now that they're in place, they do a fine job of soaking up the sun that spills in through the south-facing glass in both rooms. Long after sunset, the toppers are warm to the touch.

Because the living room is a touch more formal, because it gets less traffic, and also because it has no southern exposure, we opted for the traditional oak floor, which didn't cost an arm and a leg, because the 14' $\times$ 16' room just isn't that large. Upstairs, where we walk around in our bare or stockinged feet most of the time, we went back to pine. I do love the way it looks, and I'm partial to its relatively low cost. What with the rugs we have down in the places where we walk the most and the shoes-off traffic, I'm betting it will be a great deal longer than three years before this pine begins to show its age.

Well, Charlie, you should have an inkling of what I'm going to say next. You've been through it so many times, not only as a guide and instructor to others but with the fine places you have built for yourself and your family. By this time you know that when a home builder begins talking about putting rugs on the newly finished floors, those folks have just about stopped being builders and are on the brink of becoming homebodies.

And believe it or not, that's what we are, Jean and I, just the two of us. I'm not certain I can believe it myself, not yet. It's all too new. It's been something of a long haul, and there is still a good deal of work to be done. But we won't be driving over here to do it: That's the big difference. We'll be waking up here — waking up with the kitchen cabinets that need to have their shelves prepared and papered; waking up with the deck that hasn't yet been properly planted so it harmonizes more with the landscape; waking up to the hundreds of little jobs that every new home-owner must deal with for six months or so.

But we're homeowners. That's the magic word.

Yes, we still have the garage to build. And by the way, Jean has decided we will have a sun space glassed in on the garage's south wall so she can grow flowers almost year-round. And I'll be

110. John and Jean's dream house (for complete plans see list of reference materials)

fretting for days, waiting to see just how long it takes the grass
seed to sprout, but we're here. We're here, at last.

It seems like years instead of months have gone by since we
first drew those bubble diagrams, since we listed those activity

spaces of yours. But I found the bubble diagram, the first one, the other day when we were moving, and it's amazing how closely the final product fits our initial ideas.

I think that's because we began — you, myself, and Jean — with such a clear vision of what we agreed we wanted. We said we wanted a compact place, a house built primarily for two, with some room for a guest, for one or two of the children if they came to visit. We did not want a place planned for expansion. Rather, we wanted a place of stability, of predictable costs, of low overhead. We wanted a home, in other words, that would represent security on several levels, including the snug feeling we'd get when inside.

But we also wanted a place in harmony with nature. We weren't about to settle for a cell or some urban apartment in the country. We wanted to be able to track the seasons from our windows, to know the equinox, to perceive spring's arrival. And we learned we could have these natural presences without sacrificing efficiency, without sealing ourselves in. Indeed, the solar orientation you helped us attain not only provides our registry of the seasons, it helps warm us and our home. Because we are closer to nature, we are helped by it.

Design has achieved this. Design has given us the Zen landscapes we can see from almost every window. Design has given us our quiet garden, our trees greening on our deck, our great sense of privacy granted without a sense of isolation. These are fine balances, yet they are rendered here with simple designs, with basic solutions to basic problems. In several senses we have our cake, and we can eat it, too.

When I realize that we did all this within budget, when I look at the numbers and see that we are still within a few dollars of the original $50,000 you said we could do this for, I am so gratefully surprised. I ask myself, How can so many other well-intentioned home builders of all ages and all situations be spending so much more and getting less for their money? Why can't everyone have the compact home, the long-lived, low-maintenance, surprisingly elegant, low-overhead, sunny, sparkling sort of place this is? I'm sure it's what they all would want if they could see it.

That is, I think, the answer to my questions. Most would-be homeowners don't really "see" their home before they begin building it or having it built. They come at it with a general idea, a picture from the pages of a magazine, a picture that shows just one dimension and one perspective, and that is quite without the introspection that must precede activity charts and bubble diagrams. Most homeowners just don't take the time to go through the process you led me and Jean through; they start without really knowing precisely where they will end or how much it will cost.

We have much to be grateful to you for: your patience, your thorough explanations, your attention to detail. But primarily, we have you to thank for showing us how to think about a house, how to organize ideas so they become steps toward a livable reality. It's a process anyone can use, but it's a step a great many people never take.

Thanks to you, they needn't be without a compass any longer. Like Jean and me, they can begin by knowing where they are headed and where they will end up. We did, and — as I've told you before — if we can do it, anyone can.

Stop by when you can and see what you made possible.

Your friend,
John

References

TO BUILD OR NOT TO BUILD

Cole, J. N., and C. Wing. *From the Ground Up*. Boston: Atlantic–Little, Brown, 1976.

Roskind, R. *Before You Build — A Preconstruction Guide*. Berkeley: Ten Speed Press, 1981.

DESIGNING YOUR OWN SPACE

Alexander, C., et al. *A Pattern Language*. New York: Oxford University Press, 1977.

Curran, J. *Drawing Home Plans*. Bakersfield, Calif.: Brooks Publishing, 1979.

Syvanen, B. *Drafting: Tips & Tricks*. Brewster, Mass.: Bob Syvanen, 1981.

SITE AND CLIMATE

National Oceanic and Atmospheric Administration. *Climates of the States*. Washington: Superintendent of Documents, No. 003-017-00211-0, 1973.

U.S. Department of the Interior. *Plants/People/Environmental Quality*. Washington: Superintendent of Documents, No. 024-005-00479-3, 1972.

MATERIALS

American Plywood Association. *APA Design/Construction Guide, Residential & Commercial*. Tacoma, 1982.

Forest Products Library. *Wood Handbook — Agriculture Handbook No. 72*. Washington: Superintendent of Documents, No. 0100-03200, 1974.

FOUNDATIONS

American Plywood Association. *All Weather Wood Foundation Systems*. Tacoma, 1978.

FRAMING AND SHEATHING

U.S. Department of Housing and Urban Development. *Reducing Home Building Costs with OVE Design and Construction*. Washington: HUD-PDR, 1979.

Wing, C. *From the Walls In*. Boston: Atlantic–Little, Brown, 1979.

INSULATION

Wing, C. *From the Walls In*. Boston: Atlantic–Little, Brown, 1979.

Wing, C. *HouseWarming with Charlie Wing*. Boston: Atlantic–Little, Brown, 1983.

SOLAR HEAT

The Hawkweed Group. *The Hawkweed Passive Solar House Book*. Chicago: Rand McNally, 1980.

Mazria, E. *The Passive Solar Energy Book*. Emmaus, Penn.: Rodale Press, 1979.

WIRING

Richter, H. *Wiring Simplified*, 33rd ed. St. Paul: Park Publishing, 1981.

PLUMBING

Do-It-Yourself Plumbing Handbook. Chicago: Sears, Roebuck and Co., n.d.

GENERAL CARPENTRY

McCormick, D. *Against the Grain: A Carpentry Manual for Women*. Iowa City: Iowa City Women's Press, 1977.

Plans Available

If John and Jean's house appeals to you, we can provide you with full sets of working drawings. The drawings also show many design options and, at the very least, provide you with an excellent starting point for the design of *your* dream home. We suggest four complete sets (the contractor package): one for you, one for your banker, one for your contractor, and one to be split among subcontractors.

For your plans, send a check for:

- $85 for one complete set of drawings, or
- $145 for the contractor package of four sets
  to: Breaking New Ground
      P.O. Box 4531
      Portland, ME 04101

Index

mildew, 161
mill-certified wood products, 92
mineral wool insulation, 148–149, 150
mobile homes, 104
moisture, 161–162, 164
see also water
moisture content (MC) of wood, 84
movable window insulation (MWI), 179, 181–182, 192, 196

National Electric Code, 60, 202, 205, 207, 208
National Research Board, 93
nonmetallic corrosive cable (NMC), 207
nonmetallic sheathed cable (NM), 207

one-way glass, 166
open attics, 157
open floor plans, 193
organic horizon, 57
outdoor areas, 23–24, 33
outhouses, 70–71
outlet boxes (electrical), 209
owner-builder schools (list), 9

panels
    nonplywood, 91–92
    plywood, 91–93, 129
PASSIVE SOLAR DESIGN program, 180, 196
passive solar heating, 98, 180, 184
    design, 196–199
    functioning of, 190–192
    types of systems, 188–190
    use of the building itself for, 192–193
    see also solar heat and radiation
patio-door replacement glazing, 172, 182, 192, 196
    installation procedure, 182–183
patio-door windows, 171
patios and decks, 18, 21
people ventilation, 176
perlite insulation, 150
petcock, 69
phloem (trees), 80
picture or fixed windows, 171–172, 174, 177
pier foundations, 104, 111–112
    concrete, 113
pine, 140, 141, 229–230
pipe(s)
    composition of, 217–218
    cutting procedure, 224
    drainage, 104–106, 108, 112, 164
    installation procedure, 224–227
    insulating (freeze-proofing), 68–69, 104, 219
    internal diameter, 216–217, 222, 223–224
    sizing, 220, 222–224
    waste, 223–224

pith (trees), 81
plumbing, 213–215
    codes, 215, 219, 220
    systems, 216–224
plywood
    panels, 91–93, 129
    sheathing, 123, 124
    subfloor, 124, 198
point-of-source vents, 176
polyethylene pipes, 226
polyisocyanurate foam insulation, 151–152
polystyrene
    extruded, 68, 105, 107, 109, 150–151, 152
    molded, 150–151
polyvinyl chloride (PVC) pipes, 108, 222
    installation procedure, 224–226
positive outdoor space, 24
post-and-beam construction, 4
posts (frame), 126
    corner, 130
    dashed, 140
privacy, 16–17, 29, 55
P-trap (plumbing), 220, 221–222
pumps
    submersible, 69
    sump, 226

quadruple-glazed windows, 181

radiation. *See* solar heat and radiation
rafters (top chord), 88, 89, 123, 124, 127
    clear span for, 140
    vs. trusses, 136
rays (trees), 81
rebars, 110
reflection, 4, 50
roads, 57–59
rock wool insulation, 148–149
roof(s), 27, 139–140
    overhangs, 179, 180
    trusses, 127, 135–136, 137, 140
    weight of, 102, 103
rot (lumber), 89
roughing in (plumbing), 223
rough lumber, 133
rubble trenches, 112–113
R values, 144–152, 159, 197
    defined, 146–147
    of heat-loss surface, 190
    of insulation, 192
    modifiers, 160
    of window glazing, 182

sapwood, 81
savings through owner involvement, 6–7
septic system, 70–72, 74
    tanks, 220
    see also waste disposal (sewage)

underground feeder cable, 207
utility heat gain, 191
utility or basement windows, 171

ventilation, 164, 172, 175–177
vents (plumbing), 220–222
vent system, 216, 220–224
   fittings, 222
   layout, 222–223
vermiculite insulation, 150
vertical ventilation, 177
voltages, 204–205

waferboard, 152
wallboard, 144
wall(s)
   basement, 158
   exterior, 158–159
   insulation, 124, 127
   interior, 127
   life-cycle cost of, 156, 158–159
   load-bearing, 126, 127, 129
   sheathing, 126
   waterproof, 164
   weight of, 102
wane (lumber), 89
warp and warping (lumber), 83, 89
waste disposal (sewage), 40, 55, 69–72, 74
   fittings, 222
   layout, 222–223
   system, 216, 220–224
water, 55, 63–69, 105
   amount needed, 67–68
   filtering of, 220
   hammer, 219
   hardness, 64
   levels and cellars, 105–106
   pollutants, 64–65
   supply system for plumbing, 216–220
   table, 65–66, 101
   vapor barriers, 161–162
   vein, 66–67
   see also drainage pipes and system
water closet (toilet) trap, 220
Watts, Alan, 14
wells, 63, 65–67, 74

wind, 42, 47–48
   anchoring a building against, 103–105, 123
   barriers for, 51–52
   direction, 47–48, 51
   load, 121–122
window(s), 4, 19, 165–168
   areas of, 192
   cost of, 173, 180
   dormer, 26
   and energy, 177–179, 180
   /floor ratio, 192
   functions of, 168–169
   insulation, 179, 181, 192
   openable, 172, 177
   picture, 25
   placement of, 26, 141, 174–175, 184, 185–186
   shading of, 179
   size, 26
   sized for framing, 129
   small-paned, 25–26
   as solar collectors, 180–183
   storm, 168
   types of, 169–173
   view through, 174–175
   see also skylights
windowsills, 26, 126
winter
   design temperature, 44
   diurnal temperature, 194
wires in foundations, 110–111
wiring. See electricity
wood and lumber, 4, 76–80, 83–84, 118–119
   air drying, 86–87
   clear spans for, 132–133
   cutting (sawmills), 89–93
   defects, 87–89
   dimensions, 84
   drying and shrinkage, 84–86, 92
   foundations, 104
   framing, 131
   as fuel, 80
   properties of, 81–83, 123, 127
   see also trees
working areas, 29

Zen view, 24
zero-energy houses, 197